GRAMMATICAL MAN

Information, Entropy, Language, and Life

By Jeremy Campbell

A Touchstone Book
Published by Simon & Schuster, Inc.
New York

10   9   8   7   6   5   4   3   2
10   9   Pbk.

Library of Congress Cataloging in Publication Data

Campbell, Jeremy, date.
  Grammatical man.
  Includes bibliographical references and index.
  1. Information theory.   I. Title.
Q360.C33   001.53'9   82-3272
ISBN 0-671-44061-6   AACR2
ISBN 0-671-44062-4 Pbk.

For Pandora,
a matchless information source

Contents

Foreword

This book is an attempt to tell the story of information theory and how it evolved out of the ferment of scientific activity during the Second World War. The results of this wartime research were not simply to redefine a word which had long remained tantalizingly vague. Rather, an entirely new science was born, making it possible to examine intractable problems from a higher vantage point of knowledge. The laws and theorems of this science stimulated exciting ideas in biology and language, probability theory, psychology, philosophy, art, computers, and the study of society. Just as the principles of the new science of energy yielded fresh insights extending far beyond the horizons of engineering, so information theory opened windows onto a domain of knowledge as broad as nature, as complex as man's mind.

Biologists as well as philosophers have suggested that the universe, and the living forms it contains, are based on chance, but not on accident. To put it another way, forces of chance and of antichance coexist in a complementary relationship. The random element is called entropy, the agent of chaos, which tends to mix up the unmixed, to destroy meaning. The nonrandom element is information, which exploits the uncertainty inherent in the entropy principle to generate new structures, to inform the world in novel ways.

Information theory shows that there are good reasons why the forces of antichance are as universal as the forces of chance, even though entropy has been presented as the overwhelmingly more powerful principle. The proper metaphor for the life process may not be a pair of rolling dice or a spinning roulette wheel, but the sentences of a language, conveying information that is partly predictable and partly unpredictable. These sentences are generated by rules which make much out of little, producing a boundless wealth of meaning from a finite store of words; they enable language to be familiar yet surprising, constrained yet unpredictable within its constraints.

Sense and order, the theory says, can prevail against nonsense and chaos. The world need not regress toward the simple, the uniform, and the banal, but may advance in the direction of richer and more complex structures, physical and mental. Life, like language, remains "grammatical." The classical view of entropy implied that structure is the exception and confusion the rule. The theory of information suggests instead that order is entirely natural: grammatical man inhabits a grammatical universe.

PART ONE

Establishing the Theory of Information

1

The Second Law and the Yellow Peril

What do the codes used for sending messages back from space-craft have in common with genes on a molecule of DNA? How is it that the second law of thermodynamics, a physicist's discovery, is related to communication, so that we can speak of the "entropy" of a musical score, or a page of text, or a conversation? Why are knotty problems in the mathematical theory of probability connected with the way we express ourselves in speech and writing? The answer to all these questions is "information," and the very fact that a single concept can link so many diverse ideas is an indication of its great generality and power.

Information is a word which has never been easy to pin down. In its most familiar sense today, information is news, intelligence, facts and ideas that are acquired and passed on as knowledge. But in medieval times it had various popular and literary uses. In addition to the ones we would recognize, the word was used also with a more active, constructive meaning, as something which gives a certain form or character to matter, or to the mind; a force which shapes conduct, trains, instructs, inspires, or guides.

It was not until the 1940s that information was defined as a scientific term, and this definition was quite new, unlike any in the standard dictionaries. Yet in a curious way, the concept of information, by being described precisely enough to satisfy mathematicians and telecommunications engineers, became increasingly fascinating for nonscientists. The word began to recapture some of its other meanings which had fallen into disuse. The view arose of information as an active agent, something that does not just sit there passively, but "informs" the material world, much as the messages of the genes instruct the machinery of the cell to build an organism, or the signals from a radio transmitter guide the intricate path of a vehicle on its journey through space.

Thus information emerged as a universal principle at work in the world, giving shape to the shapeless, specifying the peculiar character of living forms and even helping to determine, by means of special codes, the patterns of human thought. In this way, information spans the disparate fields of space-age computers and classical physics, molecular biology and human communication, the evolution of language and the evolution of man.

Evidently nature can no longer be seen as matter and energy alone. Nor can all her secrets be unlocked with the keys of chemistry and physics, brilliantly successful as these two branches of science have been in our century. A third component is needed for any explanation of the world that claims to be complete. To the powerful theories of chemistry and physics must be added a late arrival: a theory of information. Nature must be interpreted as matter, energy, and information.

Information became a scientific concept when the age of electronic communications dawned, in the first part of this century. Scientists did to it very much what their nineteenth-century predecessors had done to the concept of energy. They fashioned it into a theory, provided it with laws, festooned it with equations, and, as is their practice, wrung as much of the vagueness and mystery out of it as they could.

In its pure form, information theory was an engineer's discovery. Its most conspicuous practical successes were in color television transmission, the design of early-warning radar systems, the recovery of intact messages from distant spacecraft. It was presented to the world in the form of two papers by Claude

Shannon of the Bell Telephone Laboratories, published in the *Bell System Technical Journal* in July and October 1948. Essentially the papers consisted of a set of theorems dealing with the problem of sending messages from one place to another quickly, economically, and efficiently. But the wider and more exciting implications of Shannon's work lay in the fact that he had been able to make the concept of information so logical and precise that it could be placed in a formal framework of ideas.

By treating information in clearly defined but wholly abstract terms, Shannon was able to generalize it, establishing laws that hold good not for a few types of information, but for all kinds, everywhere. While his papers may appear quite abstruse and technical at first reading, they offer new ways of looking at world processes which seem incomprehensible when viewed through the lens of classical ideas. Their full meaning still has not been exhausted. In spite of the fact that the theorems of information theory were intended chiefly for radio and telephone engineers, they can be used to investigate *any* system in which a "message" is sent from one place to another.

Just as Newton's laws of motion are not restricted to particular sorts of motion by special kinds of bodies, Shannon's laws of information are universal, and in this way compel scientists and other thinkers to confront the fact that information itself is universal. Indeed, so liberally were his theorems interpreted that Shannon, uneasy at the aura of glamor which had grown up around the subject and uncomfortable about the bandwagon of publicity it had set in motion, took to print in 1956 to warn that information theory "has perhaps ballooned to an importance beyond its actual accomplishments. . . . Seldom do more than a few of nature's secrets give way at one time." Yet it was clear from the very beginning that the theory shed light on deep, fundamental questions well beyond the scope of radio engineering. It intruded into many intellectual domains, bearing on paradoxes unsolved for centuries, suggesting a new perspective on problems that philosophy had wrestled with all through its history.

Shannon's papers dwelt on matters which were common intellectual concerns: order and disorder, error and the control of error, possibilities and the actualizing of possibilities, uncertainty and the limits to uncertainty. Scientists are still actively exploring the riddle of why nature's products are so improbable, why they display so much order, when the most probable state for them to be in is one of muddle and error, a surrender to the forces of disorder in the universe that seem so overwhelming and natural. This is still thought of as being one of the disturbing paradoxes in science. It is first cousin to the perennial question of philosophy: "Why is there something rather than nothing?" In his 1948 papers, Shannon proved that, contrary to what we might expect, "something," a message, can persist in the midst of "nothing," a haphazard disorder, or noise.

Most striking of all, Shannon's expression for the amount of information, the first precise, scientific measure, the first satisfactory definition of this distinctively twentieth-century commodity, was of the same form as the equation devised many years earlier, in the nineteenth century, for that most peculiar and fugitive of physical laws, the entropy principle. Shannon had set out to solve a specific problem in radio and telephone communication, and the solution he arrived at, by strict, deductive methods, was essentially identical to the formula for entropy that had been established in the physics of Victorian times. That equation was a mathematical expression of the tendency for all things to become less orderly when left to themselves; for energy to undergo certain transformations in the natural course of events, making it more disorganized and not so useful, degrading its quality without diminishing its quantity. Entropy had been an enormously appealing idea for nonscientists in the nineteenth century and afterward, suggesting as it did that chaos is the ultimate destiny of all things. It led to many flights of dubious speculation and inspired cranks as well as respectable thinkers. It became a reference point, a metaphor, to which philosophers, theologians, and historians of that period returned again and again, with more enthusiasm than caution. This "law" of physics, announcing that the universe is running down into a state of complete disorder, had a visible impact on intellectual fashions. And now, here, in Shannon's work, this same concept made an appearance in a different guise, a new context.

Shannon's entropy equation suggested, at the very least, a

powerful analogy between energy and information. Entropy was the connecting link. In this way it unified two worlds of thought, two eras. Energy was the ruling theme of Victorian science, as machines increasingly harnessed the forces of nature to do man's work. The concept is also present in the art and literature of the age, notably in the poems of William Blake. The Romantic movement was much interested in energy and its various transformations. Even later its residue can be seen in the work of Freud, who thought of instincts and urges as gusts of energy swirling through the brain. The steam engine was the emblem of the industrial revolution, just as the computer is the emblem of the information revolution. Unlike as the two may seem, they are linked by Shannon's theory.

Shannon's papers were published only five years before James Watson and Francis Crick unraveled the secrets of DNA at the Cavendish Laboratory at Cambridge. The double helix of DNA was revealed as an information system, though the larger consequences of this discovery were not explored for several years. Shannon himself, even in his published warnings to workers in other fields to beware of applying information theory indiscriminately, conceded that it might have an important bearing on how the genes and nervous system work, and left open the possibility that "the human being acts as an ideal decoder." Information theory rode a roller coaster from euphoria to disenchantment in the decade that followed its first appearance. Soon after the publication of Shannon's theorems, *Fortune* magazine trumpeted:

> Great scientific theories, like great symphonies and great novels, are among man's proudest—and rarest—creations. What sets the scientific theory apart from, and, in a sense, above the other creations is that it may profoundly and rapidly alter man's view of his world. . . . Within the last five years a new theory has appeared that seems to bear some of the same hallmarks of greatness.

Later, in an overreaction, information theory was rated a disappointment. It was said to have led to no great illuminations. But in the 1970s it began to mature and deepen, regaining some of its earlier luster. The most penetrating investigations into the structure of genetic information came at this time, and brought in their train important new perspectives on the unfinished theory of evolution.

Shannon's personality is quiet and self-deprecating. He is unassuming, slow to push his ideas before the public, and seemingly indifferent to applause and recognition. He is famously unprolific. Some of his work remains unpublished to this day, though colleagues have implored him to put it into printable form. Robert Fano, professor of electrical engineering at the Massachusetts Institute of Technology, said of Shannon:

> There is a significant body of work he did in the 1950s that has never been printed. He doesn't want someone else to write his papers for him, and he won't write them himself. It's as simple and as complicated as that. He doesn't answer letters. He doesn't like to teach. He doesn't like giving lectures. His lectures are beautiful, jewels all of them. They sound spontaneous, but in reality they are very, very carefully prepared.

Shannon was born in Petoskey, Michigan, in 1916. He was an undergraduate at the University of Michigan and a graduate student at MIT. He has told me that the notion of an information measure with an entropy form came to him when he was a research fellow at Princeton in 1940–41, studying under the supervision of Hermann Weyl, one of the great mathematicians and mathematical philosophers of his time. But few of the scientists around Shannon knew of the ideas he was quietly developing. J. R. Pierce, an electrical engineer who had a close relationship with Shannon soon after the Second World War, when they were both at the Bell Telephone Laboratories, remembers asking him if he had proved any new theorems, and if so, to write them down in a notebook. Pierce is certain that the notebook, which is now lost, contained few theorems. Thus Shannon's theory, when it appeared, Pierce says, "came as a bomb, and something of a delayed-action bomb."

Another colleague, Edward Moore, now at the University of Wisconsin, described Shannon as a perfectionist who worked at a very fast pace but could not bear to surrender a paper for publication until it had been refined and polished to the highest gloss. "He would let a piece of work sit for five years, thinking it needed to be improved, wondering if he had made the right choice of variable in this or that equation," said Moore. "Then, while he was still contemplating improvements, someone else would come out with a similar result which was correct, but so lacking in formal elegance that Shannon would have been ashamed to have done such a shoddy job."

As time went by, Shannon edged imperceptibly out of the academic world. He had no taste for its routine. "By 1960–61, he had begun to fade, and was seen less and less in his office," remembers Fano, who had arranged for Shannon to come to MIT, as Donner Professor of Science, in 1956.

> By 1963, he was hardly there at all. In the late 1950s he started playing the stock market. He became interested in it while working on an important scientific problem, the partition of an independent time series. The stock market average is a good example of such a series, because its fluctuations over the course of time are influenced by a variety of different factors. Shannon tried to find techniques for separating the various influences, and he chose the stock market as an illustration. I don't believe he got anywhere with the mathematical problem, but he became good at playing the market.

A second figure, also at MIT, who made important contributions to the origins of information theory was as unlike Shannon as it is possible to imagine. This was Norbert Wiener, a florid and eccentric character, a blower of fanfares for his own accomplishments, which were considerable. Shannon, in fact, had taken some of Wiener's courses as a student in the early 1930s.

In 1947, a year before the publication of Shannon's theory, Fano was working on his doctoral dissertation at MIT. At intervals, Wiener would walk into Fano's room, puffing at a cigar, and say: "Information is entropy." Then he would turn around and walk out again without another word. Clearly Wiener had grasped something of the relationship between information and entropy. Many other people had the same general idea; it was in the air. At least half a dozen research centers in the United

States and Britain had been working on the mathematics of communication and the separation of messages from noise since the early 1940s. But most efforts to solve these problems were decidedly *ad hoc*, with little sense of how the various parts of the subject might fit together into a coherent whole. Julian Bigelow, a colleague of Wiener's at MIT, describes these earlier investigations as "mathematical carpentry," whereas Shannon was unique and catalytic in his perception that what had until then been treated as a collection of separate topics really comprised "different aspects of a new and emerging science."

Wiener wrote a review of Shannon's papers, but the review suggested a curious lack of comprehension of what Shannon had accomplished. This apparent obtuseness may have been connected with Wiener's unusual and highly egocentric personality. His daughter, now Mrs. Barbara Raisbeck, remembers that Wiener generally avoided reading the work of rival mathematicians. "He was a very vain and a very complex man, who worked best on his own," Mrs. Raisbeck said. "He had a feeling that if he failed to notice his competitors, they would just disappear. Also, he was afraid of using someone else's ideas inadvertently." Gordon Raisbeck, Wiener's son-in-law, thinks Wiener did read and understand Shannon's results, but pretended he had not understood. "Understanding them would have meant admitting that he had not already invented them himself," Raisbeck said. "Norbert Wiener did not want to do that. I heard him lecture several times on information theory without mentioning Shannon at all, which was quite a feat." Wiener had been very helpful to Shannon during the war years at MIT, when they were both working on military projects, and Shannon had been especially interested in statistical thermodynamics. But Julian Bigelow, who was close to Wiener at that time, told me, "I am quite sure Wiener was not fully aware, as Shannon was, of the need for a comprehensive theory of communication, nor of the fact that it was about to be born anyhow, one way or another."

Wiener is best known as the founder of cybernetics, an extremely wide-ranging discipline which includes information theory as one among several complementary sets of ideas. Cybernetics is the science of maintaining order in a system, whether that system is natural or artificial. Since all things in the world have a tendency to become entropic, disorderly, their random deviations from order must be corrected continually. This is accomplished by using information about the behavior of the system to produce different, more regular behavior. By such means the system is kept on course. The term cybernetics comes from a Greek word meaning steersman, and it carries the sense of stability, of constant, correct functioning. Illness is entropic, irregular, an error in the living system, while healing is cybernetic, restoring the body to its original state, correcting the error. Natural selection is also cybernetic, disallowing genetic mutations which deviate from the norm in undesirable ways. Wiener regarded a human society as a self-regulating system kept orderly by the cybernetic mechanism of its laws. Cybernetics enforces consistency. It permits change, but the change must be orderly and abide by the rules. It is a universal principle of control, and can be applied to all kinds of organization, just as Shannon's theorems apply to communication of all kinds. It does not matter whether the system is electrical, chemical, mechanical, biological, or economic.

Wiener's temperament was quite unlike that of the scrupulous and self-effacing Shannon. He was an ambitious, playfully self-promoting mathematician of world stature at a time when America was conspicuously lacking in such native-born eminences. He was a former child prodigy whose early precociousness had left a decided stamp on his personality. He lived in a state of notorious insecurity as to the day-to-day condition of his own genius, and needed continual reassurance from his colleagues. Physically clumsy to a point where even the act of writing was an inconvenience, neurotic, proud, a bad listener, a speaker of several languages who was difficult to follow in nearly all of them, a hopeless administrator by his own admission, Wiener was nonetheless a highly competitive mathematician, one of the finest the United States had produced. He brought glory to the MIT mathematics department, which was no better than mediocre when he joined it.

As a child, Wiener was coached by his father, Leo Wiener, a Slavic languages scholar capable of feats of superhuman intellectual exertion, who expected the same of his son. After long spells of study, the young Wiener would be set to work in the family vegetable garden, while his father walked up and down reading aloud from the works of Tolstoy, selecting passages which commended the ennobling effects of hard manual labor.

Wiener plunged into scientific reading at the age of four, was an undergraduate at ten, received his degree at fifteen, proceeded to study philosophy at Cornell, and by the time he was eighteen had completed a doctoral dissertation on the relationship between mathematics and philosophy. He then took a traveling fellowship to Cambridge, where he studied under Bertrand Russell and G. H. Hardy, the number theorist.

At Cambridge, Wiener came under Hardy's influence in some respects but not in others. The questions on which they parted company are perhaps more interesting than the ones on which they agreed. Hardy was a passionate believer in the purity of mathematics. He subscribed to the notion that a mathematical equation is more likely to be true if it is beautiful, and almost certain to be untrue if it is ugly. The idea that mathematics should be used for worldly purposes was offensive to Hardy. In some cases, he was incredulous that such purposes could exist at all. He wondered if Wiener's claim that problems in physics had inspired some of his best mathematical work was not a "pose." Indeed, Hardy's refusal to take part in the First World War, Wiener believed, arose only in part from feelings of revulsion at the misery it caused. Another motive, perhaps inseparable from the first, was an abhorrence of war's perversion of the beauty of mathematics to military ends.

Wiener did not share this donnish belief that mathematics exists for the sake of its own chaste self. He deplored the modern tendency to divide knowledge into separate fiefdoms, each with its own jargon and declared out of bounds to scientists from other fields. He regarded Leibniz, in the seventeenth and early eighteenth centuries, as the last man to have had a full command of all the important ideas of his time. Wiener himself felt very strongly that the abstract power of mathematics—and he was the quintessence of the pure mathematician in all matters of technique—should also touch the real world of events and living things. At Cambridge, Russell had impressed on him the need for a mathematician to have a keen physical sense. And at

Göttingen, Wiener's admiration for David Hilbert, a giant of German mathematics in the early decades of the twentieth century, was due in part to Hilbert's down-to-earth temperament.

Wiener had very broad intellectual interests. He had worked as a hack writer for the Encyclopedia Americana, and was a reporter on the old Boston Herald, where he lasted only a few months. He had also written a novel, The Tempter. Biology was his early interest, and in mathematics he was actually a late bloomer rather than a child prodigy. He was a highly independent and eclectic thinker who found religious orthodoxy and political totalitarianism equally distasteful. When the Second World War began in Europe, his nearsightedness and general physical unsuitability ruled him out for military service, but he sought ways of making himself useful to the war effort by research. He obtained a small grant to work on an aspect of antiaircraft fire control, then a military research project of the highest importance.

At that time, existing weapons were nearly powerless against German bombers, which flew higher and faster than those in the First World War. In October 1940, three months after the bombing of England had begun, it was estimated that more than 10,000 rounds of ammunition were fired from three-inch antiaircraft guns for every enemy plane shot down over London. That October, when British guns were spraying ammunition almost at random at the attackers, the Bell laboratories suggested an idea which had appeared to one of its engineers in a dream: an electrical gunsight to compute and predict where the plane would be seconds after the gun was fired. An intense research effort was begun, using scientists from the Bell laboratories and from MIT, where Wiener then was, to design automatic devices which could track a plane, compute its position, direction, and speed, and predict where it would be by the time the antiaircraft shell had traveled from the gun to the target area.

The problem of trying to hit a distant, waywardly moving plane was one immediately familiar to any gambler: how to make winning choices in circumstances which are carefully arranged so as to be unpredictable. British gun crews, attempting to shoot down German bombers, were bedeviled by at least two kinds of uncertainty. To make a hit, they could not simply aim the guns directly at the enemy plane. Since the target moved across the sky about as fast as the shell could travel from the antiaircraft gun, the crews needed to aim ahead by as much as thirty lengths of the plane. If the missile was to find its mark using this new device, the radar signal would have to be as precise as possible and the flight of the bomber would have to be as predictable as possible. Yet on a radar screen, the blips which trace the path of a plane are distorted by random electrical interference in the atmosphere, and the pilot of the plane naturally does his best to confuse the gun crews by flying as idiosyncratically and unpredictably as he knows how.

Into this wartime work Norbert Wiener threw all his intense, neurotic energy and drew together the threads of a working lifetime's interest in the interconnected concepts of probability, uncertainty, and what he called "the highest destiny of mathematics, the discovery of order among disorder." The imperfect state of the art of radar early in the war presented scientists with the task of separating the orderly message from the disorder of the unwanted electrical interference, or "noise." In communications parlance, noise is anything which corrupts the integrity of a message: static in a radio set, garbling in a printed text, distortion of the picture on a television screen. When a radio signal from the ground is bounced off an enemy plane in the sky, it scatters, and comes back to earth in a much weaker form. The weaker it becomes, the more it is contaminated by random noise in the atmosphere and in the circuits of the radar receiver itself.

Wiener had made a special study of random behavior in his youthful days at Cambridge, where Bertrand Russell had called his attention to some of Einstein's papers, including one on Brownian motion. This opened up a vista of new ideas which Wiener found peculiarly congenial. Later he wrote that they "seemed to be in harmony with a basic aspect of my own personality." Brownian motion is named after an eighteenth-century botanist, Robert Brown, who noticed, while peering through a microscope at pollen grains suspended in water, that the grains were not still, but jiggled about continually in a kind of dance. The hotter the water became, the faster the pollen grains danced, but there was no telling which path any one grain would trace through space. They seemed as likely to move in one direction as in any other. Einstein showed that in Brownian motion, pollen grains are really buffeted by countless invisible molecules of water. A grain is pushed this way and that, not directly, by a single blow, but indirectly, as a result of the difference in the number of blows it receives on various parts of its surface.

Einstein discovered that Brownian motion is found quite generally in nature. The mathematics of it is based, not on simple cause and effect, but on chance and statistics. Herein lay its fascination for twentieth-century scientists, even for one who, like Einstein, believed that God does not play at dice with the universe.

Wiener had no qualms about the idea of a dice-playing divinity. From his prodigious childhood he had been suspicious of any formalism which smacked of certainty, completeness, or determinism. In fact, at the age of ten he had written a philosophical essay on the Theory of Ignorance, based on the conviction that no mechanism as loose as the human mind can devise a theory which is perfectly finished and leaves no room for change. As his mathematical horizons expanded, he came to realize that the power to create the new out of the old cannot exist in any proper sense in a world where everything is necessary and nothing is uncertain.

Wiener recognized, as other scientists of the period did, that noise in a radar receiver, caused by the random bunching up or thinning out of swarms of electrons as they stream along wires, was similar to Brownian motion, and was amenable to the same sort of mathematical treatment. More interesting by far was the realization that the sending as well as the receiving of messages has a good deal in common with Brownian motion. It may seem a large leap from eighteenth-century pollen grains to communication in the computer age, but the connection is striking, and the insight had important consequences. The link which relates the two concepts is statistics, a branch of the theory of probability, the master principle behind some of the most profound discoveries of modern physics.

A message, like the track of a particle of pollen, is a sequence of events spread out in time. These events are not known completely in advance. The price of a share as it moves up or down in the course of a day's trading on the stock market is a series of the same kind. Mathematicians call such a series stochastic, from the Greek word *stochos*, to guess. The series are not always totally unpredictable, but they do contain an element of the unknown. Nobody can look at a share of IBM and say categorically what it will be selling for two hours hence, though one can make an informed guess. In somewhat the same way, a sentence of English prose is a series of letters and words obeying certain statistical rules. It is internally consistent, so that if a person knows the rules, the sequence is not completely unpredictable. Given the first half of the sentence, it may be possible to guess the second half, or come near to guessing it, or at least to predict the next letter. But the whole point of a message, the whole point of writing the next sentence in a book, is that it should contain something new, something unexpected. Otherwise there would be no reason to write it in the first place.

Only the probable track of a pollen grain suspended in water, only the probable fluctuations in the price of a share of IBM, only the probable arrangement of letters and words on a page of print, can be predicted. In making such a prediction, a mathematician considers not one future, but a multiplicity of simultaneous futures, all of which can be said to coexist in an abstract sense. Statistics can do nothing with a single piece of data. An isolated event has no meaning. It needs to be part of a pattern of many possible events, each with a certain likelihood of being realized.

In Newton's mechanics, full determinism reigned. It was assumed that, given perfect knowledge of what an object is doing now, one can predict exactly what it will be doing at any time in the future. Wiener stated as his firm belief that a scientist can never, ever, have perfect knowledge of what a part of the universe is doing at this moment, while we are looking at it. It follows that there is no hope of knowing for sure and in detail what its future will be. The scientist must try to conquer uncer-

tainty about the future by considering a range of different contingencies and assigning a suitable probability to each contingency.
Then he can say what may happen, under this or that set of
circumstances.

Predicting where a German plane would be a few seconds
hence, so that gun crews can aim the shell ahead and hit the
target, is a problem for statistics to solve. The probable path of
the plane is treated as one of many possible paths. The task of
separating messages from noise is also accomplished statistically. Messages display a certain pattern, and the patterns
change in a manner determined partly, but only partly, by their
past history.

This was a clean break with determinism. At the time, it was
a surprising discovery. In a larger sense, it helped to establish
the conceptual framework of the new theory of information
which burst onto the scene three years after the war was over.
The classical theory of communication, which had begun to be
undermined in the 1920s, was deterministic, Newtonian. It
treated messages as single events. Wiener, like Shannon, deci-
sively cut the chains of this old way of thinking. He recognized
that to speak of one fixed item of information—a signal, a letter
on a page, a blip on the radar screen—makes no sense. In an
ordinary conversation, information is conveyed when the
speaker says something that changes the listener's knowledge.
This means that the listener is in a state of uncertainty as to
what message he will actually hear. We say "uncertainty" rather
than complete ignorance because he does know, at least, that
the message will be one of a range of possible messages. It may
be highly improbable, and therefore very hard to predict, or it
may be extremely probable, in which case the listener could
have predicted it with ease. But the message will not be impossible, in the sense that it violates grossly the rules of grammar or
meaning; otherwise it could not be called information at all. In
the listener's mind, as in the statistician's charts and tables, are
a number of possibilities or contingencies, some more probable
than others. When the speaker sends his message, he makes one
of these possibilities actual, excluding the others and resolving
the listener's uncertainty.

However, we should take careful note of the fact that a greater

amount of uncertainty is resolved if the message chosen is one
of a large number of possible messages and if it is one of the
more unlikely of those possibilities. For that reason, an actual
message must be considered not in isolation but in its relation
to all the possible messages, just as the actual path of a plane is
part of a pattern that includes other possible paths. This is a
point of central importance in information theory, which is statistical to its very bones. The masters of the mystery novel, to
give another example, are at pains to ensure that the reader's
uncertainty is maintained until the very last moment, when the
villain, finally unmasked, will turn out to have been a possible
suspect but a highly improbable one.

Wiener worked on the prediction problem as if the fate of the
entire war hung on his success. He popped benzedrine pills to
keep awake through marathon, all-night sessions that were not
really necessary, and then became alarmed at the likely effect of
such exertions on his already severely limited ability to keep
military secrets. (The whole antiaircraft fire control program was
highly classified.) There is evidence that other wartime researchers, more in the thick of the fray, were amused at Wiener's
enlarged opinion of the importance of his role. Edward Poitras,
one of four members of a committee directing research on the
project, remembers that Wiener would come down to an army
range at Fort Monroe, Virginia, to "get a feel" for the guns when
they were being fired. Poitras did not regard these visits with
deadly seriousness. "We took Wiener around, tongue in cheek,
led him by the hand as you would a child," he said. "He was a
very odd character. His connection with fire control was actually
quite minor and peripheral."

Wiener set out his ideas in a classified wartime report to the
National Defense Research Committee that was later circulated
among his fellow scientists. It became known in these elite circles as the Yellow Peril, in recognition of the color of its cover
and the intimidating difficulty of its contents. Wiener's technique was so rarefied that much of the report was impenetrable
for even the most advanced technician.

The Yellow Peril, which was actually written by Julian Bigelow from notes taken as Wiener wrote on the blackboard in Room 2-224 at MIT, was a major contribution to an important aspect of information theory. However, Wiener did not refer to his own work as a theory of communication.

The connection with information theory was implicit in the Yellow Peril, rather than explicit. "Wiener never became so directly practical as to discuss such questions as 'channel capacity,' 'source entropy,' or 'message coding,' entities on which Shannon built his theory," Bigelow says. "Wiener's concepts consisted of 'Brownian motion,' 'discrete chaos,' and 'linear operators.' These were more comprehensible to mathematicians than to communications scientists of that era. Two or three decades later it was realized that Wiener's work was relevant to an important aspect of communications theory, but his insights were (one might say) disguised by his need to express them in mathematical form only remotely connected with applications."

In any event, the American-designed electrical predictor for antiaircraft guns went into service on the east coast of England in August 1944, less than two months after the first wave of German buzz-bombs appeared in the sky. They brought about a startling improvement in accuracy. Before they were installed, only 10 percent of pilotless V-1's were shot down by ground fire. Afterward, 50 percent were destroyed. How large a role Wiener played in this practical success is open to question, but he had come to the conclusion much earlier in his investigations that a window had been opened onto a new intellectual landscape. "It became clear to me almost at the very beginning," he wrote in his memoirs, "that these new concepts of communication and control involved a new interpretation of man, of man's knowledge of the universe, and of society."

2

The Noise of Heat

Entropy is a word which carries a large historical freight of good physics, profound paradox, dubious analogies, and flights of metaphysical fancy. At first, Shannon did not intend to use such a highly charged term for his information measure. He thought "uncertainty" would be a safe word. But he changed his mind after a discussion with John von Neumann, the mathematician whose name is stamped upon some of the most important theoretical work of the first half of the twentieth century. Von Neumann told Shannon to call his measure entropy, since "no one knows what entropy is, so in a debate you will always have the advantage." That was intended as a witticism, but it is true that entropy has been defined in dozens of different ways at various stages of its history. The debate about its "real" nature is still unresolved after more than a century of inquiry and argument. Even so, generations of practical scientists have used the concept of entropy, just as they have used the concept of probability, without giving a moment's thought to the unsteadiness of its theoretical underpinnings.

Part of the trouble arises because, while entropy refers to the physical state of a physical system, it is a measure of the disorderliness of that system, and disorder is not a wholly objective property. The human observer cannot be excluded completely, because the idea of order is inextricably linked to the mind's awareness. Muddle, to some extent, is in the brain of the be-holder. One person's disorder may be another's order, depend-ing on how much knowledge that person possesses about the details of the apparent confusion. My desk may look like a mess to you, but I know my way around it. To me, its entropy is low. This leads to questions of the sort which have long plagued the theory of probability; is entropy material, or mental? Physical, or abstract? Olivier Costa de Beauregard, the French theoretical physicist, answers that entropy is subjective and objective, both at once. Entropy is an aspect of probability, and probability, de Beauregard asserts, "operates as the hinge between matter and mind, where one is knotted to the other, and reacts on the other."

Entropy is objective in the very important sense that when it rises to a maximum in any isolated system, that system is inca-pable of doing anything interesting, novel, or useful. Heat can only drive an engine when it is at a higher temperature than its surroundings. It must "descend" down the slope of temperature like water falling from a height to drive a wheel. This means that the heat source must be separate and distinct from the rest of the system, so that the arrangement of energy is to some extent "orderly"; high temperature here, lower temperature there, and a clearly marked contrast between the two. When the fuel is spent and the whole system reaches a single, uniform tempera-ture, all the molecules are mixed up in random confusion; the engine will not run.

In the same way that a waterwheel cannot be turned if all the water is at the same level, neither can human beings survive without the one-way flow of energy from the sun. It is the im-balance of a hot sun burning in the cool surroundings of space that powers the great engine of nature and civilization on this planet. When the sun burns out and this life-giving asymmetry of temperature ceases to exist, the sameness will wipe out bio-logical forms, with all their wealth of intricate order. The same amount of energy will exist in the universe, because energy is neither created nor destroyed, but it is disorderly energy in a state of high entropy, and as such cannot be used for any con-structive purpose. It has not been annihilated. It is simply inac-cessible.

A system in a state of maximum entropy is in a ferment of

constant change beneath the visible surface, as molecules shuffle and collide in random confusion; the system has lost its contrasts, its orderly arrangement, which gave it a potential for performing some definite task. It has lost its value. One region of the system is the same as any other region, and this uniformity renders it incapable of accomplishing anything interesting from a human point of view. The whirlwind of change beneath the surface does not produce any appreciable change at the surface itself, but merely insures that there is more of the same, for as long as someone is around to observe.

In a metaphorical sense, a thermodynamic system when it is in a state of low entropy—that is to say, containing an orderly contrast of high and low temperature—is like a message, while the same system in a state of high entropy, with all the contrasts smoothed out, is like noise. A glass of water with ice cubes in it makes a clearly marked distinction between its warm and cold parts. Its entropy is low, because the molecules of which it is composed are not as mixed up and random as they could be. At a later time, the entropy of the contents of the glass will increase to a maximum. The ice cubes will dissolve and the water will settle down to one uniform temperature.

The point is that before the cubes dissolved, there was more to say about the contents of the glass. They conveyed a "message" about the arrangement of the different parts of the system. After the ice melts, however, all that can be said is that here is a glass of water at room temperature. The molecules of the ice are mingled with the molecules of the water indiscriminately, so that all they convey to the observer is a meaningless "noise." Before, we could know where each kind of molecule was, within broad limits. An order existed. When that order disappears, the observer has less information about the system as a whole. When a radio broadcasts a news program, the listener has complete knowledge of what the announcer is saying, because words and sentences are in a specific, regular order, while the noise of atmospherics in the background is just a buzzing confusion and that is all the listener can say about it. It takes longer to describe the message than to describe the noise, because we know everything about the internal order of the first and nothing about the internal disorder of the second.

It is fascinating to see how, as the theory of thermodynamics progressed, the focus of interest shifted from what it is possible for a system to do, to what it is possible for an observer to know about the system.

_____

The first glimmer of an understanding of the entropy principle came early in the nineteenth century from a young Frenchman of brilliant promise never fulfilled: Sadi Carnot, the son of Napoleon's minister of war. Carnot, named after a medieval Persian poet, was an engineer, with a practical sense of the need to make engines do more work for less money, and a remarkable vision of what tremendous changes the new world of technology, based on energy, would bring.

At that time, no theory of steam engines worth the name existed. The best of these devices, used to pump water out of tin and copper mines in Cornwall, were able to convert only 5 percent of the heat energy in their boilers into actual work. Carnot had an excellent sense of theory, of clearing away surface clutter and going to the essence of the problem, establishing general truths. He idealized the heat engine, rather as Shannon idealized a communications system, so that his findings applied as widely as possible to any sort of engine using any sort of fuel.

Carnot presented his conclusions in a memoir, *Reflections on the Motive Power of Fire,* written in a small Paris apartment when he was twenty-eight. In the memoir, published in 1824, Carnot showed that heat can do work only when it descends from a higher to a lower temperature. A difference must exist. It is the amount of heat and the "height of its fall" that decides how much mechanical work can be accomplished.

At this point in his brief life, Carnot did not know what heat was. He subscribed, without much conviction, to the view generally held at the time, that heat was a weightless fluid which flowed in and out of solid bodies, so that the analogy with a waterwheel seemed very close to what he supposed went on inside a steam engine. Later, he abandoned the fluid theory and came to the conclusion that heat is simply the motion of the particles of matter, but this discovery was confided only to Carnot's private notebooks, which were not published until 1872, when the science of thermodynamics was well advanced. Carnot himself perished at the age of thirty-six in a cholera epidemic.

Carnot also assumed, mistakenly as it turned out, that heat flows downhill from the boiler to the condenser, without any being lost. He believed that there was as much heat at the end of the process as at the beginning. It was not until the middle of the century that science clearly established that this is not the case. What actually happens is that part of the heat is converted into the mechanical work of pushing the pistons of the engine, while another part is transferred directly to the walls of the condenser. Even in a perfectly built engine, only a certain amount of the heat energy goes into driving the engine, while the rest is wasted, falling uselessly down the temperature gradient.

As the nineteenth century advanced, it gradually dawned on theorists that energy is indestructible. The amount of energy in the universe does not change. However, it can change its form, and be converted into some other kind of energy at a fixed rate of exchange. Heat is one of these forms and work is another. Still others are light, electricity, and chemical processes. The important point, though, is that these various conversions do not all work equally well in both directions. They are not perfectly reversible. When a car brakes suddenly, its forward progress comes to an end, but the mechanical energy which moved it forward is not simply canceled. It is converted fully into heat energy in the form of friction in the car's brakes and tires. This energy is not useful because, as we have seen, heat cannot be reconverted back into mechanical work unless a contrast of temperatures is created, and even then there is some waste. Indeed, if a hot body is placed next to a cold body, heat will fall down the gradient, evening out the difference in temperature, without doing any work at all. It soon came to be understood that heat is only with difficulty, and never completely, converted into useful mechanical work, while work is all too easily converted, completely and permanently, into heat.

Rudolf Clausius was the man who brought the whole science of thermodynamics—literally, "the movement of heat"—to a

new level of sophistication by expressing the behavior of energy
in two laws. The first law of thermodynamics states that energy
is conserved. It is not created or destroyed. The second law of
thermodynamics says that while energy does not alter its total
quantity, it may lose quality. The name Clausius gave to the
measure of this loss of quality was entropy, from a Greek root
meaning "transformation." For Clausius, entropy was a relation
between heat and temperature. It was expressed as a fraction:
heat divided by temperature. When a quantity of heat flows out
of a hot body, its entropy decreases by the amount of heat divided by the original temperature of the hot body. When that
same quantity of heat flows into a cool body, its entropy increases by the amount of heat divided by the original temperature of the cool body. Since the temperature is larger in the first
case and smaller in the second, the fraction of entropy decrease
is smaller than the fraction of entropy increase; thus a net gain
of entropy occurs in the transfer. This gain occurs every time
heat flows from a higher to a lower temperature, and since nothing interesting or useful happens unless heat does make this
descent, all interesting and useful things are accompanied by an
irreversible increase in entropy. Clausius summed up his conclusions in the famous couplet:

> The energy of the universe is a constant.
> The entropy of the universe tends to a maximum.

Why did energy suffer this curious one-way decay, this loss
of value, in nature as well as in artifice? The early thermodyna-
micists were content to regard entropy as a gross, general property, like temperature or pressure. A thermodynamic system
evolved from one state into another state in the course of time,
and it was the states themselves that these workers were interested in. Later investigators tried to lift the curtain from the
mystery of what went on between one state and another, and to
understand the invisible machinery responsible for the irreversible increase of entropy. If Newton had given a mechanical
explanation of the movements of the heavenly bodies, once
thought to be guided along preordained paths by God, would it
not be possible to make intelligible the riddle of energy transformations by similar, rational methods?

In this enterprise, Ludwig Boltzmann was the most original and successful thinker. Boltzmann was a luminous and tragic figure on the landscape of the physics of his time. He was an ardent admirer of the German Romantic poets, especially Schiller, and as a child had taken piano lessons from Anton Bruckner, but his approach to the study of nature was implacably antimetaphysical. He regarded metaphysics as a mental headache and had nothing but contempt for idealist philosophers; he described Schopenhauer by turning that philosopher's own description of Hegel against him: "a stupid, ignorant philosophaster, scribbling nonsense and dispensing hollow verbiage that fundamentally and forever rots people's brains." As an atomist, he was opposed by a school of thought, extremely powerful at the end of the nineteenth century, that held energy to be a continuous flow rather than the motion of unseen particles in the microcosm. These antiatomists believed that the only knowledge possible in science is a knowledge of our sense impressions and of certain constant mathematical relations between these impressions. They held that there is no hope of discovering any deeper reality behind and beneath what can be observed and experienced. Boltzmann, a naturally quarrelsome and combative man, believed in fighting unceasingly for his atomist convictions, and he did so gallantly until old age, when, with his health and eyesight failing and the tides of scientific fashion running strongly against him, he hanged himself in a seaside boardinghouse on the Adriatic coast of Italy.

Boltzmann championed the atomic theory, not because he was convinced that it was the only possible one, or because he insisted on the actual, physical existence of atoms. The reason for his struggle to win acceptance for the theory was that he believed it offered the most powerful explanation for the behavior of matter. It is an illusion, he argued, to suppose that no one can describe nature without going beyond experience, because all equations inevitably express nature in an abstract form, stressing the common features of its various processes and neglecting their differences. "Only half of our experience is ever experience," Boltzmann said, echoing Goethe. Thinking always adds something to experience and creates a mental picture which is not a simple or single experience, but which represents a broad range of experiences. Using that picture, one can predict what will happen in the future, and describe something which has not yet been experienced.

The mental picture Boltzmann found so fruitful for explaining the second law of thermodynamics was that of invisible particles in the microcosm of matter. Heat is due to the excited motion of these particles, so that thermodynamics, the movement of heat, must actually be the movement of motion. Boltzmann built on the work of the Scottish theoretical physicist, James Clerk Maxwell, who as a young man at Cambridge had won a prize for an essay on the rings of Saturn. In this essay, Maxwell showed that the only way to account for the stability and motion of Saturn's rings in space is to assume that they are a system of separate particles, rather than a fluid or some other continuous substance, as observation might suggest. The success of his paper led Maxwell to treat gases as collections of tiny particles rushing about at varying speeds and colliding with each other. In a hot gas, the particles move very fast, while in a cool gas, their speeds are slower. Since it is impossible to establish the exact speed of each particle, Maxwell treated the whole collection of particles statistically.

In 1859, when Boltzmann was only fifteen, Maxwell brought out a paper which became a landmark in science. By calculating the most probable speeds of particles of gas at a given temperature, Maxwell proved that it was possible to obtain information about the behavior of the gas as a whole, about its large-scale, measurable properties, such as pressure and viscosity. The paper presented, for the first time, a law of nature not absolute and without exception, but only statistical. The law did not stipulate that such and such must happen, with one specific cause leading to a unique effect. It said only that in a system consisting of large numbers of parts, knowledge of the probable behavior of the parts leads to knowledge of the general properties of the whole.

Years later, Boltzmann read Maxwell's papers and used his statistical methods to arrive at a new and more general treatment of entropy, based on probability, and on probability alone. His earlier ideas on the subject had been drawn from mechanics, so that the tiny particles which make up matter were assumed to behave somewhat like Newton's heavenly bodies and to be subject to the same laws. The trouble is that such a treatment does not explain why a thermodynamic system evolves irreversibly toward a state of maximum entropy and stays there, because according to Newton's mechanics, a body may retrace exactly its original path and return to the place where it started. So if each particle in a system is capable of reversing its motion exactly, why should not the entire system return to its original state? As Boltzmann's work progressed, he resolved that dilemma by making entropy a statistical property of an enormous number of particles, so that the irreversible advance toward greater disorder is only probable, though so overwhelmingly probable that for all practical purposes it is certain. There is nothing in principle to prevent all the particles from reversing their paths and going spontaneously from disorder back to order, as in Newton's mechanics, but such an event would be as rare as a kettle freezing on a stove burner instead of boiling. It is so unlikely as not to be worth bothering about.

In the new scheme, entropy is an increase of disorder among the particles. At equilibrium, the state of maximum entropy, there is the most disorder there ever will be. More mixing up of the particles leads only to the same amount of disorder, just as there is no point in continuing to shuffle a thoroughly shuffled pack of cards. To do so will not increase the disorder, and it is overwhelmingly unlikely that further randomizing will by chance return the pack to its original order. Irreversible disorder is only probable, not certain, but the laws of probability are so powerful that in the world of experience they amount to a principle. The slight contradiction between Laws and Facts in thermodynamics is important to theorists and philosophers, but not to engineers.

Heat is inherently untidy. It is the most disorderly form of energy. However, all the other forms of energy, when used, are converted into the energy of heat, so that the tendency is for all the energy in the universe to fall into a state of disorder. Because of its random nature, heat, even when it is in a concentrated form—say in the boiler of an engine—cannot be converted one hundred percent into mechanical work. If all the molecules in the heat source could be lined up and made to move in the same direction, pushing a piston, then the entire amount of heat would be converted into work. But this can never happen. For the very reason that the molecules of a hot gas are all vibrating, rotating, colliding, and rushing about in all directions, only a part of their energy is actually applied to driving the engine. The gas expands in the cylinder, exerting a force on the piston, making it move in an orderly direction. Yet the behavior of the gas is more like the behavior of a mob of people in a confined space than that of a disciplined platoon of soldiers marching all together toward one destination. The overall effect of the mob rushing about in the confined space is to push the piston, but many individual molecules waste their energy by moving randomly in various directions.

As Boltzmann put it in an address to the Imperial Academy of Science in 1886:

> Precisely those forms of energy that we wish to realise in practice are however always improbable. For example, we desire that [a] body move as a whole; this requires all its molecules to have the same speed and the same direction. If we view molecules as independent individuals, this is however the most improbable case conceivable. It is well known how difficult it is to bring even a moderately large number of independent individuals to do exactly the same thing in exactly the same manner.

This means that producing an orderly process is unreasonably expensive. "Economists are fond of saying that 'there is no free lunch,' everything must be paid its value so that price and value always balance out," the economist Nicholas Georgescu-Roegen has written. "The entropy law teaches us that mankind lives under a harsher commandment: *in entropy terms, the cost of a lunch is greater than its price.*"

At the heart of the second law is the insight that order has value. It enables new forms to be created out of old forms. It makes life possible, and civilized societies. And it is intimately connected with meaning. When a system is at equilibrium, there is an enormous amount of change under the surface, on the small scale of its particles. But from the larger-scale, human point of view, it is useless change, banal, producing nothing of interest. Indeed, at the surface, nothing seems to change at all. Order is valuable in another sense, because it is much more difficult to produce than disorder. Chaos is the easiest, most predictable, most probable state, and it lasts indefinitely. Order is improbable and hard to create. Time is its enemy, because entropy tends to increase with time. Orderly energy can do work, but in the very process of working, it decays into disorderly energy. As a matter of fact, it creates more disorder than order in the end.

3

The Demon Deposed

A curious parallel can be detected between Boltzmann's work on entropy and the ideas of researchers into the nature of energy in the early part of the century. Implicit in Carnot's memoir was the discovery that there are limits to what human beings can make energy do for them. They cannot transform all of it into work. Implicit in Boltzmann's version of the entropy principle is the insight that there are limits to what human observers can *know* about a system in which energy is undergoing a transformation.

The change of emphasis was from work to information. When a system is orderly, and therefore improbable, when it is low in entropy and rich in a structure on the macroscopic scale, more can be known about that system than when it is disorderly and high in entropy. When it is at equilibrium, the state of greatest change beneath the visible surface on the microscopic scale, but of the greatest "sameness" as seen by the human observer, we have the least possible knowledge of how the parts of the system are arranged, of where each one is and what it is doing.

When hot water is first run into a bath of cold water, most of the fast molecules are at the hot end and most of the slow molecules at the cold end. The contrast is clear enough to be detected by our senses. That orderly structure is the "message" it conveys. At a later time, however, the entire bath is lukewarm. Fast and slow molecules are all mixed up together in a ceaselessly changing confusion, and there is no way an observer can keep track of them. Since the changes they undergo are random, they obey no rules. In this state, the bath is like noise. Boltzmann showed that human beings cannot know, and should not be interested in knowing, what each individual molecule (in the bath water, for example) is doing at a particular moment. They can know only how vast collections of particles (at each end of the bath) behave on the average. However, as a system becomes more disorderly and its entropy increases, even this limited knowledge disappears.

The relationship between increase of entropy and decrease of knowledge was not made explicit until many years later. Boltzmann himself was aware of the connection, but referred to it only casually and in passing. In 1894, he planted an intellectual time bomb with a remark that entropy is related to "missing information." With this one phrase, he crossed the bridge connecting entropy, and all its Victorian baggage of associated ideas, with information, the new concept so congenial to the late-twentieth-century mind.

Another way of looking at the second law of thermodynamics is to say that the higher the entropy, the more numerous are the possible ways in which the various parts of the system may be arranged. In this approach the connection between entropy and probability is plain to see: if there is a large number of possible ways in which the parts of a system may be arranged when the system is in a state of high entropy, then it is *improbable* that they will be found in any one special arrangement at a particular instant, just as it is unreasonable to expect a pack of cards, while in the process of being shuffled, to return to its original order, because that single, unique arrangement of the cards is one out of such an astronomically large number of possible arrangements. A muddle is more probable than an arbitrary "order" because there are more, usually many more, ways in which a muddle is created than there are ways in which an orderly structure is formed. The various parts of a piano can be strewn about at random in a myriad of ways, but there is only one way of putting them all together. It goes without saying that the assembled piano is more valuable and interesting than a litter of parts. This notion can also be applied to words in a language, which are not strung together randomly, but conform to certain rules of structure.

Consider, for example, this clue in a crossword puzzle: "Assent to change of name" (four letters). The correct answer to the clue is clearly an anagram of the word "name" and it must have the meaning of "assent." Obviously the word is "Amen." But what is the *probability* of arriving at the correct answer by shuffling the four letters about at random? There are twenty-four different ways of arranging the four letters of the anagram. Some of these form sensible words like "mean" and "mane," even though they are not the right answer to the clue. Out of the two dozen possible arrangements of the four letters, only three form sensible words and twenty-one are nonsense words. This means that in a random shuffling of the letters, the odds of forming the correct word, "Amen," by sheer accident are one in twenty-four. The chances of forming a sensible word are slightly better, one in eight. On the other hand, the chances of forming a nonsense word are very good: seven in eight.

In a thermodynamic system, where molecules instead of letters are shuffled about, the principle is somewhat the same. When heat is concentrated in one part of the system, so that it can move "downhill" to a cooler region and do useful work, there is a certain amount of order, comparable to the shuffled letters spelling out a sensible word. This is an improbable state of affairs, as we have seen, since the odds are heavily against it. The most probable state, when all the parts of the system are mixed up at random, is one of "noise" and nonsense. In the thermodynamic case, an improbable arrangement of the molecules is associated with the capacity to do work. In the case of the anagram, it is associated with the capacity to convey meaning.

Information, like entropy, is closely linked to the notion of variety. A meaningless word consists of the same four letters as a meaningful word, but a greater variety of letter sequences are possible when a word does not need to make sense. The correct answer to the crossword clue is a unique sequence of letters, so that there is only one possibility and no variety at all. The variety, the number of possibilities, increases a little if the requirement is only that the word should make sense, since there are then three possible sequences of letters. It increases a great deal when all constraints are dropped and nonsense words are permitted, at which stage there are two dozen possible sequences, all different.

If a state of high entropy means that there are many different ways in which the parts of the system may be arranged, and a state of low entropy means there are fewer possible ways, then entropy itself can be represented by some mathematical term which symbolizes these possible arrangements and measures their variety. This, indeed, was Boltzmann's approach to the second law. His basic equation, engraved on his memorial stone in Vienna, is very simple. It is

$$S = k \log W$$

in which S stands for entropy, k is a universal constant known as Boltzmann's constant, and W has to do with the number of ways in which the parts of the system can be arranged. The entropy S reaches a maximum when all the parts of the system are so thoroughly mixed up and random that there is no reason to expect it to favor one particular arrangement over any of the colossal number of other possible arrangements. Since the system is in constant motion, new arrangements are created at every instant in the invisible microworld, much as a new arrangement of a pack of playing cards is created every time the pack is shuffled. On the larger, macroscopic scale of human observation, however, there is no variety, because of our ignorance of the small-scale state of the system. Our knowledge of the system is at a minimum because of the immense variety of possible states in which it could be. There is no way of guessing which state is the actual one, because at maximum entropy each of this huge number of possible arrangements of the molecules is equally probable.

Boltzmann remarked that the higher the entropy, the less information we can have about the microcosm, the constituent

parts of matter. This is intuitively clear in everyday life. If someone goes into a large library to borrow a copy of *War and Peace*,
it will take only a few minutes to find the book if the library is
in a good state of order and everyone using it obeys the rules.
The book will be on the fiction shelves and the author's name
will appear in alphabetical order. In the catalogue, the book is
given a unique decimal number. There is only one possible way
in which *War and Peace* can be arranged in relation to all the
other books. Indeed, there is only one possible way in which the
contents of the entire library can be arranged. But then imagine
a second library, in which by some quirk of the rules books are
arranged on the shelves according to the color of their bindings.
There may be a thousand red books grouped together in one
section of the shelves. This arrangement contains a certain
amount of order and conveys some information, but not as much
as in the first library. Since there are no rules governing the
ordering of books on the shelves by title and author within the
red section, the number of possible ways of arranging the books
there is much greater. If the borrower knows that *War and Peace*
has a red binding, he will proceed to the right section, but then
he will have to examine each book in turn until he chances upon
the one he is looking for.

Then imagine a third library, in which all the rules have broken down. The books are strewn at random on any shelf. *War
and Peace* could be anywhere in the building. There is no deny-
ing that the books are in a certain specific sequence, but the
sequence is a "noise," not a message. It is only one of a truly
immense number of possible ways of arranging the books, and
there is no telling which one, because all are equally probable.
A borrower's ignorance of the actual arrangement is great in
proportion to the quantity of these possible, equally probable
ways.

Using Boltzmann's equation, $S = k \log W$, the library's S, or
entropy, is low if its W, or number of ways in which the books
can be arranged on the shelves, is small. When the entropy of
the library is at a minimum, with all the books in one unique,
prescribed order and all the information needed to find a particular book stored in the catalogue, S has its lowest value. On the
other hand, S is high if the number of ways in which the books
can be arranged is large, that is to say, if W has a high value.

In the library, high entropy means lack of information. It means uncertainty. In a thermodynamic system, high entropy means lack of information about the internal structure and a loss of capacity to harness energy for a useful purpose. By restoring the books to their proper place, the entropy of the library would be reduced. This leads to an obvious, though misleadingly simple, question: What if the molecules of a thermodynamic system at equilibrium or maximum entropy could be "rearranged" back into the orderly state they were in when the system was low in entropy? Would not that undermine the power of the second law, which decrees that entropy can never decrease unless energy is applied from outside the system to push it back uphill?

One of the most famous paradoxes in physics is based on the fantasy that a gas in a state of maximum entropy could be provided with its own "librarian" to put it back in order. If an intelligent being small and agile enough could insinuate himself into the microworld of a vessel of gas, the being might be able to sort the molecules into fast and slow, just as a librarian sorts books. The system would then be able to do work. No matter that such a feat is impossible in practice. It is thinkable in principle, and might be a way of violating the law of increasing entropy.

The creature imagined to be capable of such a feat was an idea of James Clerk Maxwell, and was called Maxwell's demon. If the demon could unmix the mixed molecules of a gas, sorting fast ones into one compartment and slow ones into another by opening and shutting a perfect, frictionless door, he could achieve the result ruled impossible by thermodynamics and reverse an irreversible process. For the sake of argument, the demon was supposed not to use any energy when opening or shutting the sliding door.

It is clear, however, that even if the demon uses no energy in working the door, he needs information to distinguish fast molecules from slow. In that case a new question arises: Is information by itself enough to reduce the entropy of a system and make its energy accessible and useful again? Can the demon perform his task merely by observing and experiencing? The answer is no, because in order to inform himself about the molecules in the dark chamber of gas, the demon would need a source of light. Perhaps he could be given a small pocket flashlight. But now a serious difficulty arises. By shining his flashlight, the demon creates a certain amount of order, a contrast between the high-grade energy of the light and the degraded energy of the unsorted molecules of gas. And the second law decrees that this order must become disorderly, increasing the entropy and tending to bring the entire system, including the demon, to a state of equilibrium.

It was not until 1922 that Leo Szilard, as a student of physics in Berlin, finally laid this paradox to rest by showing that the demon, simply in the act of obtaining information about the molecules, creates at least as much entropy as would be eliminated by sorting the molecules into separate compartments. In a memoir, Szilard recalls disposing of Maxwell's demon at a very fruitful period in his early intellectual development, about six months after he managed to surprise Einstein with a proof contradicting the view generally held at that time, that the laws governing thermodynamics must be derived from mechanics. The paper on Maxwell's demon, Szilard said, "was a radical departure in thinking because I said that the essential thing here is that the demon utilizes information—to be precise, information which is not really in his possession because he guesses it. I said there is a relationship between information and entropy, and I computed what this relationship was." What Szilard showed, essentially, was that not only work, not only order, must be paid for by the irreversible degradation of energy, but information as well—even such a seemingly simple thing as an observation. In the words of an often repeated *bon mot* of science, "There is no such thing as an immaculate perception."

Entropy is a protean concept. It measures a physical property, the transformation of energy from an accessible to an inaccessible state. It has to do with probability, since the most probable state of a system in constant, random motion is for all its contrasts to be smoothed out. When a penny is tossed a sufficient number of times, heads are likely to come up as often as tails—not more of one or more of the other, but a uniform spread of the two.

Entropy is also an irreversible process. It does not decrease unless some extra source of energy intervenes to push it back "uphill." It is thus a physical index of the one-way, irreversible flow of time. An observer can distinguish earlier from later by measuring the increase of entropy. If one photograph shows a perfect vase, and another shows the same vase smashed to fragments, it is virtually certain that the second photograph was taken later than the first. However, the statistical nature of entropy affects the knowledge we can have about the past and the future. In Newton's macroscopic scheme, perfect information is assured backward and forward in time. Knowing where an object is now, at this moment, knowing how fast it is moving and in which direction, enables an observer to predict where it will be at a given time in the future. What is more, one can "retrodict" and say where it has been in the past. In thermodynamics, where scientists deal in probability, no such perfect information is available. In terms of what an observer can know about a system—say of molecules in a gas—a particle does not follow a continuous, single track through space, but a number of possible tracks. One may predict where the particle will probably be at some moment in the future, but it is another matter altogether to say even where it probably was at some moment in the past. J. R. Lucas has pointed out that, even if we can say, with a high probability of being right, that a twenty-year-old man who smokes forty cigarettes a day will die before he is ninety, it does not follow, by any means, that a man still alive at ninety did not smoke forty cigarettes a day when he was twenty. This is similar to the case of a sand castle on a beach, blown randomly by the wind. It is quite legitimate to say, "By tomorrow it is overwhelmingly probable that this will not be a castle, but a pile of sand." On the other hand, one cannot reasonably declare, without prior knowledge, "It is overwhelmingly probable that yesterday this was not a pile of sand, but a sand castle." So it seems that when a system is described statistically, rather than in terms of direct cause and effect, not only time but information as well travel irreversibly in a single direction.

Entropy is closer to the untidiness and variety of life than previous physical laws. Oswald Spengler, in *The Decline of the West*, singled out entropy as the concept most typical of the downfall of modern science from its classical purity and certainty. He chose it because entropy is a statistical rather than an exact principle and has more to do with living things and with history than the timeless, abstract equations of the old mechanics. Spengler wrote:

> Statistics belongs, like chronology, to the domain of the organic, to fluctuating life, to Destiny and Incident and not to the world of laws and timeless causality . . . As everyone knows, statistics serves above all to characterise political and economic, that is, historical developments. In the "classical" mechanics of Galileo and Newton there would have been no room for them. And if, now suddenly the contents of that field are supposed to be understood and understandable only statistically and under the aspect of Probability . . . what does it mean? It means that the object of understanding is ourselves.

The second law has been called anthropomorphic, because of what it has to say about the limits nature imposes on the human use of energy. Spengler brooded on the "deep opposition of theory and actuality" it introduced, for the first time, into theoretical physics itself. A modern physicist, P. W. Bridgman, has said that the second law still smells of its human origins. Entropy has always tended to break out of its home territory of physics and mathematics and be taken up by economists, macrohistorians, and other speculative thinkers. It has been defined in many different ways by many different writers, seldom quite satisfactorily, and with some of the freedom novelists use to interpret human experience. William Ralph Inge, the "gloomy Dean" of St. Paul's Cathedral, incorporated the second law into theology. Henry Adams, inspired by a biography of Lord Kelvin, one of the founders of British physics, yoked it to a theory of a history. Entropy was applied to Freud's doctrine of the death wish and fashioned into an argument against Darwinism. Dorothy L. Sayers, who took a lively interest in what scientists of her day were up to, mentions the second law in more than one of her detective novels. At one exasperated moment in *Have His Carcase*, Lord Peter Wimsey remarks to Miss Olga Kohn that what he likes about the evidence she has just given in the murder of a gigolo on a deserted English beach is that it adds the final touch of utter and impenetrable obscurity to the problem which the inspector and I have undertaken to solve. It reduces it to the complete quintessence of incomprehensible nonsense. Therefore, by the second law of thermo-dynamics, which lays down that we are hourly and momently progressing to a state of more and more randomness, we receive positive assurance that we are moving happily and securely in the right direction.

In the period which followed the Second World War, entropy underwent yet another of its Merlin-like transformations when it was linked to a theory of information. This aspect of entropy, like others in the past, has taken years to explore and still is not out of the deep woods of scientific controversy. The idea of a relationship between information and entropy, implicit in the early days of the theory, is still questioned by scientists today. Some are doubtful that the connection is any more than formal, or that it will lead to any deeper insights. John Pierce, a leading communications theorist, insists that information theory is a branch of engineering and mathematics, and that its chief concern is to build better technology and understand the workings of communications devices. In his view, this is quite distinct from physics. "It's God's work versus man's work," Pierce has said. "Physics deals with the works of God, engineering with the works of men." It is interesting to note, however, that Claude Shannon, the chief originator of information theory, thinks differently. In a conversation in the autumn of 1979, Shannon told me:

I think the connection between information theory and thermodynamics will hold up in the long run, but it has not been fully explored and understood. There is more there than we know at present. Scientists have been investigating the atom for about a hundred years and they are continually finding more and more depth, more and more understanding. It may be that the same will be true of the relationship we are speaking about.

4

A Nest of Subtleties and Traps

Information is a more sophisticated combination of the abstract and the physical than might be supposed at first sight. This has to do with the connection between order and the state of one's knowledge, with the ambiguous nature of probability, and with the fact that order and probability are related, one to the other, both in thermodynamics and in the theory of information.

Even today, in spite of impressive accomplishments, the theory of probability rests on insecure foundations. It is powerful in practice but weak philosophically. A major encyclopedia article on the subject carries a paragraph which reads like a consumer-protection label affixed to an unsafe product: "The reader should be warned that the philosophy of probability is highly controversial and that the views expressed in this article would be rejected by many competent theorists."

Boltzmann's defense of the entropy principle, by which he raised the second law of thermodynamics to a new level of generality, was based on an important principle of probability called the law of large numbers. This law had been developed by James Bernoulli, a Swiss who originally prepared for the church, but whose interest in mathematics drew him into a secular life of teaching, traveling and scholarship. When Bernoulli died in 1705, he left with his young nephew Nicholas a nearly completed manuscript of a book which was finally published in 1713. The title of the book was *Ars Conjectandi*, "The Art of Conjecture." Part of it was devoted to the law of large numbers, expressed in a form that Bernoulli called his golden theorem. James R. Newman, a modern writer on mathematics, calls it "a nest of subtleties and traps."

Loosely paraphrased, the golden theorem proves that, in the long run, probabilities approach certainty more and more closely. In fact, however, the theorem is much trickier than that. If a perfectly balanced coin is tossed once, it can be assumed that the probability of heads is one in two, and that the probability of tails is also one in two. But if the coin is tossed ten times, there is no guarantee that the result will be five heads and five tails. Because each flip of the coin has no connection with any other flip, it is always possible to obtain ten heads in a row or ten tails in a row, thus confounding the hopes of a gambler who bets against such a sequence. As the number of flips increases, it is most likely that the percentage of heads will differ from the percentage of tails by only a small amount. The longer the coin is tossed, the smaller that small difference in percentage is likely to become. This statement looks reassuring, but it really is not. Notice that the word "likely" is used twice, in two different contexts, and that the theorem promises only an increasingly equal percentage of heads and tails, not an absolute equality.

Applied to a thermodynamic system, the golden theorem states that as the molecules move and collide at random, whatever contrasts there are in the system, whatever asymmetry exists between fast and slow molecules, it is most likely that these differences will be smoothed out. The longer the molecular collisions continue, the smaller the asymmetry is likely to become. And less asymmetry means higher entropy.

Irreversibility, therefore, the one-way transformation of matter so that its entropy does not decrease, is predicted by the golden theorem. Newton's laws permit individual particles to retrace exactly the path they followed through space, arriving back at their original starting point. But for a system whose elements are very numerous, the law of large numbers places it beyond the bounds of probability that all the elements will faithfully reverse their paths all at once. Just as, when a coin is flipped, an equal percentage of heads and tails becomes increasingly probable as time goes on, so also in a thermodynamic system, such as a gas, the even distribution of molecules grows increasingly probable. This likelihood moves in one direction only.

Irreversibility is not enforced by implacable necessity. We can imagine all the molecules retracing their paths without violating any of the principles of mechanics. We can also imagine a perfectly balanced penny being flipped a billion times and coming up heads each time. But these events, while possible in thought, are so unlikely to occur in actual experience that they can safely be ignored. Irreversibility is fact-like rather than law-like, in that it works well in practice but is vulnerable intellectually.

The search for certainty went on in thermodynamics, however, in the hope of banishing all traces of uncertainty. Scientists thought that if, by some ingenious means, they could follow the progress of each individual particle in a sample of gas, they would know all there was to know about the gas, directly and completely, without having to depend on the "subtleties and traps" of the large numbers law. Later it became clear that such a project was doomed to failure, and for very interesting reasons. Even if it were possible, using a supercomputer, to keep track of the behavior of each single particle, the information given by the computer would not tell us what we need to know. The significant properties of a gas include its temperature, pressure, and entropy. But these are all macroscopic, statistical properties of vast numbers of molecules. It makes no sense to speak of them as belonging to a single particle. The immense mass of data provided by the supercomputer would still need to be averaged out to obtain the macroscopic properties, and it is these properties which are the important ones from the point of view of the law of large numbers.

The origins of probability are enigmatic, and full of half-answered questions. Why was probability theory such a late starter in the mainstream of mathematics? Why did gamblers rely on guesswork and superstition for centuries, when science could have put at their disposal the means of establishing a formal theory of odds, putting mere luck on a rational footing?

Nothing worth mentioning happened in this field of knowledge until the Renaissance. The first figure of any real consequence in the history of probability theory, the Italian Gerolamo Cardano, did not appear until the sixteenth century. Cardano was a physician, algebraist, astrologer, palmist, and student of occult dreams—not exactly the sort of person to put the stamp of propriety on an infant branch of mathematics. He gambled steadily and sometimes disastrously for nearly forty years, and was an astute observer of card sharpers and their tricks. At the same time, Cardano had a mathematician's eye for the regularities underlying chance and luck. He realized that uncertainty possesses a structure, and that once one has the key to the structure, chance ceases to be an aspect of magic and becomes intelligible.

Cardano's own luck, in life as well as in cards, was from time to time abominable. At a low point in his career, he was an inmate of a Milanese poorhouse. At a high point, he was a lecturer in geometry at the University of Pavia. He was famous and respected for a decade, but lost his university post when he became embroiled in a scandal: his eldest son was executed for wife poisoning. Accident-prone, Cardano fell into a canal in Venice and was thrown from a fast-moving carriage in Bologna. He underwent ordeal by falling masonry and by mad dog. As an addicted gambler, he had runs of appalling luck, and despised himself for engaging in such a low activity, one that he classed with "architecture, lawsuits, and luxury" as a pursuit likely to bring a man to bankruptcy. Yet even this wretched vice conformed to certain abstract principles. That was part of its fascination for a mathematician of Cardano's caliber. Indeed, his successes as an algebraist far outweighed his performance at the card tables. Some of his work was genuinely original. For example, he brought negative numbers into the main body of mathematics for the first time.

Cardano stated some of the laws of chance, as he saw them, in a treatise, *Liber De Ludo Aleae,* "Handbook of Games of Chance." Written in about 1526, but not published until nearly a century and a half afterward, the book dealt with questions which were to be of considerable importance in the later history of probability. Astonishingly, Cardano had a grasp of some basic concepts, such as equally likely outcomes of a chance event, and the law of large numbers, that were not properly established for another 150 years. He knew how to add probabilities together, and was able to calculate the chances of drawing certain hands in a game called primero, an ancestral version of poker that enjoyed a great vogue in Renaissance Europe. In retrospect, it may appear that Cardano's discoveries were minor and could have been made much earlier by almost any mathematician with an interest in gambling. In fact, they were fresh and original insights, and were neglected for many years as probability made its curiously reluctant, crabwise advance. This neglect is a major enigma in the history of Western science.

Games of chance suggested the problems which started mathematicians thinking seriously about probability. Many theorists were also gamblers, of varying levels of addiction, even into the twentieth century. Émile Borel was a student of contract bridge. John von Neumann, creator of the theory of games, was a poker player. Claude Shannon is an amateur of the stock market. Lord Keynes, an important innovator in the field, knew his way around the European casinos. Once, on an impulse, he caught the night boat to Ostend with three friends after hearing that roulette was being played there without a zero.

The modern theory of probability can be said to have started in earnest in the middle of the seventeenth century, when a longstanding problem in games of dice was subjected to rigorous mathematical treatment and led to a result not in agreement with the accepted lay view of the day. Not for the first time, theory proved to be at odds with intuition. The famous event occurred in 1654, when the Chevalier de Méré, a cultivated French nobleman at the court of Louis XIV, went to Pascal with a question about gambling: Is it in the interest of a gaming establishment to bet that a player will throw at least one double six in twenty-four throws of the dice? According to venerable gambling lore, the house could afford to bet evens that any player would make at least one double six in a couple of dozen throws. De Méré

suspected that this old rule, based on common sense, was un-
sound. Pascal proved that twenty-four throws of dice is in fact a
sort of watershed. At or below that number the odds are slightly
against a double six. Above it, the odds turn favorable.

The question again arises: Why did such a seemingly elementary discovery wait so long to be made? Gambling had existed
for six thousand years before Pascal solved the Chevalier's problem. All that was needed, surely, was to synthesize a few well-
established ideas. Thinkers had long been aware of the inherent
uncertainty of the world. The Jaina philosophy of ancient India
was based on the idea of indeterminism and a range of possibilities. Indeed, some of its statements sound surprisingly congenial to modern ears. The seven categories of Jainan logic include
one or two that make the late Sam Goldwyn's "a definite maybe"
sound like the last word in finality. The categories are as follows:

Maybe it is.
Maybe it is not.
Maybe it is, it is not.
Maybe it is indeterminate.
Maybe it is and also indeterminate.
Maybe it is not and also indeterminate.
Maybe it is and it is not and also indeterminate.

The fifth category, "Maybe it is and also indeterminate," is
one which a present-day mathematician, Leonid Maĭstrov, sees
as a forerunner, a very long way ahead of its time, of the modern
concept of a probability field. Jainan logic assumes that the complexity of the world is unlimited, and that parts of it are always
changing. Nothing we say about it at a given moment is entirely
true. Like Shannon's information theory, Jainan logic treats error
as intrinsic and fundamental.

One of the most attractive explanations for the mysteriously
delayed appearance of fully developed laws of probability in
Western science has been offered by the philosopher Ian Hacking, who argues that nobody could begin to devise a formal
treatment of probability until its double aspect—its subjective-
objective, inner-outer properties—was clearly recognized.
Hacking believes that modern probability emerged from the

"low sciences" of the Renaissance—alchemy, geology, astrology, and medicine. It was only in these sciences that the necessary ideas were born, because in gathering information on which to base new knowledge of the world, exponents of the low sciences resorted to what was called the "testimony of nature." This testimony was not to be looked for in the so-called external evidence provided by experts and written down in books but in the forms of nature herself. In medieval society, external authority meant an opinion approved or accepted by intelligent people. Books were the main sources of this authority. In the early Renaissance the printed word was treated with exaggerated reverence and regarded as the fountainhead of truth. But during the Renaissance period a new approach to knowledge arose, one which moved away from excessive reliance on written authority, turning instead to the unwritten, internal evidence of nature. The concept of internal evidence was a break with tradition, and it arose for the most part in the low sciences.

The champions of internal evidence rebelled against the bookish doctrine of "approved opinion." Paracelsus, the sixteenth-century astrologer, alchemist, magus, and healer, a transition figure in the passage from the low to the high sciences, adopted as his slogan: "The patients are your textbook, the sickbed is your study." Paracelsus took the most famous book of medieval medicine, the *Canon* of Avicenna, and threw it on the fire, replacing it with the book of nature, or what is known as the "doctrine of signatures." According to this doctrine, information about nature can be found in nature, but only if she is read in the proper way. The age of a stag can be known by looking at the ends of the antlers. A certain flower has the power to rejuvenate because it blossoms in the winter, the season which is a metaphor for old age. Handwriting reveals character, as may also the lines and creases in the hand. The doctrine of signatures led to homeopathic medicine, in which like cures like. Poison in large doses causes sickness, but poison in very small doses can effect a cure. In some cases there were real, scientific reasons, unsuspected at the time, for these analogies and metaphors. In the eighteenth century, willow bark was thought to be beneficial for agues, because willow trees like wetness, and wetness causes chills and fevers. Later, it was found that willows contain chemicals called salicylates, on which modern aspirin (acetosalicylic acid) is based.

Ian Hacking argues that the new kind of testimony provided by signatures was an authority to be read, as the authority of books was to be read. Whereas the written word was thought to be infallible, however, the internal testimony of nature was not infallible although it could frequently be relied upon. It was likely rather than certain. It was the emergence of this different type of evidence, internal evidence which was often right but sometimes wrong, that set the intellectual stage for the belated arrival of probability theory, with its dual character, in the middle of the seventeenth century.

One of probability's two faces was turned in the direction of testimony. The other face looked toward the frequency of events, toward stable regularity, statistics. So the two kinds of probability, subjective and objective, were combined, thanks to the low sciences, in the concept of internal evidence. If this thesis is accepted, the rise of probability theory was delayed for a good reason. All the necessary ideas were *not* in place until the Renaissance.

Many attempts were made, in the years which followed, to separate these two aspects of probability, to make it exclusively objective, "out there in the world," or exclusively subjective, "in here in the mind." Much of the subsequent history of probability, its veering course between respectability and disrepute, its slow start and periods of stagnation, reflects the dilemma that theorists confronted when trying to make sense of probability's duality, its Janus face.

Bernoulli's theorem, as we have seen, rested on the assumption that a coin is equally likely to come up head or tail. But this is a highly elusive notion. Is a head really just as likely as a tail on each throw? Or do we only think it is equally likely? If the answer to the first question is "yes," then equal likelihood is objective and external, independent of the mind. However, if it arises from the fact that we think there is no reason why heads should not come up as often as tails, then equal likelihood is internal and abstract.

The objectivist view of probability emphasizes the material nature of chance events, their impersonal and public character. By flipping a coin for a sufficiently long period of time, and recording the frequency of heads relative to the frequency of tails, the probability of heads and tails becomes external, almost a physical property of the coin. The result of all these repeated trials is a set of statistics which stands on its own, whatever the observer's knowledge, making it possible to predict the probability of subsequent trials.

During the nineteenth century this relative-frequency interpretation emerged as an alternative to the classical theory, which had not externalized probabilities to such an extent and therefore seemed more ambiguous. The full flowering of this later approach to probability came in the twentieth century, in the work of Richard von Mises, who left Germany during the Hitler period and taught aerodynamics and applied mathematics at Harvard. Von Mises took it for granted that probabilities come into existence only as a result of experience, of experiment. The probability of throwing a double six with a pair of dice cannot be defined until the dice have been thrown repeatedly. One cannot speak of the probability of a single event. There must be many events. The experiment must go on and on until there is sufficient reason to believe that the relative frequency—say the percentage of heads—would approach a fixed limit if the experiment were continued indefinitely. The value of this limit is the probability.

The weakness of the von Mises approach is that an infinite series of trials is impossible in practice, and he does not specify how long a series ought to be. There is a difference between the abstract, mathematical theory and its actual use in real situations. And by saying that the series continues until there are good reasons to suppose that it will approach a certain limiting value after an infinite number of trials, von Mises allowed subjectivity to enter, surreptitiously, by the back door.

The von Mises interpretation deals with events which can be repeated indefinitely. But what about events which can be observed only a few times? What is the likelihood that a particular man and a particular woman will make a success of their marriage? Will a new author's first novel be a best seller? These are questions whose probability cannot be established by repeated trials. They seem to require a subjective interpretation of probability, one in which there is not enough evidence for near-certainty, but enough to permit a reasonably good conclusion. The English mathematician I. J. Good has defined such a subjective probability as "a degree of belief that belongs to a body of beliefs, from which the worst inconsistencies have been removed by means of detached judgements."

The subjectivist interpretation is exemplified in the work of Lord Keynes, whose A Treatise on Probability was written in 1911 but not published until 1921. Lord Keynes set out to do for probability theory what Bertrand Russell and Alfred North Whitehead had tried to do for mathematics in Principia Mathematica, namely, to deduce it logically from a small number of basic premises. Keynes held that every proposition has a certain probability, and that this probability is represented by the degree of belief that a rational person, using all the evidence available, attaches to the proposition. There is no essential difference between probability and credibility, in this view. A given amount of evidence results in a degree of belief in a statement, and there is a logical relation between the evidence and the statement. This is called the probability relation. While more general than the von Mises interpretation, the Keynes method is also unsatisfactory because "rational belief" is a quantity not easy to measure.

In the past few years, a different approach to probability has been emerging, one which avoids, to a large extent, the philosophical quagmire into which pure subjectivists and pure objectivists have often tumbled. This newer interpretation begins with the premise that a theory of probability is simply a method of encoding partial knowledge. In other words, it encodes "missing information."

According to this view, probability, which is at the root of information theory, is inextricably connected with the amount and type of knowledge we possess about any given event or series of events whose outcome is uncertain. Serious difficulties arise when scientists try to separate the idea of probability from the idea of information, because the first cannot be defined without the help of the second. In Shannon's theory, entropy is a probability distribution, assigning various probabilities to a set of possible messages. But entropy is also a measure of what the person receiving a message does *not* know about it before it arrives. Entropy is an index of his uncertainty as to what to expect. If the entropy is a maximum, that is to say, if all the possible messages are equally probable, then his ignorance is also a maximum. The receiver knows the range of possible messages, just as a roulette player knows the number of possible outcomes of a given spin of the wheel, because he is already in possession of a certain amount of prior information about the general properties of the message system itself: its alphabet of symbols, the dictionary of words, the rules or grammar for combining these in various ways. Such knowledge means that certain arrangements of symbols and words are more probable than others.

Suppose the "message source" is a professor giving a lecture on economics, and the receivers of the professor's messages are three students sitting in the audience. The first of these students is Japanese, and understands no English. Since the lecture is in English, his uncertainty is as great as it could possibly be. For him, the messages are all equally unpredictable; none of them makes any sense. They are indistinguishable from noise. The second student knows the English language, but is completely ignorant of economics. In his case, not every word the professor speaks will come as a total surprise. Because of the structure of the language, certain words and sequences of words are more likely to occur than others. The third student, an English speaker with a thorough knowledge of economics, has even less uncertainty. In many cases, he can guess what phrases or even sentences the professor is about to speak, on the evidence of what the professor has just spoken. This third student's pre-existing knowledge makes the messages more probable, less surprising.

Since the whole purpose of communication is to send messages which are not fully predictable, it must share certain properties in common with any process whose outcome is uncertain, whether it be a roulette wheel, a presidential election, or the running of the Kentucky Derby. We know enough to be able to assign probabilities to possible outcomes, and these probabilities should reflect everything we know in advance of the actual outcome. The betting odds on a horse running in the Derby are determined by information, however incomplete, available to the bookmakers. Myron Tribus, of MIT, puts it this way:

> Any theory of probability is concerned with taking information and encoding it in such a way that it enables us to act on the information without presuming more than we know, or failing to use all that we know. It gives us a way of talking about things of which we do not have complete information.
>
> Probability is essentially the assigning of a numerical value to each possible event, a number which represents knowledge. But that knowledge may be different for different people. We invent certain kinds of situation in which everyone has the same information: cards, dice, coins. The mistake lies in trying to reduce all uncertain processes to this category. The task of a theory of probability is to find a way of encoding different kinds of knowledge, assigning probabilities to them, in just the right way. And that is also the task of a theory of information. For example, if the person I am talking to knows a great deal about science, I can tell him facts more easily. I use fewer words. For a person who knows very little, I would have to say more. My code will not be the same as your code if I know more than you do.

The fruitless debate over subjective versus objective interpretations of probability, Tribus says, is "a snare and a delusion." It is made obsolete by an understanding of the deep relationship which exists between probability and information. This understanding has come in large part out of Shannon's work, even though Shannon himself adopted a relative-frequency approach.

———————

Any assignment of probabilities must reflect the uncertainty of the observer, and be "maximally vague" about that uncertainty. But it must also make full allowance for the information already in the mind of the observer. Tribus has given me a beautiful example of a message encoded in a way which enabled him to predict its full information content on the basis of knowledge already in his possession, but not in the possession of another person who read the same message. One day, a Western Union operator telephoned with a cable from Tribus's daughter, who was traveling in Europe. The cable had been sent from Paris. The operator read the message over the telephone as follows:

PLEASE SEND ME FIFTY DOLLARS AMERICAN EXPRESS
NICE LETTER OF EXPLANATION FOLLOWS LOVE LOU.

This message presented no problem to Mrs. Tribus, although the word "nice" was a little strange, a little improbable. It seemed a straightforward request for money to be sent to Paris. To Tribus himself, however, it looked wrong. He knew that there were three American Express offices in Paris, and the cable should have specified which one. It should have contained more information. Then he realized that "nice" was not an adjective describing the expected letter, but the name of a town on the French Riviera. The code of the message was not the correct one for someone who did not know that there are three American Express offices in Paris. It did not enable such a person to predict, on the basis of probability, that the word "nice" should really have been "Nice." For Tribus, the message encoded neither more nor less than he knew. Because of his prior information, Nice was more probable than nice in the context of the whole message.

So probability measures both knowledge and ignorance, just as Shannon's entropy does. The physicist Edwin Jaynes believes that, for this reason, we are on the threshold of some quite new approach to the interpretation of probability, entropy, and information, one that will be more general than anything that has gone before. It was an accident of history, Jaynes believes, that thermodynamics was connected for so long in people's minds with matter and with physical particles obeying the laws of mechanics. Although Boltzmann interpreted the second law of thermodynamics in terms of pure probability, this fact was not fully recognized for almost a hundred years. Now the entropy principle is seen as a special case of a more general method of reasoning which does not depend on the laws of physics or mechanics at all.

In the same way, it was a historical accident that information was connected with thermodynamics. Eventually, Jaynes thinks, that connection will be broken. The concepts of information and entropy will converge, leading to a wider, all-embracing theory. They will stand revealed as just a special case of the broader concepts James Bernoulli wrote about in the eighteenth century. Jaynes believes that

> We are coming round to see that Bernoulli's book, *The Art of Conjecture*, had exactly the right title. Because that's just what we are doing, even though we give it fancy names like "estimates," or "significance tests." We are conjecturing, on the basis of what we know and do not know, of information we have or do not have. And this interpretation will make the subject much more intelligible to the layman, because this is how he has seen probability all along.

5

Not Too Dull, Not Too Exciting

Shannon had done some work on secret codes during the Second World War, and the experience helped him to clarify his ideas about a new theory of information. In particular, it suggested new approaches to the problem of how to separate messages from noise, or order from disorder, in a communications system.

This is a more interesting, less parochial issue than may appear at first sight, because communication is not confined to radios, telephones, and television channels. It occurs in nature, wherever life exists. The genes are a system for sending chemical messages to the protein factories of the cell, instructing them to make a living organism. The human being is the most complex communications network on earth, and language is a code which preserves the orderly structure of the messages of speech in ways so ingenious that they are still not fully understood. The problem is so general that asking how messages and noise are kept separate in information theory is equivalent to the question which arose in connection with the second law of thermodynamics: "Why is the world full of the most improbable kinds of order, when the most probable state for the universe to be in is one of pure chaos?"

Messages are immersed in noise, because noise is disorder,

and it is an axiom of classical thermodynamics that disorder is easier and more permanent than order, which is difficult and temporary. Noise always tends to add itself to messages, randomizing and distorting them, making them less reliable. Some way must be found—and nature evidently has succeeded in finding such a way—whereby this tendency can be resisted, or at least reduced, so that the sequences of symbols sent by the message source reach their destination more or less in the original form.

In nearly all forms of communication, more messages are sent than are strictly necessary to convey the information intended by the sender. Such additional messages diminish the unexpectedness, the surprise effect, of the information itself, making it more predictable. This extra ration of predictability is called redundancy, and it is one of the most important concepts in information theory. Redundancy is essentially a constraint. It limits the value of W in the entropy equation $S = k \log W$, reducing the number of ways in which the various parts of a system can be arranged.

A message conveys no information unless some prior uncertainty exists in the mind of the receiver about what the message will contain. And the greater the uncertainty, the larger the amount of information conveyed when that uncertainty is resolved. Herein lies the profound relationship between information and probability. When a roulette wheel is spun, uncertainty is created, and the uncertainty continues until the instant when the ball comes to rest in one slot or another. At that moment, the uncertainty is resolved. It becomes information. Now consider information of a different kind. A page of English text also creates and resolves uncertainty, but the uncertainty is not the same as in games of chance. To begin with, there is less of it. Under normal circumstances, the roulette player cannot predict the outcome of the next spin of the wheel. A reader of English prose, on the other hand, is not in such a state of innocence. He may be able to predict the next letters or words in a sentence on the basis of what he has already seen. Given half a word, he can often predict the other half, or make a reasonable guess at it. The reason for this is that language, unlike coins and roulette wheels, is not a system in which all outcomes are equally probable.

A written message is never completely unpredictable. If it

were, it would be nonsense. Indeed, it would be noise. To be understandable, to convey meaning, it must conform to rules of spelling, structure, and sense, and these rules, known in advance as information shared between the writer and the reader, reduce uncertainty. They make the message partly predictable, compelling it to carry extra luggage in the form of superfluous symbols. Rules are a form of redundancy, and they are responsible for making the messages of language different from the "messages" conveyed by the ball coming to rest in a roulette wheel. The roulette messages, as we have seen, are all equally probable. However, the rules of language make certain letters and groups of letters, and even certain sequences of words, more probable than others, and therefore more predictable.

In nearly every passage of English prose there are words which could be deleted without preventing the reader from understanding what the author intends to say. And many words would still be intelligible if one or more of their letters were eliminated. In newspaper classified advertisements, for example, words and letters may be dropped from a sentence so as to squeeze the largest amount of information into the smallest space, yet still allow the sentence to perform its function of sending a message to the reader. A message like

lge liv rm, 2BR, basmt

conveys all the sense of a much longer sentence, provided it is printed in exactly that form.

In English, as in other languages, the redundancy is of more than one kind. One type of redundancy consists of rules of spelling, and the effect of such rules is that certain letters appear more often than other letters over a fairly long stretch of text. The letter e, for example, appears very often in English text, more than three times as often as it would if sentences were constructed by stringing letters together at random. This unequal probability in the average use of different letters was recognized by Samuel Morse when he devised his Morse code. Morse was an important precursor of Shannon and Wiener, in that he was aware of the statistical regularities of English, the consistent patterns by which some letters appear often and others less often. That is why he assigned very short sequences of dots and dashes to the commonly used letters of the alphabet, making it easier and quicker to transmit them in his code, and longer sequences to the letters which are relatively uncommon. He coded the letter e, for example, in the briefest possible way, representing it by a single dot.

A second type of redundancy arises from the fact that the probability of a certain letter occurring in a word depends, to a greater or lesser degree, on the letter or letters which precede it. An example of such a rule is "i before e except after c." Often, it is very easy to predict the letter which will follow a given sequence of letters. The letters th . . . are very likely, but not absolutely certain, to be succeeded by a vowel. And in any English text, if q is printed, probability approaches certainty that it will be followed by a u.

Both types of redundancy are restrictions on the freedom of the language to be perfectly arbitrary or random, but the second type leaves it freer than the first does. The difference between these two methods of constraining choice has what scientists call "nontrivial" consequences. Its full importance will be seen when we come to consider the information system of the genes.

―――――――

Shannon tried several ways of estimating the amount of redundancy in English text. He used his knowledge of secret codes to compress a passage of prose, squeezing all the surplus predictability out of it. He composed sentences of pure gibberish by typing sequences of letters completely at random and then progressively programming in rules of redundancy, so that the statistics of the sequence resembled the statistics of English prose more and more closely.

He also played various games, in which a book was opened at random and the first letter of a sentence read aloud. Players of the game would then be asked to guess the next letter and the next, to the end of the sentence. If a player made a wrong guess, he would be given the correct letter as a cue, and then be asked to continue guessing. Here is the result of one such game. A line underneath a letter or letters in the sentence indicates that the player guessed correctly. Where the letter is duplicated on the second line, the player made a wrong guess and had to be corrected.

THE ROOM WAS NOT VERY LIGHT A SMALL OBLONG
- - --ROO - - - - --NOT-V- - - --I - - - - --SM - - --OBL- - -

READING LAMP ON THE DESK SHED GLOW ON
REA - - - - -- - - --O - - - - - --D- - - -SHED-GLO - -O -

POLISHED WOOD BUT LESS ON THE SHABBY RED CARPET.
P - L-S - - - - - O - --BU --L- S--O - - - - --SH - - - -RE --C - - - - -.

There are 103 letters in the full sentence but the player needed
to be told only 40 of them. Given these cues, he was able to
predict the rest of the sentence in its entirety. In other words, 63
of the letters were redundant, from the player's point of view,
because they were predictable given a knowledge of the rules of
spelling, structure, and sense.

Shannon decided that English is about 50 percent redundant
when we consider samples of eight letters at a time. If the length
of the sample is increased, the redundancy is much greater.
For sequences of up to 100 letters it rises to approximately 75
percent. The figure is even higher in the case of whole
pages or chapters, where the reader is able to get an idea of
the long-range statistics of a text, including its theme and literary style. This means, Shannon said, that much of what we
write is dictated by the structure of the language and is more
or less forced upon us. Only what little is left is of our own
free choosing.

Just how severely a writer's freedom of choice is restricted
may vary from one author to another. James Joyce extended his
freedom by throwing overboard some of the rules of language in
an exuberant search for novelty. In *Finnegans Wake*, he allowed
himself a much wider variety of possible messages than, say,
Jane Austen, who observed the rules more scrupulously. Letters
and words are not easy to predict in a passage like

> The howsayto itishwatis hemust whomust worden schall. A dark-
> tongues, kunning. O theoperil! Ethinop lore, the poor lie. He askit of
> the hoothed fireshield but it was untergone into the matthued heaven.

A great deal of uncertainty has been created.

Here a most important point arises. In the lines above, from

Finnegans Wake, it is hard to guess what comes next. It is also difficult to detect misprints and errors. The passage is less reliable, for that reason, than a passage from Jane Austen. We do not trust its accuracy so much. Joyce shares this unreliability with the philosopher Alfred North Whitehead, whose books are full of idiosyncratic, newly minted words and phrases. Once he had finished a manuscript, Whitehead washed his hands of it. He refused to see it through the editing and publishing process, considering all that a waste of his valuable time. The result was that his books were riddled with mistakes undetectable by anyone but an expert. Even after many years had passed, allowing ample opportunity for the correction of printer's errors, a group of Whitehead scholars found more than 200 inaccuracies in *Process and Reality,* one of Whitehead's major works, and still others have come to light since.

Redundancy reduces error by making certain letters and groups of letters more probable, increasing predictability. Words usually contain more letters than are strictly necessary for understanding. In fact, it is possible to test the unpredictability of a sequence of symbols by trying to compress them, expressing them more compactly. If the sequence cannot be compressed, it is perfectly unpredictable. If it can be compressed, it contains some redundancy. However, compression destroys the built-in safeguards against error found in all languages.

The recently fashionable arguments in favor of "Black English" in the United States are based in part on the premise that ordinary English prose can be compressed and still retain its information content. Professor William Lasher has given some examples of Black English in which redundancy has been reduced. Among these are the sentences "We was at the ball game last night" and "Mary had five card." Lasher argues that in the first sentence the speaker had decided that the distinction between "was" and "were" is not essential, since it is clear from the context that the verb is plural, and a plural noun with a plural verb is redundant. In the second sentence, the speaker drops the final "s" on the word "card," since the use of the word "five" has already told us that there was more than one card. Lasher sees this as a logical attempt to simplify language. On the other side of the debate, John Simon, an acerbic guardian of the integrity of the English tongue, complained that by violating the rules in this way, we are asking for confusion. "Five does indeed indicate plurality, but the final 's' confirms it," Simon commented. "After all, the speaker may have said 'a fine card,' and it is the final 's' that ensures that we have not misheard him."

There is yet another aspect of redundancy which is of great interest. This is the role it plays in enabling systems, both biological organisms and artificial intelligence machines, to become complex. Thanks to the work of mathematicians and engineers in recent years, ideas about the nature of complexity have undergone a change. Complexity is such an important concept, and its properties so unexpected, that it deserves a chapter to itself. In the meantime, it is sufficient to note this central fact: redundancy makes complexity possible. John von Neumann pointed this out in his papers on the computer, papers which are full of insights into the nature of information processes that others developed after his death. Von Neumann recognized that the structure of living organisms and of machines is dictated to a great extent by the way in which they fail and become unreliable. Failure, von Neumann said, must not be thought of as an aberration, but as an essential, independent part of the logic of complex systems. The more complex the system, the more likely it is that one of its parts will malfunction. Redundancy is a means of keeping the system running in the presence of malfunction. Redundancy, von Neumann declared,

> is the only thing which makes it possible to write a text which is longer than, say, ten pages. In other words, a language which has maximum compression would actually be completely unsuited to conveying information beyond a certain degree of complexity, because you could never find out whether a text is right or wrong. And this is a question of principle. It follows, therefore, that the complexity of the medium in which you work has something to do with redundancy.

Shannon himself has told me that he believes the most promising new developments in information theory will come from work on very complex machines, especially from research into artificial intelligence.

Redundancy makes probabilities unequal, instead of smoothing them out evenly across the whole range of possibilities. It means that the parts of a system are not wholly independent of one another, but are linked statistically, in a pattern of possibilities. Redundancy in a message system holds information in a loose balance between total constraint and total freedom. As Fran Lebowitz, the New York essayist, once remarked of communism and fascism: "The first is too dull, the second too exciting."

But while redundancy constrains, it also may lead to great complexity within the constraints. Rules, which are a form of redundancy, generate enormous richness of expression in language. They also seem to be connected, in a most unexpected way, with creative freedom and the heights of artistic expression in many fields. In a 1980 interview, the violinist Isaac Stern talked about the relationship between constraints and the ability to produce great music:

> People very rarely realize the real happening in the arts comes out of the most enormous discipline, because when you've disciplined yourself thoroughly, you know what is possible. That's when you let your imagination move, because you know that by discipline and study and thought you've created the limits . . .
>
> When you're really disciplined, and you know what the possibilities are beyond which you don't dare go because of taste and knowledge, that's when something really begins to happen, when you throw away all the rigidities and simply make music.

6

The Struggle Against Randomness

Shannon chose as his unit of information the binary digit, or bit. A bit is a measure of amount of information, just as a gallon, an ounce, and an inch measure volume, weight, and length. One bit is simply a choice between two equally probable messages. It is a "yes" or "no" answer to the hypothetical question: "Is it this one?" The answer "yes" resolves all uncertainty in the mind of the person receiving the message, because he knows which of the two possible messages is the actual one. The answer "no" also resolves his uncertainty, because he knows the actual message is not the first, but the second alternative.

This is a highly versatile code, because it needs only two symbols,

1 for "yes"
0 for "no"

A 1 could be sent along a radio or telegraph channel as an electrical impulse, a 0 as no impulse. Or they could be represented by a switch in an on or an off position. If it is just as likely to be raining as not raining, only one question needs to be asked: "Is it raining?" The transmission of a 1 or a 0 will supply the answer. The same is true in the case of a choice between head and tail when a penny is tossed, or between red and black or odd and even in roulette (assuming there is no zero). The transmission of one binary digit gives complete information about the state of the various systems.

If there are more than two possibilities from which to choose, more bits are needed to resolve the uncertainty about which has actually been chosen.

Suppose there are not two, but four alternatives for the outcome of a spin of the wheel: red and even, black and even, red and odd, black and odd. Now the uncertainty is measured by two binary digits instead of one, since two questions must be asked, each halving the uncertainty. These questions are, "Is it either red and even or black and even?"

If the answer is 0, or "no," the next question becomes, "Is it red and odd?" If the answer is still "no," then all uncertainty is resolved, because we know the actual outcome was the fourth possibility, black and odd. Thus, doubling the number of possible messages increases the uncertainty by one question to which there is a "yes" or "no" answer. In other words, by one bit.

The procedure is less simple, however, when all the possibilities are not equally probable, and the system contains some redundancy. If a penny is tossed repeatedly, information about the outcome of each toss can be encoded as a string of bits, each one resolving uncertainty about the result of each toss, because heads and tails are assumed to be equally probable. But when the message is a sentence of English prose, quite a different situation arises, because each letter in the sentence is not equally probable. Certain letters or clusters of letters which occur infrequently—which are "improbable"—require a larger number of bits, or yes-or-no answers, to encode them. The often-used pair of letters th can be coded into only two bits, while a seldom used pair like lc would need seven or eight times as many. The reason for this is that the probable takes up more "space" in the spectrum of possibilities than the rare.

Suppose a fat man is seated on the left half of a park bench and two thin men are sitting on the right half. Only one question needs to be asked about the fat man: "Is he sitting on the right half of the bench?" The answer "no," encoded as a 0, resolves all the uncertainty. However, the uncertainty as to the whereabouts of one thin man can be resolved only by asking two questions. To the first question, "Is he sitting on the right half of the bench?" the answer would be "yes," encoded as a 1. But a second question must follow: "Is he sitting on the left half of the right half?" Only when this question has been answered with a "yes" or a "no" has all the uncertainty been resolved. The fat man, being more "probable," is encoded into one bit, 0, but each thin man, being less probable, is encoded into two bits, 1–0 or 1–1.

This simple procedure can be elaborated to quite sophisticated levels. In the transmission of television programs, for example, a problem in which Shannon was keenly interested, many of the tiny dots which make up the picture on the screen do not change for quite long stretches of time, even though other parts of the picture change. The unchanging dots are more probable, and can be coded in a shorter, simpler form than the less predictable dots, which do change a great deal.

One of the most important questions Shannon set out to answer was whether a message, coded into strings of binary digits which reflect its partly predictable, partly unpredictable character, can be sent along a channel without having its order thrown into disorder by noise. His wartime work in military ciphers gave him some insight into this problem, because in a secret code, the key to the code is added onto the message, rather in the same fashion as noise is added onto a message in ordinary communications. In the first case the addition is useful, in the second case a nuisance. To decipher a secret military message, one must separate the key from the message, and the idea is to design a code which makes that a very difficult task for the enemy to accomplish. A code for normal, peacetime radio broadcasts, on the other hand, aims at exactly the opposite goal. That code must be designed so as to make it as *easy* as possible to disentangle the message from the noise.

It was Shannon's achievement, in his 1948 papers, to show that in any type of communications system, a message can be sent from one place to another even under noisy conditions, and be as free from error as we care to make it, as long as it is coded in the proper way. Nature does impose a limit, but the limit is in the form of the capacity of the communications channel. As long as the channel is not overloaded, then the code guarantees as high a degree of accuracy as we choose. Shannon proved that such codes must exist in the most famous of all his theorems, which deals with a noisy channel. It is usually known simply as Shannon's second theorem, and was one of the major intellectual discoveries of the time, because it seemed to run counter to common sense. By showing that reliable information is possible in an unreliable world, the second theorem had the status of a universal principle, because "information," as defined in the new way, is universal. It is an aspect of life itself, not merely of communications engineering.

Error-correcting codes may need to be extraordinarily ingenious, but, in principle, they can insure perfection in the midst of imperfection, order in the face of disorder, by adding redundancy of exactly the right kind. A very simple form of code is used when a clerk writes down the number of words in a telegram at the end of a message. When the cable reaches its destination, a rough test can be made to see if any words have been lost in transit. A self-healing code is a more advanced form of redundancy. It is able to correct errors without having to go back to the source for more information, as in the case of the telegram. If a message encoded into binary digits, 0's and 1's, is sent along a channel, it is possible to control the amount of errors in the message by adding an extra digit to the end of each string, as a sort of brief description of the string. A 0 added to a string, for example, might mean that if all the digits in the string are added up, they come to an even number. A 1 would mean that they come to an odd number. If the total is odd when the code says it is even, an error has been detected. A more complex version of this idea enables errors to be traced to individual digits by various forms of cross-checking. Once a digit is shown to be wrong, it is the easiest thing in the world to put the mistake right. Since a digit can only be in one of two states, either 0 or 1, if one state is incorrect, the other must be correct. The message is then self-healing.

At first sight, it might seem that in order to have superreliable communication under very noisy conditions, so many redundant bits would need to be added to the message that there would not be time to transmit them all. However, this is not the case. There is a way of coding messages so that they can be sent both rapidly and accurately. In fact, the second theorem guarantees that information can be transmitted over a noisy channel at the fastest rate permitted by the capacity of the channel, and still contain as few errors as we wish.

Some of the most elaborate codes, which evolved out of Shannon's work, were devised for the U.S. space program, where scientists were faced with the problem of recovering very distant, very weak signals from beyond the earth's atmosphere. In 1962, when the program was in its infancy, only about 2,000 bits per second could be transmitted. Today such a message can be sent at far faster speeds. So advanced is the technique, in fact, that a rate of 500 million bits per second, or half a "gigabit" (a gigabit is one billion bits per second), will probably be attained within five years.

The redundancy of these especially complex codes is large, but not unmanageably so. For the Voyager II mission, which in 1981 sent pictures of the rings of Saturn back to earth, the redundancy was 100 percent; in other words, one redundant bit was sent for every bit which conveyed information. The rate of error in the Voyager II code was one in 10,000 bits. The space telescope, due to be launched into earth orbit early in 1985, uses a code in which there are three redundant bits for every information bit. The reason why unusually high redundancy is needed for the space telescope's transmitter is that it is designed to gather and report information about such phenomena as galactic temperature and background radiation, information which itself contains a large amount of randomness, and therefore uncertainty. Ultimately, these relatively high levels of redundancy are necessary because space vehicles are too small to carry large, powerful transmitters. Thus their signals are weak and prone to disruption by noise. Coding requirements for the radio link from ground control, which can send as powerful signals as desired, to the space vehicle, are much less stringent. Here a redundancy of only 14 percent is sufficient for accuracy.

Shannon proved that an ideal code exists which can give as much accuracy as we like within the constraints of the channel capacity. He did not actually describe this code, which has been called the Holy Grail of information theory, but he showed that even if the ideal code is too complicated and expensive for practical use, it represents a perfect limit which engineers may approach as closely as they wish. If a certain code permits one wrong digit in ten million, it is always possible to find another code which gives one error in twenty million, by adding redundancy in the right way. When engineers find that the messages they send are slow and unreliable, they know they cannot blame nature for this poor performance. They must blame themselves, for not devising a sufficiently ingenious code.

The second theorem proves that the price of safeguarding the integrity of information is not so restrictive that it prevents a wide variety of messages from being sent. If the only way of adding redundancy were to repeat the same sequence of digits over and over again, very few messages could be sent. Carried to the extreme, the redundant bits would swamp the information bits. To obtain infinitely few errors in this way, the sender would have to repeat the same message an infinite number of times. The result would be perfect monotony, whereas the whole purpose of communicating is to transmit many different messages. There must be some constraints, but there also must be some freedom.

The second theorem permits variety and accuracy to coexist. It enables novelty to flourish and yet be reliable novelty. The question scientists are now asking is whether nature herself has designed similar, redundant codes to protect the reliability of living forms. Evolution has produced an immense amount of variety. It is an "inventive" process. On the other hand, there is also a large amount of underlying uniformity in the animal kingdom. There are limits on the amount of variety natural selection permits. Lila L. Gatlin, an American biophysicist, has suggested that the big breakthroughs in evolution, the moments at which really promising creatures emerged from primitive forms, were also the moments when the message system of the genes combined an optimum amount of variety with an optimum amount of error control. Gatlin calls this process "second-theorem evolution," in acknowledgment of Shannon's most elegant and profound discovery.

PART TWO

Nature as an Information Process

7

Arrows in All Directions

The "arrow of time" is a metaphor invented by Sir Arthur Eddington to express the idea that there exists a purely physical distinction between past and future, independent of consciousness. Such a distinction is based on the entropy principle, which asserts that as time goes on energy tends to be transformed from an orderly into a less orderly form. In Eddington's view, earlier is different from later because earlier energy is more highly organized. There is no need to appeal to our intellectual sense of the passing of time to explain why *now* is not the same as *then*. It is all a question of degree of organization. If there is more and more randomness along the path of the arrow, it points toward the future. If there is less and less randomness, it points toward the past. Unlike space, which has no preferred direction, time is asymmetrical, always moving forward, never backward, and it behaves in this fashion whether human beings are there to experience it or not. Time's arrow is irreversible, because entropy cannot decrease of its own accord without violating the second law of thermodynamics. A reversible arrow would be like a movie run backward. The scenes in the movie are not impossible by the laws of classical mechanics, but they are patently absurd. Only the one-wayness of physical time, from more to less organization, Eddington said, insures that the world makes sense.

However, ordinary common sense tells us that something is wrong here. If time's arrow follows the path of increasing randomness, it wipes out information. Yet history is not a record of things unraveling, descending into chaos, but of new types of order and a richer store of information. As it moves through centuries and millennia, history is a chronicle of novelty—new structures, new organisms, new civilizations, new ideas. Information, which is a measure of novelty, increases rather than diminishes with the passage of the years.

David Layzer, a Harvard astronomer, has recently presented a theory which suggests a universe starting from simplicity, but growing more complex and richer in information as time goes on. At each successive moment of its history, there is something in it that is entirely new. Here Layzer is speaking, not just about the planet earth, with its wealth of living forms, but about the cosmos as a whole.

There is certainly a paradox here if, as Eddington claims, the arrow of time is supposed to point in the direction of increasing entropy and disorder. For, as new and highly detailed accounts of the birth of the universe, split second by split second, show, time might just as well be said to flow in the direction of *greater* order and complexity. A second paradox arises from the fact that underneath the surface of matter, in the microcosm of particles and forces, the fundamental processes of physics, with one very minor exception, are reversible. The backward-running movie may be nonsensical, but the events it portrays do not violate these microscopic physical laws, which are very nearly time-symmetric. They breach only the statistical, "fact-like" assumptions that follow from the entropy principle.

Layzer looks for a way out of these paradoxes by proposing not one, but three arrows of time. One of these is the arrow of cosmic expansion, pointing away from the initial state of the universe, a state which was infinitely condensed and uniform. The second is the arrow of history, defined by all the rich, evolving structures of galaxies, stars, planets, life, civilization, and mind. The third is the thermodynamic arrow, the arrow of increasing entropy, which is generated by the unraveling of macroscopic structures.

In Layzer's theory, the arrow of history points irreversibly in the direction of increasing complexity, increasing information. Unlike some contemporary astronomers, Layzer does not believe that the universe began in a state of disequilibrium and is running down into a state of equilibrium, or maximum entropy. In his view, there was no need for the universe, at its birth, to have any structure whatever. If the big-bang theory of cosmic genesis is correct, the universe could have started out totally devoid of information, both on the very small scale of its microscopic particles and on the large, macroscopic scale of its visible appearance. Uniform disorder prevailed at the beginning. Information, regarded as a measure of the nonuniform, orderly properties of physical systems, evolved out of that initial state of perfect confusion.

Cosmic expansion was the reason why the infant universe departed from a state of maximum entropy. As long as the processes which randomized the distribution of energy and the concentrations of various types of particles were very fast, faster than the rate at which the cosmos was expanding, equilibrium could be maintained. Bits of atoms smashed into one another in the confusion of that very dense undifferentiated state with such frequency that no structures could arise. But this state of affairs lasted only for a brief fraction of a microsecond. The speed of the cosmic expansion was not constant, and once it became greater than the speed at which the forces of disorder could degrade information by collisions, chemical equilibrium was broken. As encounters between particles became less frequent, due to the greater distances between them, the equal distribution of different kinds of particles could not be maintained.

Thus the chemical composition of the universe changed from a state of equilibrium to one of disequilibrium as the expansion proceeded, and this change was to have momentous consequences. For it is the chemical disequilibrium of the sun that is the source of free energy on which all life on earth depends. If the cosmos had expanded at a slower speed than was in fact the case, all the matter in it would have become pure ash, as if a coal fire burned away every scrap of its fuel with complete efficiency. However, because the forces of equilibrium did not keep pace with the expansion, the universe could not consume all its fuel, thereby enabling long-burning stars like our own sun to evolve, and ultimately the kingdoms of animal and vegetable life. So the cosmic expansion created a set of initial conditions that made possible two quite different kinds of order-generating processes: cosmic evolution and biological evolution. The direction of this latter process is also irreversibly away from uniformity and toward new forms of structure and greater complexity. It traces a path in time that is described by the arrow of history. Along this path, too, points the thermodynamic arrow, because entropy arises naturally as a result of the very processes which give rise to living systems and drive the engine of human civilization, with its increasing dependence on the energy-degrading machines of modern technology. But the arrow of history and the thermodynamic arrow are complementary, not in conflict. One is not more natural or more fundamental than the other. The view Layzer challenges is the one that says the growth of entropy is a necessary feature of the world, while the growth of order is somehow an accident. This is not the case. Both follow logically from events which took place at the first instant after the big bang.

Entropy is missing information, as Boltzmann observed more than a hundred years ago. Where, then, does information go when it disappears? In closed systems, missing information on the large scale of the macrocosm is converted into increasing information on the small scale of the microcosm. An analogy may be helpful here. Suppose we have a pack of playing cards, in which the four suits, hearts, clubs, diamonds, and spades, are in their original order in the pack, but each suit has been shuffled. A player has no way of knowing exactly where, say, the ace of hearts is, although he knows for certain that it is somewhere in the top fourth of the pack. Then imagine that the whole deck is divided up into four stacks of cards. These four stacks are cut in half, and in half again and again, forming smaller and smaller stacks until all fifty-two cards are spread out face down on the table. At this stage, macroscopic information about the state of the pack as a whole has disappeared completely. Microscopic information about individual cards is all that remains, and to obtain this information the cards must be turned face up, one by one.

Macroscopic information, Layzer argues, decays into microscopic information, as in the example of the pack of cards cut into smaller and smaller stacks, so that in principle the total amount of it remains constant. What is "uniform" on the large scale may be highly nonuniform on the small scale. But in the real world, this second kind of information is not preserved, because of the mixing processes at work in the universe. It is dissipated and jumbled up through indiscriminate buffeting by stray, random particles and forces outside the system. Entropy increases, and information vanishes.

Maxwell's demon can obtain perfect information about all the molecules in the whirling microcosm of his vessel of gas, but only because he is an ideal, mythical being. His chamber is immaculately sealed against all kinds of chance impacts and influences from the outside world. The demon inhabits a perfectly closed system, but no such system exists in the real world, where, for example, the effects of a nonlocal force such as gravity must be taken into account. It has been estimated that the microscopic state of a gas in a laboratory would be altered significantly in a fraction of a second if a single gram of matter as far away as Sirius, the dog star, were to be moved a distance of only one centimeter. If a nonmythical scientist wanted to have complete information about the exact behavior of all microscopic particles in an enclosed volume of gas at a given instant, so as to predict how they would behave at some instant in the future, he would need to know about the disturbing influences surrounding the chamber. Then he would need to know about the influences disturbing those influences, spreading his net of inquiry wider and wider until it became necessary to be informed in the minutest detail about every particle and force in the universe.

This stupendous task of description, ridiculously ambitious for ordinary mortals, might be undertaken by some cosmic Maxwell's demon, some fantastic universal intellect along the lines suggested by the Marquis Laplace in the eighteenth century, a period when there seemed no bounds to knowledge. Laplace supposed that a vast mind, which could know, without breaking any of the laws of physics, all there is to know about the behavior of every particle in the universe, would be able to describe the whole history of the cosmos from the first day to the last:

"Nothing would be uncertain and the future, as the past, could be present to its eyes."

———————

Today, Layzer's very radical conclusion is that, even for a Laplacean superintelligence, total information about the whole universe on the scale of its individual molecules is impossible. Here he is not speaking of the uncertainty of quantum mechanics alone, but also of certain irremovable restrictions on the kinds of knowledge that can be specified about the universe. These restrictions are due to a cosmic symmetry principle which occupies a place of central importance in his theory.

It is true that the microcosm of a bounded, finite physical system can be described completely with a finite amount of information. However, it turns out that the universe itself has certain unexpected properties, setting it apart from the smaller, local systems it contains. For one thing, the universe is assumed to be unbounded, although it is still an open question in science as to whether it is finite or infinite. Another unusual feature of the universe, unlike other systems, is that it conforms to what is called the Cosmological Principle.

According to this overarching law of cosmic symmetry, the universe looks the same from any vantage point to a typical observer. The same statistical patterns of galaxies recur again and again throughout the cosmos. Thanks to the Cosmological Principle, nothing, nobody is able to occupy a privileged, special place in it. And as a consequence of these peculiar properties, Layzer argues, information about the microcosm of the universe as a whole simply is not there. It cannot be specified, nor can it be acquired. This fundamental indeterminacy rules out the possibility of complete knowledge of the universe on anything but the large scale. A general macroscopic description can never be expanded by adding to it details of the fine inner structure. The meaningful properties of the cosmos, therefore, are all statistical, dealing with great collections of small particles.

The classical view was that in any unbounded system there is as much order at any one time as at any other time, and in principle we can have full knowledge of it. It does not matter how mixed up the system may be. When a new pack of playing cards is taken out of the wrapper, we know where all the cards are without looking. They are in the conventional sequence they are always in when they leave the factory. If someone shuffles the pack, the cards are no longer in the same sequence, but it is possible to discover the new sequence by looking at each card and memorizing it. The whole pack does possess a unique order that is knowable. It is even possible to predict the order of the cards after they have been shuffled, assuming that the shuffling is deterministic. A crooked poker player, for example, can shuffle a deck so that the cards do not lose their original order. This is similar to the classical idea of a cosmic superintelligence keeping track of all the particles in the universe even though they are moving about all the time.

Layzer concludes:

> My view, however, is that the order is unknowable even in principle. Imagine an unbounded stack of playing cards, topless and bottomless, deck piled on deck without limit. Information about the order of the cards in one section of the stack is of no help, because any given sequence is repeated an infinite number of times elsewhere, in the same way that patterns of stars and galaxies are repeated throughout the universe. It is meaningless to say that you are at such and such a place in the stack, even when you have full information about the order of cards at that place. You still don't know whereabouts you are in the stack, any more than the typical observer knows whereabouts he is in the cosmos. The Cosmological Principle says he doesn't know, and he can't know.

The universe, Layzer finds, is not running down, as generations of thinkers assumed. Agreed, the thermodynamic arrow of time points toward increasing entropy, because large-scale information decays into smaller-scale information, which in turn is dissipated by the effects of random disturbance from outside. But the cosmic expansion, moving away from the uniform disorder of the primal explosion toward a more highly ordered physical universe, continually creates macroscopic information. Its arrow describes the direction of a process which starts from uniformity and leads to more and more variety. So little information is needed to describe the first instant of the universe *completely* that it could be written down on a small sheet of paper. It would contain the laws of physics, which are very broad and general, and define what is possible, and a set of constraints, which apply more narrowly, and place limits on the possibilities.

Seen from this perspective, the universe generates its own novelty as it goes along. It is law-like, but unpredictable. There is always more information in it than there used to be. "In Laplace's world, there is nothing that corresponds to the passage of time," Layzer has written.

For Laplace's "intelligence," as for the God of Plato, Galileo and Einstein, the past and future coexist on equal terms, like the two rays into which an arbitrarily chosen point divides a straight line. If the theories I have presented are correct, however, not even the ultimate computer—the universe itself—ever contains enough information to specify completely its own future states. The present moment always contains an element of genuine novelty and the future is never wholly predictable. Because biological processes also generate information and because consciousness enables us to experience those processes directly, the intuitive perception of the world as unfolding in time captures one of the most deepseated properties of the universe.

8

Chemical Word and Chemical Deed

Once the genes are seen as information first and chemistry second, once their all-important role as symbols is recognized, then the barriers dividing one science from another come down. Chemistry no longer owns exclusive rights to the genes. They become one of many different kinds of symbol system, including the very rich and expressive system of human language.

One important property of language is that, while its symbols may be used to bring about physical results in the "real" world of substance, they need not be used for that purpose. Symbols can be decoupled from physical reality to a greater or lesser extent. Words are not deeds, though they often lead to deeds. Symbols can be manipulated more freely than substance, and they can be manipulated to form new statements and expressions which are only tentative, playful, figurative. Symbols are at liberty to be a little irresponsible and experimental. We might logically ask then whether this abstractness, this nonphysical aspect of language is also a feature of the genes. B. G. Goodwin, an English biologist, gives an affirmative answer to this question:

> Aristotle was correct to insist that something like formative "ideas," different in some sense from ordinary physical matter, must guide the intricate and extraordinarily varied formative processes of or-

ganic nature. We now recognize this difference to lie in the symbolic nature of the genetic code and the remarkably elaborate system cells have for its translation. It is genetic symbolism that enables living matter to step outside the constraints imposed by physical laws . . . The symbolic nature of the genetic material is what provides a virtually inexhaustible reservoir of potential genetic states for evolution, since symbols can be juxtaposed in very many different ways, to provide new "statements," new hypotheses, which can then be tested.

There are certain basic resemblances between genes and language that are beyond dispute. A gene is a segment of the DNA message, about a millionth of its total length in humans. It is made up of a sequence of chemical symbols, much as a sentence is constructed from letters of the alphabet. Of course, this alphabet is much shorter than that of English. It consists of only four letters: A for adenine, G for guanine, C for cytosine, and T for thymine.

As it happens, this system is closer to Shannon's binary code, which consists of just the two digits 0 and 1, than to the alphabet of any human language, making it easier to apply the principles of information theory, and to establish how much information is contained in a DNA molecule. Another reason why information theory has interesting and highly general things to say about living creatures is that it does not have to deal with a multiplicity of alphabets. The genetic alphabet of a mouse is the same as that of a rabbit or an elephant. With very minor exceptions, the code is universal. When a virus invades a cell, the conquest is easy, because the virus, although an outsider and a foreigner, uses the same symbol system as the cell it infects. It is able to use its own information to subvert and take over the information of the cell, which proceeds obediently to produce the energy and materials needed for the virus to reproduce itself. It is as if Napoleon's soldiers, at the gates of Moscow, had all spoken flawless Russian.

The sequences of chemical symbols, the bases A, G, C, and T, which are strung out along the DNA molecule, are possibilities. Proteins are these possibilities made actual. Genes are linear, one-dimensional, like words on a page. Proteins are not linear, but three-dimensional. They are the substance, the reality, for which the symbols stand. Proteins are very complex and quite fragile. They are assembled by stringing together chains of amino acids as specified by the chemical code of the gene in a complex process of copying and translating. The twenty different kinds of amino acids can be arranged in an enormous number of different sequences, and it is the order of the sequence that decides what the particular protein is, and what role it will play in the living organism.

Proteins are the "meaning" of the genetic message. They are closely coupled to reality, because they are the essential stuff of which flesh and bones are made, and it is on proteins that Darwinian natural selection acts. One might say that DNA is the word, while proteins are the deed, and deeds are more directly engaged, run more risks, confront life more irretrievably, than do words.

The message of DNA is intrinsic. If we speak in metaphor about the "ideas" contained in it, then those ideas are innate. They do not come from outside, from the environment, even though external chemical messages certainly play a role in the development of the living system. The original script of the DNA message, the organism's lifelong store of information, specifying its structure and growth, is placed for safekeeping in the nucleus, at the quiet center of the cell, and is housed in long, thin strands called chromosomes. It has no direct traffic with the world outside. Its symbol sequences are communicated to the chemical factories in the outer, working domain of the cell by another kind of nucleic acid molecule called messenger RNA, which carries a copy of sections of the DNA message to a place where proteins are assembled. These sections are read by the translation machinery of the cell in frames of three symbols at a time, called codons.

If the relationship between DNA and proteins were one-to-one, perfectly direct and simple, then the symbols would have no very interesting part to play in evolution. Natural selection, as an external, controlling force, accepts or rejects proteins as fit or unfit, or in some cases may ignore them if they have no special function. If the information in the DNA message is merely a description, in another language, of the proteins themselves, then the changes which have taken place in DNA over millions of years of evolution would correspond to the changes which have taken place in proteins. Knowing one would be the same as knowing the other. We might as well study the history of substance, proteins, and ignore the history of the symbols, DNA.

But the system is not as literal-minded, not as banal, as that. On the contrary, the relationship between DNA and protein is quite complex and sophisticated, and certainly not a simple reading of the sequences of letters codon by codon, from one end of the sequence to the other. As a result, more possibilities exist than can ever be expressed. And information theory wants to know about possibilities as much as it wants to know about actual events. This insight, that there are nonsimple connections between symbols and substance in certain kinds of information systems, is an overarching theme of this book. Here, it leads to new ideas about evolution. In later chapters, it will be indispensable to an understanding of the various codes and information processes in the brain.

Certain parts of the DNA text are structural. In other words, they code for a specific functional product. They are instructions for making proteins, and the message is on a literal level, like a recipe for shortcake. The message means exactly what it says. But other parts of the text are not to be taken so literally. These may consist of a kind of commentary on the structural genes, or contain hypothetical recipes for proteins which are not manufactured, or programs for editing and rearranging structural sections. They may represent information about information. If this is so, it would be quite a startling departure from earlier, simpler ideas about the gene.

Evolution is a more complicated process than was formerly supposed. Chance mutations alter the genetic message by replacing one letter with another, so that the meaning of a sequence is changed. In the case of the structural genes, a mutation may lead to the manufacture of a different protein. However, a mutation in a "nonliteral" part of the text would have another kind of effect altogether, because it would bring about a change in the commentaries, or programs, resulting perhaps in very significant modifications to the organism.

This way of looking at evolution elevates the symbols to a place of high significance in the scheme of biology. Until recently, proteins have tended to capture star billing as the most glamorous players in the vast theater of organic life. That is understandable. Proteins are acrobats, twisting themselves into a fantastic variety of shapes, each shape having a specific meaning in terms of a protein's function, of what it is and what it does in the chemistry of the organism. Lately, however, DNA, rather than proteins, has become the main focus of attention.

This change of perspective in biology is curiously similar to the shift of emphasis in modern linguistics, where the surface appearance of sentences is only part, and for some the least interesting part, of language. Below the surface are abstract principles, some of them universal, and grammars, which are devices for generating sentences with a certain structure. A grammar of this kind is intrinsic and defines what a speaker knows about a language rather than what he actually does with it. Such knowledge, which is partly hidden and unconscious, generates an enormous quantity of outgoing information in the form of spoken sentences, while relying on relatively little incoming information, in the form of what others say. A generative grammar provides in language what B. G. Goodwin believes the DNA information system provides in the cell, namely a "virtually inexhaustible reservoir" of possibilities.

This approach to language, developed by Noam Chomsky at MIT in the 1950s, was a radical departure from old ways of thinking, because it came to grips with the question of why language is creative, and creative not just for poets and other professional word spinners, but for the man in the street. We do not need to copy sentences others have already spoken, although we often do. The point is that we are always capable of inventing new sentences of our own, and we do so spontaneously, in the most casual of conversations.

We shall examine Chomsky's theory of language in more detail later on. Suffice it to say now that the theory offers a coherent explanation of why language can always surprise us with its fresh, original forms of expression. Chomsky proposes that sentences are generated by means of internalized rules, used again and again on a finite vocabulary of words. This makes possible an unlimited variety of properly formed grammatical sentences, more than any one person could speak in a lifetime. Because the possibilities are virtually inexhaustible, it is hopeless to expect to be able to describe them all, one after the other, in terms of their surface appearance. Nobody could write down all the sentences a language contains, since in principle there would always be more sentences to add. The project would never come to an end. It would be as futile as trying to make a list of all the whole numbers, from one to infinity. The only way to describe the series of whole numbers, as far as it can be described, is to make a list of the basic ten digits, from 0 to 9, and then give the rules for forming one number after another, without limit. The same few rules, used on the same few digits, generate the entire body of whole numbers. In this way, much is made out of little. The only way to describe a language fully is to identify the rules, and the conditions on those rules, and then throw in the dictionary. This means going down below the surface of language to discover its hidden principles.

The living organism must be the product of rules built into the DNA text and used repeatedly on the same set of symbols. Here too, nature appears to make much out of little. The number of genes on a DNA molecule is limited, as are the words in the vocabulary of a language. But by means of the rules, an unboundedly rich variety of products can be generated in the form of many different combinations of proteins. The comparison with Chomsky's generative grammar is not as outlandish as it looks. Some biologists actually encourage it as a way of explaining the creative processes in the cell.

Perhaps this is the moment to juxtapose two fundamental questions, one arising out of linguistics, the other out of biology:

How is it that a child can acquire something as complex as a language, so quickly, by being exposed to random samples of adult speech?

How is it that something as complex as a human being can evolve in a relatively short period of time, by random mutations of the genes?

Chomsky has already given his answer to the first question, though what he says is still open to vigorous debate. Innate principles are supposed to prevent a child from acquiring wrong rules and lead him to acquire the right ones. They predispose the child to form a correct theory of his language. That means he is not wholly dependent on information about the language given by parents and teachers. But Chomsky also has an opinion on the second question. He suggests that natural selection, acting on chance mutations, is not sufficient to explain the elaborate creations of nature. In a recent conversation he told me:

> As soon as you begin to take seriously the actual character of biological systems as they develop in the maturing individual—and language is just a biological system—you realize that they are highly structured and they develop on the basis of a very small amount of external conditions, external input. Consequently, they must be predetermined in very large measure. In my view (in this respect I may be a little more heretical), natural selection in itself does not provide anywhere near enough structure to account for what happens in evolution. That is pure speculation, I should say.

The theory of evolution, as it stands, is an incomplete statement about the origins and transformations of living organisms.

In countries outside the Anglo-Saxon orbit, where Darwin is held in less high regard, eminent men can sometimes be outspoken in claiming that this emperor wears no clothes. Pierre-Paul Grassé, France's leading zoologist, is a polemical anti-Darwinist who protests that Darwinism cannot account for the most striking and obvious aspect of evolution, namely its inventiveness. He writes:

> The powers of invention in the living world are immense. In our opinion, they are nothing but the capacity to process information in a given direction and perhaps toward a given goal. We do not know their inner mechanism and their underlying sources: biologists grope in darkness.

One major difficulty is that the central argument of Darwinian theory circles back on itself, explaining nothing. To say that evolution is the survival of the fittest, and then to define the fittest as the ones who leave the largest numbers of descendants, is not too far from saying that those who survive, survive. Even the modern form of Darwinism, the so-called synthetic theory, which explains evolution as the natural selection of random mutations of genes, still relies on the principle of the survival of the fittest.

The primary obstacle to accepting these arguments is that they depend so heavily on randomness. There does not seem to have been enough time in evolution to generate highly complex beings through a process in which chance plays such a prominent role. Murray Eden, a mathematician at MIT, tried to simulate the emergence of the human species by simple mutation and selection on a computer. He reached the conclusion that the chance of that happening is about the same as the chance of typing a library of a thousand books by hitting the typewriter keys at random. What is more, the typist would have to begin with a meaningful phrase, retype it with a few random errors, make it longer by adding letters, reorder smaller sequences, and finally take a look at the result to see if it made any sense. So much for mere accident!

But if the internal, generative principles of DNA are taken into account, new questions can be asked. Rules constrain, but also make rich expression possible. Purely random changes in letter and word sequences in a written language destroy sense and lead to gibberish. But if the changes are random, yet grammatical at the same time, interesting new sentences may result. Possibly some similar process is at work in evolution. Grammar is an antichance device which still allows plenty of room for novelty. It leaves the system of language essentially open and unbounded. If the rules of this grammar evolve and change over time, then important transformations take place in its products. Mutation of a single letter in a DNA sequence is one thing. Mutation of a rule is quite another, and the consequences are likely to be more interesting. A change of rule could lead to an innovation, a burst of originality, so easy to explain in terms of language, but so hard, until now, to make plausible in terms of Darwinian evolution.

9

Jumping the Complexity Barrier

Language and living systems, it is clear, have at least one thing in common: they are complex and stable at the same time, and they achieve this by means of internalized rules. They do not surrender to the randomizing effects decreed by the second law of thermodynamics, and they depend less than might have been expected on chance and accident. Their complexity is self-regulating.

What is more interesting, these features have clear connections with information theory and thermodynamics. "Complexity," "novelty," "variety," "constraints on possibilities" are all terms which arise continually in the work of Shannon and his successors.

It is one of the curious facts about languages that they are always rich in structure, no matter what their time and place in the history of known tongues. The languages that "backward" people speak are not primitive. In fact, there is no such thing as a primitive language. All are highly complex. Nor does language decay and fall into disorder, as one might suppose. Languages tend to preserve intelligibility, so that what may appear to be decay at a present time is not really decay at all. It is the replacement of one kind of structure by another kind. The linguist Edward Sapir called this process "drift."

A language which seems to be regressing toward simplicity or becoming disorderly actually remains complex, but in a different way. Robin Lakoff, a modern scholar of language, says,

> Languages have an internal rationale for what is going to change and in what way. As the case system went out of Latin, for example, Latin started to impose a fixed word order, and these changes went inexorably together, because there must be a way of giving information about structure, and if cases no longer do so, then the order of the words in the sentence must take on that task. And this is consistent. Even though speakers looking at their language might feel that distinctions are being lost, in every case another way is found of saying the same thing, preserving intelligibility. There is no reason why language should decay, any more than the human mind should decay. The conceptual structures of the mind that are responsible for the universal forms of grammar do in fact keep language running. And those things do not really change over time. Every language has about the same number of rules. Indeed, we can be reasonably sure that our own language has the same amount of syntax, the same amount of structure, as Proto Indo-European.

The notion of structures in the mind, in larger part universal, which "keep language running"—in other words, preserve its variety and complexity—is typical of much present-day thinking in linguistics. We could say that an antichance device inside the brain prevents language from becoming entropic or noisy as time goes on, so that it does not rely completely on the accidental, time-dependent features of experience to maintain its orderly structure. Language, Lakoff points out, has an "internal rationale" which keeps the number, if not the types, of rules fairly constant. Some modern biologists look at the language of the genes in somewhat similar terms.

The science of thermodynamics is still shedding new light on just this central question of why the world becomes increasingly organized rather than increasingly simple and random. One of the most effective thinkers in this field is Ilya Prigogine, who has been called "the poet of thermodynamics." Prigogine, who won the Nobel Prize for chemistry in 1977, believes that organized systems arise *naturally* out of unorganized matter rather than being extraordinary flukes or arriving on the earth from elsewhere in the universe. He proposes the existence of a hitherto unrecognized principle which pushes living organisms, even human beings themselves, to states of greater and greater complexity, whether or not that is the direction in which they want to go. Prigogine observes:

> This is something completely new, something that yields a new scientific intuition about the nature of our universe. It is totally against the classical thermodynamic view that information must always degrade. It is, if you will, something profoundly optimistic.

The tendency to move forward toward a highly organized state, rather than backward toward a simpler state, is a property of open systems, those that exchange matter and energy with their surroundings. Open systems do not behave in the same way as closed systems, which for a long time were the chief objects of study in physical chemistry. Under certain circumstances, open systems reach a steady state in which they are far from equilibrium, or maximum entropy, and they maintain that state. They are highly "improbable," highly complex. What is more, such a steady state can be reached from different starting points, and in spite of disruptions along the way. The state is what is called "equifinal."

Prigogine sees these open thermodynamic systems as beginning in a state of disorder, becoming unstable, and then entering a stage in which energy accumulates and structure develops. He calls this the creation of order by fluctuations. A fluctuation is a chance affair, a variation from average behavior that is normally smoothed out, but under special conditions grows larger and becomes established. Fluctuations are always occurring, but some grow large, while others are eventually smoothed out again. If fluctuations reach a critical size, they stabilize in the "equifinal" state. The creation of structure depends on how far the system is from equilibrium, and this in turn depends on the rate and amount of exchanges of matter and energy with the surroundings. The distance from equilibrium will be great if there are many exchanges, and very small or nonexistent if there are few. The same laws of physics apply in both cases, but near equilibrium. Prigogine says the laws lead to "doom or destruction," whereas further from equilibrium they may become processes of construction and organization. In this latter case, he adds, probability theory breaks down. Nonequilibrium can therefore be a source of order in open systems, whether these systems are chemical or biological, revealing a fundamental kinship between life and nonlife. Complexity is maintained in both types.

The whole question of complexity is one which has proved surprisingly subtle when investigated by modern theorists. Complexity is not just a matter of a system having a lot of parts which are related to one another in nonsimple ways. Instead, it turns out to be a special property in its own right, and it makes complex systems different in kind from simple ones, enabling them to do things and be things we might not have expected. Chomsky suggests that human language competence, which must be among the most complicated structures in the universe, arises uniquely in evolution at a certain stage of *biological* complexity. In other words, it appears when, and only when, evolution has led to an organism as complex as a human being. Chomsky goes on to say,

> This poses a problem for the biologist, since if true, it is an example of true 'emergence'—the appearance of a qualitatively different phenomenon at a specific stage of organization.

Emergence is not a popular word in modern science. But it is not absolutely taboo, and it is usually associated with complexity. Artists, on the other hand, feel quite at home with the idea. T. S. Eliot did not hesitate to define a poem as emergent, a new thing which defies explanation in terms of cause and effect, even when all the necessary information about its causes seems to be known. Scientists are a little more circumspect. The American physicist John Wheeler has remarked upon the way completely new concepts come into being when a system is made up of a very large number of parts, as in the cases of temperature, pressure, and entropy itself, which are all properties of thermodynamic systems consisting of an immense number of microscopic particles. Ilya Prigogine notes that there are chemical reactions in which molecules adjust their behavior not only to local circumstances but also to the larger parent organism, "which increases in complexity and grows to be something vastly different from the mere sum of its parts."

One of the great names of twentieth-century science is associated with the problem of emergence. John von Neumann, the son of a prosperous Budapest banker, was a child prodigy who as a young man made important discoveries in the foundations of mathematics and logic. Von Neumann was capable of extraordinary intellectual feats, being able to recite whole chapters of books from memory and to develop new mathematical concepts in the distracting atmosphere of a night club or the back seat of a taxi. His colleagues, in semiserious jest, suggested that von Neumann's brain might itself be an emergent organ, of a different order of complexity from those of ordinary mortals.

Von Neumann came to Princeton as a young man in his twenties. When American scientists began to build the first atomic bomb, his copious knowledge of the theory of shock waves made him invaluable to the Manhattan Project. At the bomb laboratory in Los Alamos, New Mexico, he was mainly responsible for devising the implosion method of detonating nuclear fuel, a method in which a substantial mass of the stuff is squeezed evenly in on itself from all sides at once. Implosion speeded up the development of the bomb by at least a year. It had to be precise to within a millionth of a second, otherwise it was no good, and the theory was beset by horrifying mathematical difficulties, in which von Neumann naturally rejoiced. To cope with the myriad calculations needed, Robert Oppenheimer, the director of Los Alamos, told von Neumann to order the most sophisticated calculating machines he could find. Punched-card machines made by IBM, whose calculators also helped break the Japanese code at a critical stage in the war, were brought in, to the delight of the other scientists, who used to play with them in the evening. Von Neumann quickly became fascinated by the logical structure of these machines and he began to pursue ideas about this property of complexity which computers share with the human brain. He was still working on the problem up to the time he died of cancer, in 1957.

A theory of complex systems, von Neumann thought, would be quite unlike a theory of simple systems. No theory of the former type existed at the time. The whole concept of high complication was ill defined and vague, meaning different things to different people. Von Neumann made a start at defining complexity by describing those characteristics of which he was reasonably sure. To begin with, he believed complexity belonged to the more general subject of information, and to what he called "quasithermodynamical considerations." Complexity, he said, displays "critical and paradoxical properties," properties such as entropy, which are found only in systems which are non-simple.

Moreover, to understand complex systems, such as a large computer or a living organism, we cannot use ordinary, formal logic, which deals with events that definitely will happen or definitely will not happen. A probabilistic logic is needed, one that makes statements about how likely or unlikely it is that various events will happen. The reason for this is that computers and living organisms must function reliably as a whole, even though their component parts cannot be expected to perform perfectly all the time. The parts function correctly only with a certain probability, and this probability must be built into the logic of the system. The aim is to insure that even if single parts are very likely to malfunction, the chance of the entire system breaking down is reasonably small. As systems become more complex, this statistical property of overall reliability, as opposed to the reliability of individual parts, becomes increasingly important.

Another property of certain very complex systems is that they are able to reproduce themselves in such a way that the offspring do not lose, and may in fact gain complexity. Living creatures reproduce themselves, but they do more than just reproduce. As time goes on, simple organisms evolve into more elaborate ones. The amoeba led eventually to human beings. The obvious question is: How could simple ancestors have possessed, in the text of their DNA, enough information to produce more sophisticated descendants? Machines in a factory do not behave in this curious fashion. It takes quite an elaborate machine to make a simple engineering part. Far from increasing, complexity is drastically reduced when a mechanical parent produces an off-spring. A machine tool cannot make another machine as sophisticated as itself, let alone one more sophisticated. If a robot is to make a second robot, it must contain not only a description of that robot, but also a set of rules for building it.

"How can machines reproduce themselves?" Queen Christina of Sweden asked her tutor, Descartes, after he informed her that the human body, though not the soul, could be explained in mechanical terms. Good question. Three centuries after the Queen asked it, John von Neumann suggested an answer. He proposed that in living organisms, and even in machines, there exists a "complexity barrier." Beyond this barrier, where systems are of a very high complexity, entirely new principles come into play. It is possible, von Neumann said, for a machine to make another machine more elaborate than itself once it attains a certain level of organization—once it breaks through the complexity barrier. Complexity is a decisive property. Below the critical level, the power of synthesis decays, giving rise to ever simpler systems. Above that level, however, the synthesis of more elaborate systems, under the right conditions, becomes explosive.

For our purposes, the important feature of complexity is that it is made possible by redundancy and generated by rules, which are a form of stored information. The power of a small number of fixed rules to produce an *unpredictable* amount of complexity is very striking. A slightly playful way of illustrating this power can be seen in some of the ingenious games that computer scientists play. These games mirror in odd and surprising fashion some of the patterns of growth of living organisms. Stanislaus Ulam, a mathematician who was a close friend of von Neumann's and also worked on the Manhattan Project, devised some intriguing versions of these games on an imaginary flat sheet of paper of unlimited size. In one version, a pattern of squares can be made to grow, almost like an organism, by adding new squares onto existing ones according to a set of rules agreed in advance. One rule of the game might be that a new square can be added so that it is in contact with a single square, but cannot be added if it is in contact with two existing squares (neighboring squares which touch only at their corners are not considered in contact). The moves of the game, according to this particular rule, result in a symmetrical pattern. This is how it looks (the numbers inside the squares refer to the successive moves, or generations of growth):

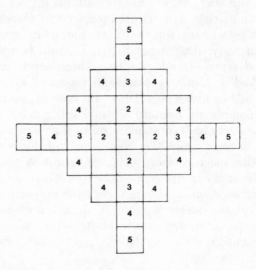

The patterns can be made to move in space if a rule is added that squares more than a certain number of generations old must be erased. Sometimes these patterns split into separate parts which resemble the parent shapes. Ulam calls this process self-reproduction. His computers simulated the growth of offspring using a new rule: when two offspring are both trying to occupy the same space, a new square is not added. The rule leads to a fight for survival between the offspring, and in some cases both die out.

Ulam was struck by the complexity and richness of the patterns that could be formed by using the same few rules over and over again on an object as simple and unexciting as a square or cube. Lovely and elaborate coral shapes appeared, and their evolution was very hard to predict. The physical appearance of all these figures could not be fully described, yet the rules that generated them could be described completely.

John Conway, an English mathematician whose special field is the theory of numbers, developed these computer patterns into what he calls the Life Game, which is played with colored counters on a checkerboard of unbounded size. The rules of the Life Game are devised so as to make the behavior of the patterns unpredictable. A counter is allowed to stay on the board if there are two or three other counters on neighboring squares. It survives and so is "fit" in an evolutionary sense. However, if the counter has four or more such neighbors, it is unfit and must be removed from the board. In this way the game allows for death, but it also provides for renewal. Each empty square adjacent to exactly three occupied squares is ruled to be a birth cell and a new counter is placed on it at the next move.

What makes these games so interesting is their capacity to surprise the player. The rules are simple, but their products are highly complex, so that they present serious difficulties to mathematicians who try to analyze them. Martin Gardner, who presented Conway's Life Game in *Scientific American* (October 1970), showed that patterns of counters, as they change according to the rules, assume exotic, sometimes beautiful, and always unexpected forms. Unsymmetrical figures tend to become symmetrical, and the symmetry is not only preserved but becomes richer. Most show remarkably stable behavior over long periods of time, or oscillate in a constant pattern. Strange incidents were observed in the course of some of the games. Clusters of five counters gave birth to a new, identical cluster every thirty moves. If one of these newborn clusters came into contact with another figure, called a pentadecathlon, made up of twelve counters, the pentadecathlon ate it up. Two pentadecathlons could shuttle a five-counter figure back and forth between them indefinitely. Another pattern of counters turned itself upside down every seven moves. A long, thin formation, a "barber pole," could be stretched to any length, and a "Cheshire cat" cluster vanished every sixth move, leaving only a string of counters behind, in the form of a grin. On the seventh move, the grin disappeared and only a pawprint remained.

Some of these games are cartoon versions of biological processes in the living world. A counter introduced into regular, stable figures behaved like a virus in a host cell. If it was placed on certain squares, it began to break up the whole pattern. Yet when it touched the corners of four blocks of counters, the host cell eliminated the virus and repaired itself in two moves.

These are really quite strange results to obtain from such simple sets of rules. The Life Game, Martin Gardner thinks, may in fact be much more than a game. It may mimic the effects of rules built into the structure of matter and these rules may have generated self-reproducing, moving automata in the primordial soup of amino acids before life existed on earth.

So a common theme begins to emerge from these investigations. Rules are the link between the new biology and the new linguistics. A modest number of rules applied again and again to a limited collection of objects leads to variety, novelty, and surprise. One can describe all the rules, but not necessarily all the products of the rules—not the set of all whole numbers, not every sentence in a language, not all the organisms which may arise from evolution. Ulam has told me that Chomsky's theory of generative grammar was the point of departure for his own work on computer games, yet at the same time he believes the games may lead to a new understanding of how living systems develop, much as gamblers' questions prompted mathematicians to devise a theory of probability in the seventeenth century.

There is still another idea of great importance arising from the Life Game. This is the notion of incompleteness, a famous crux of twentieth-century science and logic. Can a system governed by axioms or rules ever be complete, and if not, why not? Ulam sees computer models of organic processes as an aspect of this fundamental question. He links them to von Neumann's theory of complexity and also to one of the most revolutionary of all modern discoveries in logic, the Incompleteness Theorem of Kurt Goedel.

Goedel, born in Czechoslovakia in 1906, was a permanent member of the Institute for Advanced Study at Princeton from 1938 until his death in 1978. At the age of twenty-five, in Vienna, he published a paper so radical, so disturbing to the foundations of logic, that its full implications were not developed for many years, and the theorem itself became fashionable and widely known to the general public only in the 1970s. Goedel's paper does not apply to mathematical logic alone, but touches on much broader questions about the completeness of all formal systems of knowledge. It deals with the perennial, rock-bottom problem: What can the human mind know? It suggests that there are unavoidable restrictions on knowledge. Above a certain level of complexity, there are intrinsic limits to a logical system, if that system is consistent. There will always be true statements which can neither be shown to be true nor proved to be false within the confines of the system, using the axioms and rules of the system. Moving outside the original system, enlarging it by adding new axioms or rules, might make the statement provable, but within this wider metasystem there would be other statements that could not be proved without further expansion, and so on without end. Perfect completeness is never reached.

For Goedel's theorem to apply, the system must be of sufficient complexity, but this requirement is not extraordinarily high. Ordinary arithmetic is complex enough to qualify. It contains an endless number of true statements that cannot be deduced using a closed set of rules of inference. In other words, the rules by which the truths of arithmetic are established are not completely defined, and never can be.

Goedel's discovery means that logic, mathematics, and perhaps other kinds of knowledge are richer than can ever be described and defined exhaustively at any one time. This is the essence of the new approach to linguistics which began with Chomsky: Language will always be capable of surprising the reader or listener with its freshness, its power to rise to the level of new ideas when called upon to express them. The figures generated by the Life Game are unexpected. Matter itself, in the subatomic realm, is unpredictable, in that the observer cannot say exactly what state matter will be in at some time in the future, using his equations. He must ask a new question of matter, and by asking the question he disturbs the system he observes uncontrollably, changing its state.*

* Aage Petersen has reminded us that the word "nature" in classical mechanics was used in the special sense of information not already contained in the mathematical formalism. But this information was needed only for the starting conditions of the system being observed. Knowing exactly what a planet is doing

Goedel's theorem caused something of a scandal among logicians and those interested in theories of knowledge. It portrayed the truths of arithmetic, and perhaps of much else besides, as a continent for explorers to discover. And the exploring goes on indefinitely, because the continent is without bounds. The final map will never be completely drawn. However, this picture is not at all strange when applied to works of the imagination—plays, novels, poems, which are all essentially unfinished.

No poem above a certain "level of complexity" can have the last drop of meaning wrung from it, even by generations of critics. T. S. Eliot warned against too much reliance on a "causal" explanation of poetry, very much in the manner of modern quantum physicists rejecting cause-and-effect accounts of the behavior of matter at the subatomic level. Eliot had been irritated by the publication of two biographies of Wordsworth, both offering external reasons for the decline in quality of Wordsworth's later work. One of these biographies purported to explain the change as the result of the poet's affair with Annette Vallon. The other suggested that the drying-up of inspiration came about because of Wordsworth's thwarted love for his sister, Dorothy. Eliot considered both these hypotheses inadequate, because they fail to explain the essential nature of the forces which produce poetry. He wrote:

> For myself, I can only say that a knowledge of the springs which released a poem is not necessarily a help towards understanding the poem: too much information about the origins of the poem may even break my contact with it . . . I am even prepared to suggest that there is, in all great poetry, something which must remain unaccountable however complete might be our knowledge of the poet, and that is what matters most. When the poem has been made, something new

---

makes it possible to know what it will be doing at any time in the future, using Newton's equations of motion. These equations do not wipe out existing information about the planet, nor do they generate new information, since everything essential was known in the beginning. They merely "translate" the information forward into the future or backward into the past. However, in the case of matter at the subatomic level, "nature" takes on a very different meaning. The result of an experiment gives information not already contained in the starting conditions, which specify only the probability of this or that event being observed. The outcome of the experiment is undecidable, but "nature" makes a decision just the same.

has happened, something that cannot be wholly explained by *anything that went before.*

No final, wrapped-up, all-inclusive theory of reality will ever be perfected. The nature of language, the forms of logic, the duality of matter beneath the surface we observe, the power of rules to generate new structures, the limits to knowledge, the special character of complex as opposed to simple systems, all point to this conclusion. In this respect, science and art, philosophy and politics, history and psychology, meet on common ground, so that the barriers between the cultures break down under the recognition that all are incomplete and always will be; that no single discipline or school of thought has a monopoly on the truth. The truth itself has become more difficult to define as a result of the last half-century of discoveries in what used to be known as the exact sciences, making them richer, but not necessarily more exact, and disturbing them to their foundations.

10

Something Rather Subtle

One of the most perceptive attempts to shift the focus of interest in evolution from substance to symbols was made by the biophysicist Dr. Lila L. Gatlin, in the late 1960s and early 1970s. At the time, her ideas looked fairly heretical, but in the few years since they first appeared, advances by other molecular biologists have given her arguments new force and weight.

Dr. Gatlin's approach is radical by the normal standards of thinking in her field, because she begins by assuming that biology ought to be very much richer than it is in the sort of powerful theoretical concepts found in physics, just as Chomsky regards linguistics as being particularly weak in this respect. Most biologists tend to see themselves as describers of nature, collectors of facts which will lead to a good experiment. Yet if DNA is an information process, and a theory of information exists, then it is reasonable to suppose that scientists can at least make a start at sketching out a theory of living organisms, in the full sense of the word. This is exactly what Gatlin sets out to do.

She proceeds on the assumption that when the symbols of DNA are translated into the substance of proteins, communication takes place. This is more than just another metaphor. Gatlin is using the word in the sense intended by Claude Shannon in his 1948 papers on the mathematics of communication.

Since Shannon's work was highly abstract, and for that reason extremely powerful and general, it can be applied to any kind of information system in which messages are sent from a source to a receiver. And since information in the living system is transmitted from DNA to protein along a channel of biochemical processes in the cell, it can be subjected to Shannon's theorems and equations.

DNA is regarded as the source of the message and proteins are at the receiving end of the "communications channel." Here, at once, is a contradiction between the doctrines of classical evolution and the principles of information theory, because, while evolution is primarily concerned with the output of the channel, the proteins, information theory attaches great importance to the source, and the way the information is structured there.

In Shannon's theory, the essence of successful communication is that the message must be properly encoded before it is sent, so that it arrives at its destination just as it left the transmitter, intact and free from errors caused by the randomizing effects of noise. This means that a certain amount of redundancy must be built into the message at the source. Only in that way can the sender be sure that the message will reach the other end ungarbled and in its original orderly state. In his second theorem for the noisy channel, Shannon proved that codes do exist that preserve order in the face of general disorder. These codes insure the transmission of messages as nearly perfect and free from error as the coder cares to make them, provided the ideal code is used. Shannon's remarkable theorem shows that messages need not come unraveled, even when subjected to the mixing effect of the second law of thermodynamics.

In organic evolution, natural selection is an antichance agent, imposing order on the haphazard changes and mutations of living forms. Information theory, however, suggests that a different kind of antichance device can be built into the genetic message *at the source.*

In Gatlin's new kind of natural selection, "second-theorem selection," fitness is defined in terms very different from and more abstract than in the classical theory of evolution. Fitness here is not a matter of strong bodies and prolific reproduction, but of genetic information coded according to Shannon's principles.

The codes that made possible the so-called higher organisms,

Gatlin suggests, were redundant enough to insure transmission along the channel from DNA to protein without error, yet at the same time they possessed an entropy, in Shannon's sense of "amount of potential information," high enough to generate a large variety of possible messages. It should be remembered that, in information theory, entropy is a measure of how many messages might have been sent but were not. If an actual message is selected from a great number of possible messages, then it resolves a lot of uncertainty and so conveys a large amount of information. With the proper use of codes, the need to prevent errors in the transmission of genetic messages does not inhibit too severely the wide range of "meanings" those messages are able to express. Such is Gatlin's view.

In the course of evolution, she argues, certain living organisms acquired DNA messages which were coded in this optimum way, giving them a highly successful balance between variety and accuracy, a property also displayed by human languages. These winning creatures were the vertebrates, immensely innovative and versatile forms of life, whose arrival led to a speeding-up of evolution.

Vertebrates were agents of novelty. They did more than just adapt. They revolutionized their anatomy and body chemistry, evolved more rapidly than other animals, and exerted an impressive mastery over their surroundings. The first vertebrates known completely from the fossil record, the ostracoderms, were cumbersome and slow. These bottom-dwelling fish flourished some 350 million years ago. They were covered with heavy, waterproof armor plating from head to tail. The weight of their external skeleton kept them anchored to the floor of fresh-water lakes and estuaries. But later on they began to change in striking and significant ways. Spiny parts of the tough armor evolved into pairs of fins. In some, true bone appeared for the first time in evolution, and soft cartilage was invented. The armor around the head was transformed into a skull, with openings for the sense organs of smell, sight, and hearing. There was a space to house the brain. Primitive gill slits were modified to become jaws, and conveniently placed armor plates became teeth. In one type of jawed fish, now extinct, bony supports in the fins evolved into limbs, and the stage was set for the rise of the amphibians.

In the history of vertebrates, we see nature at her most inventive. Looked at over the immense stretch of time in which they evolved, vertebrates seem to make leaps toward the new. Even when they did not migrate to new habitats, they became more complex, and the stages of transition were not smooth or steady. What kind of error-correcting redundancy did the DNA of these evolutionary prize winners, the vertebrates, possess? It had to give them the freedom to be creative, to become something markedly different, for their emergence was made possible not merely by changes in the shape of a common skeleton, but rather by developing whole new parts and organs of the body. Yet this redundancy also had to provide them with the constraints needed to keep their genetic messages undistorted.

The four chemical letters of the genetic alphabet are arranged in different sequences in different species and in different individuals of the same species. These sequences clearly are not random, any more than the words in a sentence or the bricks of a house are arranged at random. Each sequence possesses a certain structure. Not all the letters appear in the sequence equally often. More than that, the probability that a letter or letters will appear at a certain place in the sequence may be affected by the preceding letter or letters. In other words, a letter is not necessarily independent of the preceding ones in the chain. As in ordinary language, these rules of redundancy act as constraints, limiting the number of ways in which the message source can arrange symbols into sequences. Without the rules, any sequence of letters would be possible, and language would be wholly private and arbitrary, free to string letters together at random and therefore unable to communicate meaning.

Redundancy, of course, increases the probability that certain letters will appear and decreases the probability that certain other letters will appear. In this way, it lowers the entropy of the message source by reducing the variety of possible messages from which the actual message may be chosen. However, and this is the important point, redundancy does not lower the entropy in one way only.

Some idea of how this procedure works can be seen in a variation of the hypothesis that if a monkey had unlimited time and an endless supply of typewriters, it might, by a sheer fluke, type the complete works of Shakespeare. The whole idea is slightly foolish, because it approaches language from a purely mechanistic point of view. Even Shakespeare would not write the works of Shakespeare if a modern scientist sat him down at a typewriter. In its usual form, the conceit is merely a picturesque way of saying that the second law of thermodynamics, because it is based on chance, is not absolutely certain and necessary, but only overwhelmingly probable. It is not forbidden in principle for a kettle to freeze instead of boil when placed on a stove burner, but the contingency is so fantastically remote that it is not even worth discussing. The same is true of the likelihood of monkeys becoming writers of Elizabethan blank verse.

A Yale professor of engineering, William R. Bennett, Jr., using computers, has calculated that if a trillion monkeys were to type ten keys a second at random, it would take more than a trillion times as long as the universe has been in existence merely to produce the sentence "To be, or not to be: that is the question." However, Bennett has also shown that by applying certain quite simple rules of probability, so that typewriter keys were not struck completely at random, imaginary monkeys could, in a matter of minutes, turn out passages which contain striking resemblances to lines from Shakespeare's plays. He supplied his computers with the twenty-six letters of the alphabet, a space, and an apostrophe. Then, using Act Three of *Hamlet* as his statistical model, Bennett wrote a program arranging for certain letters to appear more frequently than others, on the average, just as they do in the play, where the four most common letters are e, o, t, and a, and the four least common letters are j, n, q, and z. Given these instructions, the computer monkeys still wrote gibberish, but now it had a slight hint of structure:

NCRDEERH   HMFIOMRETW   OVRCA   OSRIE   IEOBOTOGIM   NUD-SEEWU . . .

Next, Bennett programmed in some statistical rules about which letters are likely to appear at the beginning and end of words, and which pairs of letters, such as th, he, qu, and ex, are used most often. This improved the monkeys' copy somewhat, although it still fell well short of the Bard's standards:

ANED AVECA AMEREND TIN NF MEP FOR'T SESILORK
TITIPOFELON HERIOSHIT MY ACT . . .

At this second stage of programming, a large number of indelicate words and expletives appeared, leading Bennett to suspect that one-syllable obscenities are among the most probable sequences of letters used in normal language. Swearing has a low information content! When Bennett then programmed the computer to take into account triplets of letters, in which the probability of one letter is affected by the two letters which come before it, half the words were correct English ones and the proportion of obscenities increased. At a fourth level of programming, where groups of four letters were considered, only 10 percent of the words produced were gibberish and one sentence, the fruit of an all-night computer run, bore a certain ghostly resemblance to Hamlet's soliloquy:

TO DEA NOW NAT TO BE WILL AND THEM BE DOES
DOESORNS CALAWROUTOULD.

A computer monkey programmed to reproduce the statistical structure of groups of letters as they appear in Ernest Hemingway's novel *A Farewell to Arms* started straightaway with an improper proposal.

Bennett's four levels of programming, which resulted in a closer and closer approximation to Shakespearean blank verse, added redundancy to the message source in progressive stages by constraining the freedom of all letters in the alphabet to appear with equal probability. The redundancy lowered the entropy of the message source at each stage, but not always in the same way. At the first level, the imaginary monkeys were typing entirely at random, with every key just as likely to be hit as any other key, so that the entropy, or freedom of choice, was at a maximum. This also meant that the uncertainty of the reader was at a maximum, since he was not able to predict, even as a probability, which letter would appear next in the sequence. As the programs became increasingly complex, however, this freedom of choice became more and more restricted. At the second level, some letters were made to appear more often than others, so that it was as if the monkeys were randomly hitting typewriters which had a large number of "e" keys, a slightly lesser number of "c" keys, and so on down the scale of letters according to the frequency of their use in Act Three of *Hamlet*.

At the next stages of programming, the probability of a single letter was not considered on its own, but was affected by the one, two, or three letters preceding it. It is clear that the probability of the three letters DOE being followed by the letter S was very high. Bennett's computer was not powerful enough to deal with groups of five letters, but as the monkey texts proceeded up through the levels of redundancy, they acquired more structure—looked more familiar—even when the words made no sense. They became easier to predict. The electronic monkeys had considerable freedom of choice in the keys they could hit, but they did not have complete freedom, because the program had made the probabilities unequal. This is reminiscent of the difference between a thermodynamic system being at equilibrium, where all possible arrangements of the molecules are equally probable, and being far from equilibrium, where certain arrangements are more probable than others.

Gatlin points out that in cases such as that of Bennett's monkeys, we are talking about two different kinds of redundancy. Both kinds lower the entropy, but not in the same way, and the distinction is a critical one. The first kind of redundancy, which she calls D_1, is the statistical rule that some letters are likely to appear more often than others, on the average, in a passage of text. D_1, which is context-free, measures the extent to which a sequence of symbols generated by a message source departs from the completely random state where each symbol is just as likely to appear as any other symbol. The second kind of redundancy, D_2, which is context-sensitive, measures the extent to which the individual symbols have departed from a state of perfect independence from one another, departed from a state in which context does not exist. These two types of redundancy apply as much to a sequence of chemical bases strung out along a molecule of DNA as to the letters and words of a language.

Increasing D_1, the context-free redundancy, Dr. Gatlin shows, is a safeguard against error, because it makes the sequence more predictable. If a page of print has a larger proportion of x's than of e's, it is clear that something is amiss. The statistical structure of English has been violated. All the same, context-free redundancy is expensive, because if it is increased too much, it places severe limits on the variety of messages which can be sent. The price of accuracy becomes extremely steep. It is as if a printer found himself with too few sorts of certain letters and too many sorts of others in his type box. If the printer has millions of a's and t's, but scarcely any of the other twenty-four letters of the alphabet, just about the only word he will be able to set up in type is "at," repeated millions of times.

Context-sensitive D² also makes the sequences of symbols more predictable, because it sets up a relationship between letters. As a result, it is often possible to guess what the next letters in the sequence will be, on the evidence of the letters which have already appeared. Yet context-sensitive redundancy is not as expensive as context-free redundancy. It can be increased by a reasonable amount without cramping the message source too severely. It does not restrict the message to only a few letters, as does the context-free type. It permits greater variety, while at the same time controlling errors. English is higher in context-sensitive than in context-free redundancy, which accounts for the rich variety of the language, coupled with its excellent readability, even when distorted by misprints and mistakes. It can always communicate new ideas, but within the framework of familiar rules of structure and sense.

Bennett programmed in context-free redundancy at an early stage in his computer experiment, and held it steady, but he had to keep on increasing context-sensitive redundancy to the limits of his equipment before the computer began to write sentences which were roughly similar to sensible English, let alone to Shakespearean verse. Even at the highest level of programming, when the probability of a single letter was dependent on the three letters preceding it, there was too much randomness left in the message source.

Lower organisms, Gatlin suggests, may have more context-free redundancy in the information system of their genes than context-sensitive redundancy, insuring that the signals sent along the channel from DNA to protein are low in errors, but at the same time limiting the system to a very narrow range of simple messages, as if a book were to contain the same few words repeated over and over again. The DNA of primitive creatures may be so high in context-free redundancy that it attains freedom from error, but only at the cost of sacrificing freedom of expression.

This is not a very clever strategy to adopt. It makes no attempt to exploit the possibilities of Shannon's second theorem, which promises an optimum blend of variety and accuracy if the message is made redundant in just the right way at the source. Phage, for example, little virus particles which infect bacterial cells, are able to copy themselves in the host cell dozens of times an hour with such astonishing accuracy that Leo Szilard, when he first saw phage in action at the Cold Spring Harbor laboratories on Long Island, had to go outside and pace up and down on the porch of his guesthouse until he could recover his composure. Such errorless reproduction may be due to the fact that phage are very extravagant with context-free redundancy in their DNA, as are bacteria and invertebrates as a whole. However, vertebrate DNA, Gatlin argues, is more like a human language, in that, while the total amount of redundancy is quite high, it is richer in the context-sensitive than in the context-free type.

Gatlin regards context-sensitive redundancy, which measures the divergence from independence of the symbols in the DNA message, as an evolutionary index, marking the dividing line between creatures with backbones and creatures without backbones. It is a sort of information barrier, which, once surmounted, leads to increasing biological complexity. If this is correct, evolution is not simply a matter of random changes in proteins, selected for fitness by purely external factors like ecology, population clusters, food supply, and competition among and within various species. It has an internal, abstract side to it, which must be understood in terms of the laws of information and communication. The environment still plays an important part in the survival of the fit, but the fit are defined in a less external way and are selected by more than one kind of anti-chance device. Once the right balance has been struck between too much freedom of expression for the message source of DNA, and too little freedom, then the range of choices open to organisms expands. It was this extra freedom, safeguarded by redundancy, that moved life forward to more complex forms. Like the acceleration of Western civilization after the invention of printing, evolution may have acquired a forward momentum of its own.

Variety and control of variety, the essence of the modern computer revolution, are also at the heart of the information system of the genes. Gatlin writes:

> The vertebrates and their ancestors were the first living organisms to achieve the stabilization of D_1, thus laying the foundation for the formulation of a genetic language. They then increased D_2, while allowing D_1 to increase from zero only up to the optimal boundaries fixed by the genetic code. Hence they increased the reliability of the genetic message without a great loss of message variety. They achieved a reduction in error probability without paying too great a price for it, and an information theorist would recognize this as the utilization of Shannon's second theorem.

The Gatlin scenario is as follows: If molecules carrying information copy themselves, then those which make the largest number of copies with the fewest mistakes are likely to win the competition for survival. In the first, primitive stirrings of prelife on the planet earth, it is possible that short sequences of chemical symbols tended to survive because they had a high redundancy. Then this simple information system, with its high level of accuracy, could be expanded into something more complex by making the sequence longer. Entropy increases, as it does in all local systems, in obedience to the second law of thermodynamics. Redundancy, which lowers entropy, must consequently decline. The range of uncertainty broadens, "vocabulary" becomes richer, variety increases. Context-sensitive redundancy reaches its minimum value.

It is at this point, Gatlin believes, that life in the accepted sense of the word began. Until this moment, evolution followed the thermodynamic arrow of time, the direction of increasing entropy. But when context-sensitive redundancy began to increase, making the DNA messages resistant to error, even while the messages themselves were still growing longer, the principle of Shannon's second theorem made its entrance. Living systems, which had been following the thermodynamic arrow, reversed their course. Evolution was no longer random, but took a specific direction, not toward maximum entropy, but toward complexity and a high degree of order. The DNA of vertebrate animals found the middle range of entropy values, between the very uncertain and the very predictable, the range in which mistakes are under control but restraints on the variety of messages are not too confining.

Here we are at the beginning of a theory of evolution as an information process. Even if some of Gatlin's ideas are speculative, they force us to look at the internal structure—one can almost say the linguistic structure—of the DNA text as a protagonist rather than a passenger in the emergence of living creatures. In a now famous paper published in 1969, the American biologists Jack Lester King and Thomas Jukes wrote, "We cannot agree . . . that DNA is the passive carrier of the evolutionary message. Evolutionary change is not imposed upon DNA from without; it arises from within. Natural selection is the editor, rather than the composer, of the genetic message."

Only a short time ago, it was an axiom of biology that the genes of all organisms, whether simple or elaborate, behave in a similar fashion. But recent research shows that this view is mistaken. At least some of the DNA messages in human beings, other animals, and higher plants are not decoded and activated in the same way as in more primitive organisms such as bacteria. All the messages, with very minor exceptions, are written in the same four-letter code. But the rules for converting symbols into substance can be different, and even in very simple organisms, information may be stored in surprisingly subtle and ingenious ways.

In 1977, amid a fanfare of publicity, Sir Frederick Sanger and his co-workers at the British Medical Research Council's molecular biology laboratory in Cambridge accomplished the remarkable feat of decoding a complete biochemical message. The team's success, widely applauded, was in deciphering the entire genetic text of one of the smallest bacterial viruses, ØX174. A mystery had surrounded this particular virus. It did not seem to contain enough information for making the nine different kinds of proteins which are in fact produced when the virus infects a healthy cell. The sequence of 5,375 chemical symbols on the DNA of the virus was too short to spell out the full set of instructions to the cell. If DNA is seen as a cookbook, containing recipes for the manufacture of proteins, this cookbook appeared to be lacking several chapters. By deciphering the entire sequence of symbols, however, the mystery was at last unraveled. There was enough information in the viral DNA, but it was stored in an unexpectedly tricky way. The words of the text overlapped, so that more messages could be squeezed into a small space.

When the machinery of the cell translates DNA information into protein, it needs to be told when to start and when to stop. Every message for making a protein begins with a codon, or triplet of chemical symbols, that consists of the "letters" ATG. The signal to stop making the protein is given by one of three codons, TAA, TGA, or TAG. All this seemed quite straightforward until the text of ØX174 was examined carefully. There it was found that a single sequence of symbols contained information for making two quite different kinds of protein, depending on the way it was read. The sequence had one meaning when read starting from the first letter and a wholly different meaning when read starting from the second letter. Genes were not neatly separated by a clear beginning and a clearly marked end. A TAA "stop" signal might overlap a TGA. Shift the reading frame by one letter and the entire sequence of codons acquires quite another significance in terms of the proteins specified by the symbols. The sense of the message is transformed. The viral DNA used the same symbols to form many different codons, rather as words across and words down overlap in a crossword puzzle, cramming more information into a tight space by making some letters do double duty, so that they appear in two words at once.

The discovery that this tiny virus stores information by means of a DNA text so cunningly composed as to tax the ingenuity of a master anagrammatist came as a revelation. It had been thought that in the genetic code, precision and accuracy were too important to risk playing clever word games to increase the complexity of the organism. Surely, evolution would insist on messages so clear that they left room for one, and only one interpretation? But apparently the structure of DNA, even at such a primitive level, is more interesting than that. It cannot be understood, any more than language can be understood, merely as strings of symbols which have a simple, one-to-one relationship with the finished product. The existence of rules for converting words into sentences, or DNA symbols into proteins, insures that this relationship is far from simple, and makes the products highly varied and sophisticated. As Sir Frederick Sanger remarked, in one of the classic understatements of biology, "Something rather subtle seems to be at work."

PART THREE

Coding Language, Coding Life

11

Algorithms and Evolution

In modern theories of language, the term "rule" needs to be defined rather precisely. The word is not used in the same sense as a rule of polite society, a convention which merely forbids people to do what they would otherwise be free to do. Quite the reverse. Linguistic rules have the effect of opening up new realms of activity. They are immensely powerful in their capacity to generate sentences. So powerful, in fact, that they need to be curbed by conditions imposed on them, and these conditions, Chomsky believes, are part of the structure of universal grammar, common to all human languages.

As the rules of chess define the game of chess, linguistic rules define the game of language, which would not exist without them. They are not strict mechanisms of cause and effect—one thing simply making another thing happen—but leave a system essentially open and incomplete, so that it is always capable of novelty. Rules of etiquette close off a system, keeping it uniform and predictable unless the rules are changed. Rules of language are indirect and can be used again and again on the same finite set of letters and words, making possible an open universe of new sentences based on the closed universe of the dictionary.

An unbounded system, governed by rules of this type, contains more information than we might expect by merely looking at its component parts. This is a way of approaching the paradoxical question of how a structure as elaborate as the human brain can be produced from the biological information on a set of chromosomes. Here the effect, the brain, seems so extravagantly much greater than the cause, the sequences of symbols on the DNA molecule. The answer to the paradox is that the symbols of the text are not read off one by one along the length of the DNA chain, but are expressed in various combinations, by means of "rules" which are used repeatedly on symbols, as the rules of language are used on parts of sentences. The information content cannot be determined by counting codons, any more than the information content of a language can be determined by counting the number of words in the dictionary.

It should be stated as emphatically as possible that language is *generated*, as well as sometimes imitated. A child does not merely store copies of heard sentences in the file cabinet of memory one at a time. Because language is generated by means of internalized rules, the child is able to be creative, and is not wholly dependent on information from outside. If DNA is not the "passive carrier of the evolutionary message," language most certainly is not the passive imitator of what other people say.

In 1957, with the publication of his *Syntactic Structures*, Chomsky exposed the folly of supposing that English, or any natural language, is a finite-state system. A finite-state grammar is the simplest and most limited of all grammars. It is like a machine which starts by printing the first word of a sentence and adds one word after another until the end of the sentence is reached, at which point the machine stops. Such a grammar has no memory; it cannot look back at previous parts of the sentence as it proceeds from end to end. Thus the grammar cannot extend a sentence by embedding clauses one inside the other, as ordinary languages do quite freely. It cannot cope with any rule which requires that the choice of words in one part of a sentence be contingent on the choice of words in an earlier part. To make such a machine as competent in a language as a human being, it would be necessary to write a separate rule for every conceivable grammatical sentence in the language, and a grammarian would die long before that task could be completed.

Linguists before Chomsky had been working with finite-state grammars, even though they may not have realized that they were doing so. Chomsky's importance lay in the fact that he introduced new principles which were very much more powerful than those of the finite-state model. His theory of transformational grammar was based on a system of internalized rules capable of generating an infinite number of grammatical sentences.

An example from logic can be used to show the power of rules to generate new information just as transformational grammar generates new sentences. The information theorist Michael Watanabe has pointed out that if the human mind is a processor of information it should be able to lose information but not gain it, in accordance with the law of increasing entropy. Yet, clearly, the mind does create information. Indeed, it floods the world with the stuff. A way out of this apparent contradiction, Watanabe thinks, might be to consider that the information stored in a law or rule is vastly greater than the information needed to specify a single event. In the famous syllogism

> All men are mortal
> Socrates is a man
> Therefore Socrates is mortal

the first sentence, a kind of rule governing the nature of man, tells us much more than the second. It reduces uncertainty about the entire class of human beings, over the whole history of the human race, whereas the second sentence reduces uncertainty only about a single individual.

When the rules of expression for DNA are discovered, they will probably resemble the same creative principles of transformational grammar, not the pedestrian operations of the old finite-state grammars. As we have noted, one of the most important discoveries of modern molecular biology is that not all sequences of symbols in the DNA text code directly for proteins. It is suspected, but not known for sure, that at least some of these other sequences regulate the action of the genes that do code directly for protein, switching them on and off in batteries in various ways and at various times, like a conductor bringing in different sections of the orchestra during the performance of a symphony. It is clear from the elaborate ways in which living creatures are transformed from embryo into adult according to an exquisitely subtle timetable of development, that a very complex system of controls and rules, a genetic grammar, must exist.

In the parlance of mathematics, some parts of the DNA message may behave more like an algorithm than a cookbook recipe or the tape in a tape recorder. The word "algorithm" is an interesting one. It is derived from the name of the mathematician and astronomer Al-Khowarizmi, a cultivated and scholarly man whose patron was Al-Mamun, son of the ninth-century Moslem ruler Harun al-Rashid, the caliph who appears in many of the stories of the *Thousand and One Nights*. Al-Khowarizmi, a member of the House of Wisdom, an academy of scientific thought in Baghdad, devised abstract rules of procedure for reorganizing mathematical expressions. He wrote a treatise entitled *Al-jebr w'al-mugabala*, meaning "transportation and removal," the transposing of terms from one side of an equation to the other, and the cancellation of equal terms on both sides. The system is known today as algebra.

In its modern sense, an algorithm is some special method of manipulating symbols, especially one which uses a single basic procedure over and over again. It converts certain quantities into other quantities, using a finite number of transformation rules. Rules of language, for example, are of this kind. In the case of DNA, the rules may enable sets of genes to be copied over and over again and to be expressed as protein in various specific ways and not in others. The algorithm would be a kind of program, instructing certain combinations of genes to turn on or turn off at specific times, and it would be stored in the DNA text as information. It may be analogous to the grammar and syntax of English. Knowing the words of the English language does not enable a speaker to form sentences, any more than knowing the genes that code directly for protein—the so-called "structural" genes—enables a biologist to understand why those genes are expressed as proteins in such elaborate ways. They seem to be switched on and switched off with the virtuosity of a pianist striking the same keys on the piano in a dazzling variety of different combinations, according to the algorithm of the musical score.

An algorithm is often a more compact form of expression than a literal description of the product for which it is an instruction. To generate the string of digits 1212121212, all that is needed is to issue the instruction, "Write 12 five times." The string can be extended to an indefinite length by changing the algorithm to read, "Write 12 a thousand times" or "Write 12 a million times." If the string of digits has a less simple pattern, the algorithm will have to be more elaborate. To specify the string 121122123124, the instructions must read something like, "Write 12 four times, each time inserting a digit starting with 1 and progressing through the series of whole numbers up to 4." This is a long algorithm, but, again, it can order the construction of a string a million digits long with only minor changes in wording.

Murray Eden, the MIT engineer who tried to simulate the evolution of humans on a computer using the classical forces of natural selection acting on random mutations of genes, found that there would not have been nearly enough time in evolution to bring human beings onto the scene. He concluded that algorithms must impose constraints on the chance mutations in the symbols of the DNA message, since the constraints of natural selection alone do not seem to be powerful enough. No language, Eden pointed out, can tolerate random changes in the sequence of letters in a sentence, because meaning would be destroyed. Any changes must be "syntactically lawful" and conform to the rules of structure. Just as a human language does not decay over time, but acquires new kinds of structure while preserving intelligibility, the genes, Eden conjectured, have a kind of grammar, which remains stable, even though it may change. And this happens in spite of the random mutations and selection pressures of evolution.

In logic, an important distinction has to be made between statements and "meta-statements," which contain information about the statements, and stand outside them. One must bear this distinction in mind or risk falling into contradiction and paradox. It is clear at once that any changes in the meta-statements, any rewriting of the algorithms, in the course of evolution, would have far more drastic effects on the organism than would mutations of this or that symbol in the parts of the DNA message that code directly for protein. Nothing very enlightening can be said about DNA if it is regarded as merely passive, simply making "statements" about the form of the organism it specifies. It makes more sense to regard DNA as dynamic, and as making "meta-statements"—statements about statements—which are on a higher logical level and may not evolve, as time goes on, in the same way that statements evolve.

A most revealing experiment, carried out at Harvard Medical School by Dr. Edmund Lin and his associates, illustrates the power of algorithms, or meta-statements, to produce significant evolutionary changes in even simple creatures. In this experiment, several billion bacteria were deprived of the carbon compounds which they used as nutrients. Under normal conditions, the bacteria readily metabolized such compounds by means of enzymes whose configurations fitted neatly into their chemical structure. But for the purposes of the experiment, the bacteria were given a very different type of carbon compound, called xylitol, which was commercially synthesized. This compound was wholly strange to them, and they were unable to metabolize it.

It happens, however, that in the DNA of the bacteria there is information for producing an enzyme called ribitol dehydrogenase. This enzyme can rapidly metabolize another sort of compound, ribitol, which has a chemical structure similar to that of xylitol. Although the surface of the enzyme had evolved so as to fit closely into the structure of ribitol, the enzyme can also attach itself to xylitol, albeit with much less affinity. And when confronted with xylitol, the enzyme is able to convert it into another nutrient, which the bacteria can use.

However, a serious problem stood in the way of such an alternative strategy. The algorithms of the bacterial DNA were such that the structural gene coding for the important enzyme was switched on only if ribitol was present in the environment. So although the bacteria had the possibility of utilizing the novel compound xylitol, this possibility could not be made actual without ribitol, and there was no ribitol.

Thus the bacteria were faced with a Darwinian situation. Only by a mutation enabling them to produce ribitol hydrogenase in the absence of ribitol could they take advantage of xylitol and be able to grow. It turns out that such mutants do indeed exist in a large population. But the mutation changes are in a meta-statement of DNA, not a statement. That mutation alters a regulatory program, so that the gene coding for the needed enzyme is expressed whether or not ribitol is present. Under continued selection, the structure of ribitol dehydrogenase is modified in such a way that it can metabolize xylitol more effectively. Mutants producing such improved versions of the enzyme would have the advantage of growing faster on xylitol. In this manner, new strains of bacteria can emerge under laboratory conditions within a matter of days. Lin was able to show that organisms with new capabilities can arise by a change in the programming of gene expression and by improvements to existing components in their genetic makeup, rather than by the construction of a completely new component.

The biologists Roy Britten and Eric Davidson pointed out in 1971 that the role played by structural genes, the "statements" of DNA, is not so very much different in a very simple, single-cell organism such as a bacterium from their role in the much more sophisticated chemistry of mammals. Such a tremendous difference in complexity between the two forms of life, these biologists argue, must have been due chiefly to the emergence of algorithms of vastly greater power to generate new biological structures with novel functions. It is the changing *pattern* of gene activity, rather than changes in structural genes themselves, that led away from biological simplicity and toward the higher forms of life. Mammals possess a DNA text thirty times as long as that of a sponge, but the extra length does not consist of genes which code directly for proteins. It has been estimated that scarcely more than one percent of mammalian DNA is of that type. Britten and Davidson think that the extensions to the text contain new sets of control programs. They conclude:

We follow the view that major events in evolution require significant changes in patterns of gene regulation. These changes most likely consist of additions of novel patterns of regulation or the reorganization of pre-existing patterns. We feel that, generally, the appearance of new structural (producer) genes represents a minor part of the changes involved.

Evolution is not a ladder, leading step by step from primitive to sophisticated organisms. It is replete with blind alleys, false starts, wrong turns, and bungled experiments. No clear connection has been established between complexity and fitness, and there are examples of creatures who became simpler in the course of time. Nevertheless, in general and over the long term, evolution has produced novel forms of life whose increasing biological complexity matches or surpasses the complexity of the environment. The German zoologist Bernhard Rensch, following Julian Huxley, calls this process "anagenesis," by which he means the progressive mastery exerted by living creatures over their surroundings, through a higher and higher level of molecular organization in the chemistry of body and brain.

How, then, is anagenesis achieved? To a certain extent, it is brought about by a more elaborate set of structural genes, coding for new and different types of proteins. But this strategy is by no means the only one, and it becomes less significant, rather than more so, in the later stages of evolution.

In the final evolutionary advance which led to the appearance of humans, mutations in structural genes do not become increasingly frequent, as traditional evolution theory would predict. Just the opposite is the case. When the reptiles finally ended their hundred-million-year reign as lords of the earth, the spaces they left vacant were filled by creatures not very impressive to look at. However, these new arrivals reproduced in a very interesting way, one that was to have momentous consequences for the future of species. These were the placentals, small animals which spent most of their growing time, not in an egg, as reptiles do, but inside the body of the mother, where they were nourished with food and oxygen from her body.

Two striking features of placentals were their larger brains and the longer time they spent growing up. The placentals dominate the age of mammals, which has lasted seventy million years, up to our own time. Yet during the period between the rise of the placentals and the arrival of man's ancestors, the rate of preserved mutations in the proteins of these advancing species slowed down sharply, even though the placentals themselves evolved at an exceptionally rapid rate.

Morris Goodman, professor of anatomy at Wayne State University, and his fellow researcher, G. W. Moore, in an investigation of vertebrate evolution, developed a computer model which compresses minor trends taking place over immense stretches of evolutionary time, speeding up the film, as it were, so that the effects of very weak natural selection, effects which might otherwise be mistaken for no selection at all, can be detected. This model shows that progress toward an increasingly complex internal chemistry is not steady and smooth, but jolts along in spurts and starts of lessening intensity.

Goodman's graph of the rates of evolutionary changes in the *proteins* of the forerunners of the human species over the last 600 million years resembles a chart of share prices on the New York Stock Exchange in the years preceding the Great Crash of 1929—a series of peaks and troughs leading to ultimate collapse. Successful mutations in proteins put on brief bursts of speed at the first appearance of revolutionary new bodily functions and organs, changes which enabled animals to spread into new spaces and complete an extraordinary saga of territorial conquest. With each new advance, however, the rate of mutation in structural genes slowed down. It raced ahead in the first vertebrates, then fell off sharply; picked up some speed with the emergence of four-footed animals; decelerated for about 175 million years; accelerated only moderately when the placental mammals came into their own; and then braked violently, almost coming to a halt over the past hundred million years except for one major upward convulsion that gradually petered out. This slowing down is especially marked in the final stages of descent, when apes and hominoids went their separate ways.

Goodman believes that this deceleration came about because, once evolution had fashioned the highly complex protein chemistry of the brain and nervous system of humans, with their long period of infancy and childhood, such a marvelously intricate structure needed to be stabilized more than it needed to be improved. That would be especially true while the child is still inside the mother's body. A great variety of gene activity, producing a wealth of different proteins inside the womb, would be dangerous, perhaps fatal, for the gestating embryo, because its chemistry needs to be as uniformly compatible as possible with the chemistry of the mother, whose immune system might otherwise reject her own offspring.

Once expelled from the luxurious sanctum of the uterus, how-ever, the newborn infant needs a variety of gene products in order to resist the myriad shocks and infections likely to be encountered as part of the unpredictable process of simply being alive in the world. Not until after birth is the immune system formed, with its tremendous built-in range of information about harmful foreign bodies. At about this time, too, the central ner-vous system also undergoes important stages of development. Its elaborate network of connections requires a high degree of variety in the molecular building blocks used for its construc-tion.

All this is under the control of subtle and highly evolved systems of algorithms, presumably of many levels of complexity, in DNA. These algorithms see to it that a child's protein chem-istry is simpler inside the womb than out in the world, by switching off certain genes before birth and switching them on as the child grows up. This means postponing many of the most important phases of human development until a later time of life, so that an extended childhood and adolescence are guaran-teed, programmed in. The opposing forces of uniformity and variety still act strongly today on the human gene pool, insuring a prolonged period of immaturity.

Thus it is the timetable which is of critical importance in the emergence of biological traits in evolution that are characteris-tically human. The more various the range of experience open to the individual, the more intense are the pressures for greater variety in the information system of the genes. This requires a long period of protected, predictable gestation, free from sur-prises and risks, enabling the intricate circuits and billions of nerve cells to be laid down in the brain under orderly, stable conditions. It also calls for a burst of genetic variety, switched on after birth. Goodman believes that this blaze of postnatal richness may be the biochemical source of the tremendous range of different talents, tastes, skills, temperaments, and divergent types of thinking that is the mark of a successful society. In recognition of the fact that humans need both phases of the timetable, prenatal and postnatal, to rise to their intellectual preeminence in the animal kingdom, Goodman christens man-kind "the conservative and revolutionary mammal."

12

Partly Green Till the Day We Die

One of the scandals of modern biology was the discovery that humans and chimpanzees are 99 percent identical as far as their structural genes are concerned. The genetic distance between them on this level is less than the distance between sibling species of fruit fly, species which are so alike to look at that one cannot be distinguished from another. This conclusion did not come as a complete bombshell when it was announced in 1975. The groundwork had been laid as long ago as 1901, at Cambridge, by rough-and-ready methods of analyzing immune reactions of different species, but the significance of those results went largely unnoticed. About fifty years later, Morris Goodman established the close molecular relationship between chimps and man by means of more refined techniques, using immunological data from serum proteins in different primate species. Goodman's tests convinced him that chimps and gorillas should not be placed in the gibbon and orangutan family, as tradition dictated, but belong in the same family with man. Finally, some twenty years after that, Mary-Claire King and Allan Wilson, both geneticists working at Berkeley, announced that the difference in the protein-coding sequences of DNA between chimp and man is only about one percent.

It is clear that in many respects the distance between the species is very great indeed. Scarcely a bone in the body is the same. The pelvis, feet, legs, arms, and fingers are different in shape, and the chimp's brain is smaller. During evolution, the changes which led to such significant differences must have taken place not in those parts of the DNA text that specify a protein directly, but in the passages containing the algorithms which control the timing and use of existing structural genes. One result of these changes, clearly, was the emergence of that most distinctively human possession, the big brain. King and Wilson declared in 1975, "Most important for the study of human evolution would be the demonstration of differences between apes and humans in the timing of gene expression during development of adaptively crucial organ systems such as the brain."

The following year, the biologist Emile Zuckerhandl reported that the brain of a human being is so similar to that of a chimpanzee in its basic chemistry that it may not contain a single protein with a genuinely novel function. "The uniqueness of the human brain must be due to structural and functional variants of pre-existing proteins," Zuckerhandl said, "and to variations in the quantity, timing, place and coordination of the action and interaction of these proteins."

It is important not to oversimplify the role of regulatory programs in DNA. Clearly, they operate at many levels and in various ways. Systems regulating genes are often affected by events in the outer domain of the cell, and by communication between cells. Also, the programs themselves depend for their functioning on the finely adapted sequences of structural genes, so that the importance of such sequences, which evolved to their present state of high efficiency over long stretches of time, should not be underestimated. In some cases, structural genes are also regulator genes: they produce protein molecules which are instrumental in switching other genes on or off.

Roy Britten has called our present ignorance of the exact nature of such control systems "abysmal." However, he and other biologists assume that there is a basic source of control, governing the timing of gene expression, and that this source is to be found in the information of DNA, in its "meta-statements." It is here that we must look for the essential biochemical difference between man and ape.

Human DNA, as its information structure evolved to produce our brainy species, apparently adopted a most ingenious strategy. A change of programs resulted in a significant change in the timetable of growing up. This timetable was rewritten, presumably by mutations, in a very curious way, making it radically different from, yet oddly similar to, the timetable of man's primate ancestors. It retained some of the features of the primate system, but turned them topsy-turvy.

When fully grown, the human male or female bears a resemblance to an ape which is still in the fetal or juvenile stage of development. Put another way, the infant ape, in some respects, looks strikingly like the adult *Homo*. This is not a regressive trend. Far from it. It is a biological feat of the highest importance, leading to the emergence of mind.

Reprogramming was the secret, changing the rules of timing. The strategic slowing down of the body's timetable arrested the growth of certain features of the primate anatomy, freezing them at an infantile stage of development. Fetal apes have flat faces, long necks, round heads, small teeth—and massive brains in relation to the weight of the whole body. The bones of the cranium are thin, the ridges over the brows undeveloped, and there is not much hair on the body. Even more remarkable, in an ape at the fetal stage, the place at which the spinal cord enters the skull lies directly under the brain, allowing an erect posture. As the ape develops, however, the place of entry shifts back behind the brain, making it impractical to stand upright. The retarded timetable adopted by humans means that this critical shift backward never takes place, and it enables the human to walk erect all through life.

This technique of slowing down maturity, retaining into grown-up life the juvenile traits of ancestral species, is called neoteny, a word coined in 1883. It means, literally, "holding youth." Neoteny is a concept made fashionable by the Dutch anthropologist Louis Bolk, who developed a theory of fetalization between 1915 and 1926. Bolk held views on evolution which were contrary to those of Darwin and are regarded as disreputable today. He believed that transformation takes place along a path determined and directed by inner forces, in a unified, coordinated fashion. For this reason Bolk's theory went into eclipse for many years, clouded by the dubious philosophy of vitalism on which it was based. In recent years, his beliefs have been rescued from limbo and given a contemporary gloss. Bolk's metaphysical speculations have been carefully sifted out and separated from his useful scientific insights.

By retarding development of the body, evolution can be "put into reverse," to some extent, so that a species which has become overspecialized, and is in danger of ending in a blind alley through being too good at doing too few things, can retreat to a less specialized form.*

Many different creatures in nature have neotenous features. The King Charles spaniel is one of the best known. Lap dogs are neotenous, as are a type of cricket, the female glowworm (but not the male), and bighorn sheep. The adult ostrich retains the soft down feathers of a nestling chick, and has lost the power of flight. Dogs are neotenous wolves.

In neoteny, not all parts of the body need to be retarded. The famous example of this partial deceleration of growing up is the tiger salamander (Ambystoma tigrinum). Individuals of North American populations develop fully: the adult loses its gills, breathes by means of lungs, and spends most of its time on land. On the other hand, individuals from the Mexican populations, known as axolotls, are neotonic: while they look like adults, they retain their gills and never leave the water. Such a strategy may provide an escape route from too much narrow specialization, so that no matter how specialized the adult form of a spe-

---

* The zoologist Walter Garstang, an endearingly combative figure, who composed several excruciating comic verses on the subject of neoteny and kindred abstruse aspects of natural history, was among the first to realize the profound impact neoteny might have on future evolutionary events. Garstang had made a special study of certain larval forms of marine life that are thrown up by organisms living on the bottom of the sea so as to spread the species far and wide in the ocean currents. These larvae had been specially adapted for their peculiar mode of existence by natural selection. Garstang realized that in the larvae there are two opposing kinds of evolutionary needs. One need is to grow up into an adult and settle down on the bottom of the sea in order to reproduce. The other, contradictory need is to remain in an infantile, floating state for as long as possible, so as to disseminate the species over a very wide region.

Garstang concluded that the infantile stages might be modified by evolutionary change just as much as the adult stages, and that these modifications could have momentous effects, not only on the adults of the species but on the whole future

cies may be, the juvenile form may still evolve into a new line, perhaps leading to a different animal altogether.

———————

In the human species generally, the most significant effect of neoteny is on the formation of the big brain. The brains of the great apes, relatives of *Homo,* do most of their growing in the first year of life, making an extended period of intellectual development impossible. A gibbon's brain is nearly three-quarters complete at birth, and is fully formed after the first six months of life. Human brains develop in quite a different way. They better than double their weight in the first year of life, then increase it by more than 25 percent in the second year and by more than 15 percent in the third.

Timing the expression of genes in the growing organism has turned out to be a process which is much more than a marvelously intricate illustration of how nature uses information to organize matter. We are talking here about something a great deal more remarkable: the hypothesis that a change in the timing of gene expression thrust *Homo sapiens* onto the stage of prehistory and made possible the massive, slow-maturing brain of a species which can do more than merely perceive its world and act immediately upon what it perceives. The human brain provides a significant space between perception and action; in this space arose complex forms of abstract knowledge and the fruits of the contemplative mind: myth, religion, art, literature, and philosophy.

Such an altered program of growth, so important for human

———————

of the species itself. Suppose a primitive invertebrate organism on the sea bed, such as a starfish or a sea urchin, sent up larvae that by neotenous strategies became able to stay afloat in the larval form for a long time, speeding up the development of the reproductive organs in relation to the rest of the body. The organism might easily acquire a strong tail, enabling it to swim more efficiently than did the feeble equipment nature had originally provided. Becoming sexually mature while still swimming, it need never settle down.

Could this active, free-moving creature, Garstang wondered, in a leap of speculation, have been the forerunner of the first vertebrates, which led on to fish, and eventually to human beings? If that conjecture turned out to be true, it would demonstrate the enormous, progressive power of neoteny as a strategy of evolution. Garstang's son-in-law, A. C. Hardy, promulgated these ideas in the 1950s, arguing that some major groups in the animal kingdom could never have evolved without neoteny, and among those that did are some of the most successful species in evolution.

uniqueness, is under the control of the algorithms, or rules, contained in the DNA message. Clearly, these algorithms have changed during the course of evolution, and they have changed in ways which enable humans to become neotenous, retarding the development of some physical features and slowing down the timetable of maturity for the brain. This means that the schedule for the formation of the brain does not come to an end immediately, or even very soon after the infant leaves the womb of the mother. The brain goes on growing after birth at a rate almost as rapid as before birth. The result is that the neural circuits are still being laid down at a time when the child is growing up and coming to terms with its world. They are open to the full impact of information pouring in from the outside.

Neoteny, by slowing down the timetable, keeps the brain developing, because it is held back to the fetal stage—and the fetal stage is one of a rapidly growing brain.

Only a fraction of our brain's development takes place inside the womb, during gestation. The rest is spread out over two decades of experiencing and learning. One obvious consequence of this singular arrangement is that humans, unlike other species, are much less bound by automatic or instinctive mental traits inherited and specified by the information in the genes. They are more powerfully affected by active encounter with their environment. By stretching out the years of childhood, the human species has become notably dependent on the social framework and relationships within the family during infancy. Yet at the same time human beings are extraordinarily individualistic. Their brains are so complex, plastic, and slow to mature, that each one is unique to the person who possesses it, and shows a marked and surprising physical variation from one individual to another.

Dr. Peter Huttenlocher, professor of pediatrics at the University of Chicago, has found that the young child has a more complex set of connections among the nerve cells in the cerebral cortex than it will ever have in later life. Contrary to what was once believed, the number of these connections does not increase with age, but declines. At the same time, the brain of a six-year-old has a slower and more irregular activity than that of an adult, and this, too, increases the child's capacity to acquire and remember knowledge. Huttenlocher says, "One of the most interesting aspects of the six-year-old brain is that a child who has had little educational experience in this crucial year has tremendous difficulty in catching up later, even with very good effort. Six seems to be a critical period, a time when the brain is especially receptive."

Neoteny slows down the rate of bodily development in humans, giving them a longer childhood than their primate ancestors and a brain which grows in early life as fast as it grew in the womb. This was a revolutionary change, resulting in a unique openness to new information at a time when the child is fully dependent on its parents, who spend much time on its care and mental enrichment. The plasticity of the child's brain, its flexibility and redundancy, enabling it to shift and reorganize its resources to meet the needs of various modes of life, make the human species the least narrowly specialized of all animals. The brain comes provided with a generous number of possible patterns of organization in early childhood. Which patterns are actually developed may depend on the experiences of each child, his or her capacities, tastes, drives, and the mental stimulation given in the critical period. The large, slowly maturing brain helped to provide an escape from the trap of overspecialization which blocks the avenue to further evolutionary advance. No single evolutionary event has had such a transforming effect on the life of the planet; neoteny is the biological principle which made civilization possible.

An extended period of growing up, made possible by alterations in the timetable of development, tends to promote a more versatile and interesting species, more varied in its mental, emotional, and physical behavior. There is a diminished sense of those urgent forces of survival and competition, of nature red in tooth and claw, that makes Darwin's world view appear so fierce and unrelenting. Indeed, neoteny does not seem to work well in the case of mammals which give birth to large litters of offspring, where the young compete intensely for space, nourishment, and attention. In a large litter, the struggle for necessities tends to shorten the period of childhood dependency and accelerate the arrival of maturity. However, when competition is somewhat relaxed, by reduced family size, an extended childhood creates a setting in which the young are able to experiment and try out new forms of behavior in the safe, predictable surroundings of the family circle.

That is exactly the sort of environment in which, modern educationalists find, children are able to learn reading, writing, and other skills at a surprisingly early age. The secret of flexible behavior is to have interesting experiences in stable conditions as free as possible from serious danger. One of the most important of these experiences is play. Play, which is the normal activity of children who feel secure, is a symptom of versatility that tends to lead to more versatility. It is an activity in which neotenous creatures typically engage.

More than a century ago, when theorists studied play, they regarded it as a vehicle for the harmless release of surplus energy. More recently, as has been the case in other branches of knowledge, a theory of play in terms of energy gave way to a theory based on information. Play began to be seen, at least in part, as an element in the process of learning.

Play is a symbolic activity, to some extent. Its rules may be broken, or new rules invented, without leading to serious consequences. It flourishes best when the consequences of an action are likely to be of less importance than the action itself. New forms of behavior can be invented without the risks which normally accompany breaches of the adult code. In play, it is possible to go to extremes, to be daring, to experiment, so that the boundaries of the permissible and the practical can be tested to the full.

Spontaneous innovation is the hallmark of play. Jerome Brunner has suggested that the use of tools in evolution may have arisen, not from Darwinian, survive-or-perish pressures, but after a long period of unforced, pressure-free existence in a terrain that did not need to be defended all the time. In this view, technology was a sort of extension of play, thriving under the same conditions and for some of the same reasons.

The timetable of human development coded into DNA allows a generous number of years for this adventurous, carefree stage of a child's life, when he is at ease with the novel and the unknown. But the period is not open-ended. Young children are often very good at improvising songs and minting new metaphors without being especially aware that they are being original. They are spontaneously, unself-consciously given to imaginative and fresh expression. Howard Gardner, a Harvard psychologist, has given examples of children's flights of fancy which rise to the level of genuine poetry. A girl describes her naked body as "barefoot all over." Another child speaks of skywriting as "a scar in the sky." Almost without exception, says Gardner, youngsters will produce drawings and paintings that, in their use of color and sense of composition, "bear at least a superficial kinship to works of Klee, Miró or Picasso."

As the child grows older, however, poetry gradually vanishes from his language, the quality of drawing declines, and adventurousness wanes in all fields of mental and artistic endeavor. Conformity sets in and play is subject to fixed rules, strictly observed. Symbols are manipulated without the same sense of daring and self-assurance. Drawings are copied, language is prosaic. Children become more receptive to the work of others. Gardner calls this stage the period of literalism, a time for mastering rules, traditions, norms, and for understanding the technical aspects of art—style, balance, and composition. Very few children can recover the gift of original expression, and they do so only after attaining conscious mastery of technique. They have lost entirely the uninhibited, unrehearsed freedom of childhood and instead must learn to be innovative again, to break the rules, not innocently, but with full awareness. Before they can become artists, they must go through a literal stage, and this stage is an essential part of their development.

There is a kind of "sensitive period" in the years leading up to adolescence, Gardner concludes, in which the future artist must pick up skills quickly, so that when adolescence comes, the possession of a good technique will be proof against the onslaught of his own developing powers of criticism. The child creates unthinkingly, the adult with a great awareness of technique, yet both share a certain openness, a willingness to explore and break new ground, so that the daring impulses of childhood persist, under a new guise, in the works of the mature artist. In his foreword to the revised version of *The Magus*, a novel about the pains of becoming adult, John Fowles wrote that the book

> must always substantially remain a novel of adolescence written by a retarded adolescent. My only plea is that all artists have to range the full extent of their own lives freely. The rest of the world can censor and bury their private past. We cannot, and so have to remain partly green till the day we die . . . callow green in the hope of becoming fertile-green.

Play, prolonged childhood, and a larger brain are interlocking themes in evolution. For as far back into prehistory as science has been able to reach, mammals have had bigger brains than other vertebrates; and primates, from the very beginning, had bigger brains than other animals relative to the size of their bodies. Primates live longer and mature more slowly than other mammals of comparable size. Monkeys leave the mother after a few months, while chimps enjoy maternal attention and protection for four or five years. Humans have a childhood and adolescence lasting twice as long as those of the great apes. And along with the stretched-out childhood goes the capacity for play. Ascending the scale of the primates, anthropologists find that play is more and more central to the process of growing up, and most essential of all in human beings.

The genetic principles underlying these special, interrelated characteristics are to be found, not so much in the structural sequences of the DNA message, though these are of great importance, but rather in the timing of the stages of development. And this timing is under control of highly complex regulatory systems, "information about information," which have yet to reveal their secrets to present-day biology. Here, it is thought, must lie the answers to many questions. We do not understand significant aspects of these systems. But when we do, says Roy Britten, "we will understand the nature of life."

13

No Need for Ancient Astronauts

Sudden accelerations in evolution, jumps from plateau to plateau, cannot be understood in terms of single mutations, one at a time, in the structural genes of man's ancestors.

This is a point worth lingering over, for it is exactly here, on the vexed question of evolutionary leaps, that Darwin's theory is weakest and least satisfying.

During the first half of the nineteenth century, most geologists accepted the view that the history of the earth was marked by a series of convulsions, arranged by God, of which the biblical deluge was a fair example. However, as an undergraduate at Cambridge, reading for a career in the church but coming increasingly under the spell of natural science, Darwin was exposed to the ideas of scholars who thought in terms of gradual transformations in the geology of the earth. For his voyage on the *Beagle*, beginning in 1831, serving as ship's geologist, Darwin took with him a copy of the newly published first volume of Charles Lyell's *Principles of Geology*, which effectively demolished the notion of successive, divinely ordained paroxysms in favor of gentler and more uniform change, brought about by forces which have not varied from the earliest times to the present day.

Catastrophism was not purely theological, but was based on scientific evidence of discontinuity in the fossil record. However, Lyell took the view that living species became extinct gradually, and that new ones were continually created. Fresh from his perusal of Lyell, Darwin made his first stop in the tropics when the *Beagle* dropped anchor off St. Jago in the Cape Verde Islands on January 6, 1832. There he saw with his own eyes a perfectly horizontal white band in the face of a sea cliff, high above the water. This white band was formed of "calcareous matter," with thousands of marine shells embedded in it. Darwin thought that the smooth straightness of this stratum of shells which had once formed the sea bottom was a sign that the island had been raised slowly and gradually, over the centuries, rather than being thrust up in a sudden, violent catastrophe. The insight, Darwin noted in his autobiography, "convinced me of the infinite superiority of Lyell's views over those advocated in any other work known to me."

The gradualist thesis had a long history of controversy and did not enjoy a clear run even in Victorian times. It has now, in the light of recent knowledge, come under fresh challenge. New research in paleontology, including the discovery of microfossils up to 3.5 billion years old, when added to the evidence already existing, poses serious questions as to the soundness of the "slow, steady" explanation of evolutionary change. There seems, for example, to have been a sharp break between life as it existed in the vast expanse of time which is called the Precambrian period of earth's history, in which the microscopic forms show little change over billions of years, and the relatively sudden emergence of larger scale, more complex organisms about 570 million years ago. The transition appears explosively sudden by the leisurely standards of the geological time frame—not more than 100 million years.

Stephen Jay Gould, at Harvard, pointing out the extreme scarcity of transitional forms between one species and another in evolution—the "missing links" in the fossil record—believes the theory of gradualism is now invalid as a description of evolution, since it fails to explain many advances which were relatively abrupt, including the size and structure of the human brain. Gould says:

Paleontologists have documented virtually no cases of slow and steady transformation, foot by foot up the strata of a hillslope—not for horses, not for humans . . . Instead, most fossil species share two features; first, they do not change in any marked way during the entire course of their existence; second, they enter the record abruptly, either replacing or coexisting with their ancestors. In short, stasis and sudden replacement mark the end of most species.

If evolution is seen first and foremost as an information process, then the reasons for the rapid emergence of evolutionary novelty that paleontologists have noted in the fossil record must be sought in the structure of the DNA message. In information theory, novelty is related to the number of possibilities in the message source. In living organisms, these possibilities may exist as unused information in the genes. Evolutionary innovation, the creation of new organs with new functions, would then be accomplished by making the possibilities actual.

Susumu Ohno, the American geneticist, thinks such possibilities were provided in evolution by the fortuitous appearance of "useless information" in the DNA of organisms. This came in the form of repetition, which is the simplest form of redundancy. Existing genes duplicated themselves, producing exact copies which at first were quite superfluous, of no use to the organism. The DNA text was extended, but the effect was like printing a book which consists of the same few pages repeated over and over again. Extra copies of these pages provide no new information.

As time went on, however, the redundant genes underwent chance mutations. They ceased to be copies and became unique sequences, new pages in the book of life. Very often these sequences were gibberish, mere genetic noise, with no meaning in terms of a protein product. Ohno suspects that the many nonsense passages in the DNA of organisms today are relics of those scrambled genes, which litter the text as the fossils of extinct animals litter the surface of the earth. In some cases, however, mutations may result in a gene copy acquiring a meaning. A structural gene would code for a useful new protein. A gene that was part of a regulatory system would alter the timing of expression of the structural genes in a way which could be of benefit to the organism. These extra pages would then add sensible new information to the book.

What is even more interesting is that a gene copy, as an extra page, is often ignored by natural selection, even when accumulating mutations, as long as the "original page" of which it was a duplicate continues to serve its beneficial function. The copy is free to change in ways which would not be tolerated in the original. Once the new gene acquires a useful meaning it may then come under the protection of natural selection and be preserved.

Explosions of gene duplication took place in evolution, Ohno argues, when the forebears of man were still swimming in the sea or alternating between water and dry land. Later, ancestral mammals were provided with many sets of copies of existing genes, and as time went on, these useless pages, containing no new information, were rewritten by mutations to become different genes with novel functions.

Gene copies provide a source of experiment and creativity in evolution. They are adventurous, supplying "new hypotheses" which are only later put to the test of natural selection, which by itself is a conservative force, only modifying what already exists. The extra pages in the script are possibilities, potential information far in excess of what the organism needs to survive.

It is a curious fact that major new steps in evolution were not usually taken by the most advanced members of a class of animals, but by one of the more primitive and simple members of the class. The explanation for this seeming paradox, Ohno points out, is clear at once if the word "primitive" is taken to mean unspecialized, not committed to narrow behavior patterns, and if "advanced" is taken to mean specialized and locked into these patterns. A simple, generalized creature is like a sheet of white paper ready to be written upon. And it was this type of species which was the original ancestor of the vertebrates. Its DNA was provided with redundancy in large quantities, and eventually the redundancy became useful information.

It was an excess of possibilities, Ohno believes, that laid the genetic foundations of the human brain. A supply of new genes in much greater numbers than were needed produced the building blocks of a brain far more complex than was needed for coping with a primitive environment. The complexity of the brain is due to the intricate network of connections among nerve cells, and these connections are thought to be determined by the attraction which exists between the proteins on the cell surface of individual cells. A constellation of scores or even hundreds of different proteins on the cell surface establishes a highly specific "lock-and-key" connection with proteins on other cells.

A tremendous variety of protein constellations is needed for such an intricate communication system. This variety was supplied, Ohno proposes, by explosions of gene copies, which mutated beyond the reach of natural selection and acquired new functions. These new genes, as we have noted, could have been either structural or regulatory.

In this view, new proteins and new programs were sufficiently abundant, sufficiently early, to make possible an evolutionary leap, producing a brain of high complexity long before the appearance of civilization, so that the capacity for human culture did not come gradually, but in a thunderclap. In particular, Ohno believes that Neanderthal man was already in possession of a brain whose chemical structure was as intricate as our own. He asks, "Did the genome [DNA text] of our cave-dwelling predecessor contain a set or sets of genes which enable modern man to compose music of infinite complexity and write novels with profound meaning? One is compelled to give an affirmative answer."

This hypothesis moves the whole discussion of genetic information into highly controversial realms, and touches on questions which are very much part of the ferment of new ideas and discoveries in the prehistory of man. The appearance of the big brain poses problems for which there are, as yet, no good answers. The notion of a brain growing to full size in primitive beings whose mental outlook was supposedly so limited, so plagued by superstition and fallacious assumptions about nature, is paradoxical. The same brain today masters the intricacies of quantum physics, unravels the genetic code, and builds ships which carry man to the moon.

———————

Ideas about the origins of culture, and therefore about the development of the human intellect, are in a period of rapid change. As the mists of prehistory begin to lift a little, culture is seen to be extremely ancient, reaching back perhaps as far as three million years ago, to the time of *Australopithecus*, a man-like ape who may have had some glimmerings of symbolism. Pebbles found near australopithecine remains bear natural markings on them resembling faces. *Homo habilis*, the tool-making "handyman" who lived out in the grasslands between 2,000,000 and 2,500,000 years ago, was perhaps capable of a form of ritual. Examples of hand-worked red ocher have been found with skeletons of *habilis*. *Homo erectus*, who arrived about 1,000,000 years later, had a brain size which in some cases approaches that of modern humans. He was the first human ancestor known to have used fire. The tools of *erectus* were carefully and precisely made to serve a number of different pur-poses. He hunted big game, including elephants, which presum-ably calls for a high degree of cooperation and communication by some rudimentary form of speech.

The first known example of the intentional use of symbolism in engraving is extremely ancient, belonging to the later period of *Homo erectus*. This was an ox rib, bearing markings in the form of festooned, double arcs, found at the site of Pech de l'Azé, in France, in a level which is about 300,000 years old. Such a discovery pushes back to a very distant date indeed the beginnings of complex symbol-making activity, with all that im-plies for the mental capacity of early man.

Neanderthal man, who appeared about 100,000 years ago, was at one time portrayed as a slouching, primitive brute, a mental incompetent hardly fit to be spoken of as human. That view has now entirely changed. Neanderthal man is known to have used sophisticated tools constructed from carefully built compo-nents. His brain was slightly larger than ours, as befitted his bulkier size. Neanderthals practiced ritual and buried their dead with ceremony and a sense of the transcendent: stone imple-ments and cooked food have been found in single graves and at least seven different kinds of flowers were laid in a shallow Neanderthal pit in Shanidar, Iraq.

Much is mysterious about the Neanderthals, but the evidence is now compelling that they were fully human, members of our own species. One eminent paleontologist, Bjorn Kurtén, has written a novel about the Neanderthal as a way of airing hypotheses about them which could not be supported by scientific proof. In *Dance of the Tiger,* Kurtén depicts the Neanderthal people as gentle and intelligent, close enough genetically to the more recent, "sapient" Cro-Magnons for the two peoples to interbreed. Such interbreeding might explain the otherwise puzzling disappearance of the Neanderthals some 35,000 years ago, when they were replaced by Cro-Magnon man. Possibly the genes of the more numerous Cro-Magnon swamped those of the Neanderthal people.

Neanderthal man used symbols and abstract notations. Intentional zigzag images and fine parallel lines have been found engraved on bones excavated at Neanderthal sites, and these are the type of markings which appear later in the more fullblown culture of Cro-Magnon, with its profusion of complex symbol and image. Evidently the capacity for intellectual activity of a high order was in place long before the first civilizations, a fact which makes it difficult to sustain traditional ideas of human culture as progressing by gradual increments as a result of slowly increasing mental competence. The British archeologist Clive Gamble has recently stated that

> It is no longer sufficient to look at human evolution over the past 300,000 years as simply a process of increasing intelligence and offer an explanation in terms of changes in the brain . . . recent studies have demonstrated the existence, some 300,000 years ago, of mental ability equivalent to that of modern man. The dramatic developments in material culture, such as the appearance of art, now seem to be more closely related to changes in the amount and kind of information needed by paleolithic societies, rather than being dependent on the evolution of the brain.

Alexander Marshack, of the Peabody Museum at Harvard, believes that Neanderthal man used a variety of symbol systems, reflecting a well-defined social structure and documenting an awareness of nature. They are evidence that "primitive" man, much earlier than was once thought, possessed powers of abstraction far beyond those of a mere tool maker and hunter. They suggest that the brain of Neanderthal man was of the same order as our own.

Some of Marshack's most important discoveries came from an

inspection of the remarkable collection of Cro-Magnon carved figures found at the cave site of Vogelherd, in southern Germany, in 1931. One set of statuettes in the collection, radio-carbon dated at 30,000 B.C. or older, must have been made by Cro-Magnon man before the Neanderthals vanished from the earth. Marshack uses advanced techniques, including infrared and ultraviolet light, to reveal subtleties of craftsmanship over-looked by earlier researchers.

Looking at these objects through a microscope, Marshack re-alized that they had been created to be used, and were not sim-ply decorations. Some bore symbolic markings. A horse carved from mammoth ivory was worn smooth by much handling and carrying. An angle had been cut into the shoulder, apparently for symbolic purposes. A roughly carved figure, with female breasts, bore three sets of marks made by different tools, sug-gesting a ritual use of the object over a period of time. On a statuette of a horse or reindeer dated 29,000 B.C. were engraved intricate geometric patterns of multiple curves and sets of straight lines of different lengths. These kinds of markings occur repeatedly during the Ice Age and after.

Marshack considers the objects and their markings part of a complex system of interrelated images and abstract notations, based on a sustained tradition. An oval plaque, carved from antler or bone and some 30,000 years old, found in the Dor-dogne, bears a most intriguing series of engraved marks, forming a serpentine chain looped and folded back on itself. The marks were made by different tools and by different styles of twisting and punching with the tools. The figure was clearly intended to have a meaning in terms of its parts as well as of its entire serpentine contour. It was a device for storing information of some kind, whether mythic, social, or having to do with the behavior of nature. To decipher its code one needs a key, and this introduces yet another awkward difficulty, for to hand on a key to a code, it seems clear that a fairly sophisticated form of communication must have been in use. The miniature scale of the engraving, requiring fine precision, suggests a tradition al-ready well established and great self-assurance on the part of the engraver. A symbol system at a primitive stage of develop-ment would surely be inscribed in a larger, more uncertain hand. Marshack concludes that there is evidence for a number of symbol systems existing simultaneously well before the departure of Neanderthal man.

Such codes, Marshack believes, are not writing or arithmetic. Writing in the accepted sense of the word goes back only about six thousand years, and arithmetic did not appear before the Upper Paleolithic period ended 10,000 years ago. But the codes do have a meaning and a function. The zigzag markings and meanders inscribed on bone objects may be evidence of a shamanistic symbolism having to do with water and the use of water imagery. They reveal the capacity to symbolize the external world in various ways.

———————

Is this Darwinian evolution? It makes no sense to talk of such epiphanies in terms of survival and fitness, or strategies of adaptation, because the richness of the imagery and symbolism seems so much greater than would have been needed to master the challenges posed by the environment at the basic level of "to subsist or not to subsist." Early man apparently was tackling more profound questions.

The tradition of abstract symbolism that shines out from the bits of bone and antler retrieved by archeologists, stretching back so many millennia, yielding so much more to intelligent inquiry than was ever suspected, is far in excess of what was needed for subsistence. Such elaborate mental activity cannot have been a mere adaptation. Marshack sees the Ice Age culture as the *culmination*, rather than the genesis, of a cultural unfolding which had been in progress over a great span of evolutionary time, perhaps as long as a million years.

The remarkable animal paintings in the Paleolithic caves of France and Spain, dated earlier than 17,000 years ago and at first dismissed as hoaxes, are not, in his view, an exceptional, isolated blaze of artistic splendor, but represent one facet of more widely dispersed and more continuous symbol-making activities. The abstract notation in other regions of Upper Paleolithic culture are equally impressive as displays of an advanced intellectual capacity. They are different in degree but not in kind. If the cave paintings are the Rembrandts of the era, other evi-

dences of symbolism represent the Leibnizes and Newtons.
These abstractions were not writing, but they were based on
mental processes as sophisticated as those which underlie writing. It is unlikely that such complex thoughts were the result of
hunting animals or gathering roots and berries. Paleolithic art
exploded in the glories of cave paintings like those in Lascaux
and Pech Merle because the seeds of the cultural—not simply
artistic—revolution had been planted long before in the biology
of human ancestors. "It's the evolution of this 'silent' capacity
that we should be interested in," Marshack has said. "It's a
generalized hominid capacity that goes back a very long way
indeed."

The idea that tool making, the technology of subsistence, was
the driving force behind the evolution of intelligence and language is open to serious question. Anthropologists have noted
the surprising stagnation of the tool industry over an immense
stretch of time. The engraved markings on bone, stone, and clay,
the zigzags and meanders, lines and indentations are no longer
regarded as random scribblings but as highly organized and systematic—as information. And they are seen increasingly as an
index of intellect in the fullest sense. In this view, codes, symbols, and rules are primary, and the practical application of such
abstract modes of thought to tool technology are secondary.
Rules for making implements certainly grew more sophisticated
with time, but the mind of early man was moving in the direction of knowledge infinitely more general and conceptual than
was needed for such utilitarian tasks as maintaining a warm
body and a full stomach.

The momentum behind the first, fullblown, preclassic civilizations in the valley of the Tigris and Euphrates came, at least
in part, from the need of people whose minds were already
predisposed to religion, art, symbolism, and ritual to express
these in a more elaborate way. An inner impulse as well as
external circumstances made it possible for the civilization of
Mesopotamia, Egypt, and the Indus Valley to "evolve." In many
ways, they were immanent in the consciousness of the people
of the Stone Age. The rise of farming and herding, the produc-

tion of more food than was needed for mere subsistence in the
fertile flood plains of wide rivers, and unlimited water all combined to support the existence of communities of people freed
from the stark struggle for survival and able to give their attention to cultural and social pursuits. Yet it is clear that culture
did not develop as an incidental overlay on top of the more basic
amenities of food, climate, and transport that are usually cited
as reasons for the rise of the preclassic civilizations.

Jacquetta Hawkes, the archeologist, wrote:

One of the underlying effects of this materialistic interpretation of
the birth of a civilisation is its apparent inevitability. Every stage
comes pat upon the one before and the whole chronicle seems to
advance with perfect logic and good sense. Yet one knows that it was
not inevitable, for on the one hand men have lived on well-watered
and fertile land without creating civilisation, and on the other have
created civilisations in apparently poor environments. As for the
logic and good sense, was not all this effort from surplus food-grow-
ing onwards and upwards to be devoted to the wildest imaginative
fantasies—to raising artificial mountains for men-gods and building
millions of tons of rock into a perfect geometric form to receive the
corpses of god-men?

With all these orderly economic and social constructions we seem
to be confronted with something like a motor car without an engine
or a suit of armour without a knight. The dynamic is missing . . . the
material advances in food production, technology and the rest make
it possible for these mental forms to find a new magnificence of
expression—to be royally dressed. That they were not new and that
they were to a very large extent universals of human self-conscious-
ness responding to what it found in its inner and outer worlds, can
hardly be doubted in the face of the evidence.

Explaining the origins of this great flowering of the human
spirit in external terms has reached the heights of speculative
folly in modern times with the hypothesis of ancient astronauts,
other-worldly messengers, bearers of information beyond the
mental reach of primitive man, descending in their chariots to
bring enlightenment and culture to the savage mind. Behind this
fantastic view of prehistory lies an all too familiar assumption
that archaic man was mentally unformed, ignorant of the unify-

ing principles and relations in the material universe. The ancient astronaut thesis is behaviorism carried to cosmic extremes. It presupposes that the human mind is passive, needing to be led rather than being able to innovate on its own terms, adapting rather than creating, copying, not originating.

Neanderthal man made tools flaked on both sides, but that was nothing earthshaking. He also used pointed fragments of bone or wood, was master of fire, prepared skins, and built huts within encampments. Much more to the point was the uniform spread of his culture across three continents, and the evidence of ritual and symbolic practices. Yet it is almost certain that he was not the first to show an aesthetic sense, to take an interest in the meaning of death and be aware of the supernatural, all aspects of the early psyche with vast implications for the higher flights of civilization which were to come much later. Archeology is continually extending the history of human consciousness further back in time.

It is not necessary to imagine that these great advances of the mind and spirit were made possible by packets of imported knowledge brought in spaceships by superior beings from other parts of the galaxy. Long before the visible traces of culture appear in the depths of the Paleolithic past, archaic man already possessed the foundation of a brain so highly organized, so various, so full of possibilities, it would enable his remote descendants to ride in fiery chariots of their own making on voyages of discovery across the boundless ocean of space.

14

The Clear and the Noisy Messages of Language

A theory of evolution which takes no account of the internal structure of the information in DNA stumbles and falters under the impact of new discoveries, new ideas, in the fast-moving science of molecular biology. It is not rich enough to accommodate them. In much the same way, a theory of language which concerns itself only with the surface appearance of the spoken or printed word has no hope of understanding its most important and essential properties. It misses the whole point of language as a human activity.

In information theory, it is the message source which is of primary importance. The source chooses a message out of a set of possible messages and codes it for transmission, sending it to a receiver, which is a sort of transmitter in reverse. In the process, some noise will add itself to the message, distorting and garbling it. Only if the message has been properly encoded at the source will it overcome the muddling effects of the noise, so that, when the message is decoded at its destination, it retains its original, intended structure and form.

Such a code must take away some of the freedom allowed the source in its selection of different messages, if fast and reliable communication is to take place. But a successful code takes away this freedom in special, ingenious ways, so that as much as possible is retained by the sender. And in finding the best way to accomplish this task, the designer of the code must consider not the observable, surface form of this or that particular message, but deeper and more general rules of structure which belong to the message system in its entirety. This approach is best described in a classic commentary on Shannon's original papers by Warren Weaver. Information theory, Weaver said, concerns itself with the "real inner core of the communication problem, with those basic relationships which hold in general, no matter what special form the actual case may take."

The modern revolution in linguistics, which began in the 1950s, roughly contemporaneously with the discovery of the genetic code, was an attempt to investigate the universal principles of all languages using a similar route, delving down beneath the observable surface of spoken sentences to the hidden, abstract structures underlying them.

Noam Chomsky has been the most original and powerful thinker in this search for tacit principles, the hidden mental operations which undergird human language. He wants above all to discover "those basic relationships which hold in general." He is firmly of the opinion that what a person says is an unreliable guide to what that person actually knows, often unconsciously, and it is knowledge of the patterns of language as a complete system, the command of all its possibilities, that interests Chomsky most. For a theory of language in the full sense of the word, what *can* be said is of more interest than what is actually said, and it is Chomsky's thesis that every speaker can say infinitely much. In this respect, his work has a close affinity with that of Shannon, in whose theory a single message is of interest only from the point of view of its relationship with all other messages which could have been sent but were not.

Chomsky regards language, at bottom, as a well-defined system, as far as its form is concerned. The input to the channel between speaker and listener is "coded" by a grammar which is beautifully regular and reliable. But as a message moves from the source in the brain on its journey to the person for whom it is intended, the message becomes distorted in various ways. At the surface, in the form of speech, the message is very often untidy, imperfect, and full of errors. It conveys messages, to be sure, but the messages are distorted by "noise," in the form of mistakes, slips of the tongue, memory lapses, repetitions, and distractions. The receiver must make sense of the message, disentangle it from the noise, reconstruct it in its original, non-random form. Unless this is done, communication is impossible.

The receiver is able to accomplish this task, Chomsky believes, because there exist, underlying the chaos of the surface appearance of language, abstract sentence forms which contain the "useful" information content of the message, in Shannon's term. At this deeper level the message is clear and explicit, free from the corruption of noise. A listener detects these clearer, uncontaminated messages without thinking about how he does so, because he, like the speaker, possesses within his brain the same coding principles. If this were not the case, a child could never learn a language rapidly and easily, but would have to rely on messy and entropic examples of adult speech. There must of necessity be more abstract principles at work, closer to the message source, which is in the child's own brain.

Chomsky's predecessors, the American structuralists, by assuming that the surface form of a sentence is the only reality, found themselves unable to explain the most striking property of language: its unlimited potential for expressing new thoughts and ideas. It is quite otherwise with Chomsky. His chief, avowed purpose is to frame a theory of language which can do justice to its inexhaustible freshness and originality, to account, in a rigorous, exact fashion, for its creative genius.

At first sight, his approach may seem paradoxical. Chomsky pays great attention to order, regularity, and form. Syntax is his prime concern. He concentrates on everything we have come to associate with redundancy, the entropy-reducing elements in an information system that separate messages from noise. He believes that a linguistic theory should deal only with an "ideal" speaker and listener, who knows his language perfectly and never makes any mistakes, never departs from grammatical propriety.

Chomsky makes a critical distinction between what he calls "competence" and "performance." Competence is the tacit knowledge possessed by a native speaker of all and only the well-formed sentences of his own language. The speaker could never actually utter all these sentences, because they are unboundedly numerous, but since he could speak any one of them if he chose to, they sit there in the message source as possibilities. Performance, on the other hand, is the actual use of language in everyday encounters among people, and for Chomsky, who finds behavior by itself a rather barren field of study, performance is much less interesting than competence.

Language does not wear meaning on its sleeve. Underneath a spoken sentence lie abstract structures, to which the sentence itself is related only indirectly. These structures are, in a sense, plans or descriptions of sentences. They exist on more than one level, and are related to one another by means of rules. If the meaning of a sentence at one level is not explicit, it will be explicit at another level, where the parts of the sentence may be in a different order. To make clear the precise relationship between parts of a sentence, as intended by the speaker, both levels of structure are needed. This is the only way to make sense of many conversational utterances.

A listener is able to grasp this relationship, because his own competence gives him access to the rules which connect the surface performance version with the other versions underlying it. The two sentences Chomsky most often uses as examples—

John is easy to please

and

John is eager to please

—are similar on the surface, but different at a more abstract level. The structure underlying the first sentence might be something like

It is easy to please John

while that underlying the second sentence would be of the form

John is eager to please someone.

Conversely, the sentences which might sound very different at first hearing

The man stopped the car

and

The car was stopped by the man

are really two versions of a single underlying structure. One is converted into the other by means of transformations, linguistic algorithms, which carry out operations on a sentence form at one level, deleting elements, transposing them, or joining them together. In this way an active sentence can be changed into a passive one, a statement changed into a question. According to this theory, ambiguity, which is really a kind of noise, obscuring the sense of the message, can be resolved by referring to the structure of which the message is a transformation.

In Chomsky's linguistics, which is constantly undergoing revision and change, a set of base rules generates "deep structure," which is the abstract plan of a sentence. Deep structure is closest to the meaning intended by the speaker, and the least affected by distortions and ambiguity. It is the structure to which all other structures can be reduced. Other kinds of rules, known as rules of transformation, change deep structure into surface structure, which, though abstract too, is the final form of the sentence before its conversion into the physical sounds of speech.

Of late, Chomsky has given up using the term deep structure, because it misled many people into thinking that language at this level is literally more profound than at others, which is not the case. He also dropped the term surface structure, for much the same reason: it suggests that in this form, a sentence is overt, actually what we hear a speaker say, whereas surface structure is still quite far from being a concrete utterance. Deep structure is now called, simply, "D" structure. Surface structure, or, in the new terminology, "S" structure, has become more abstract than it used to be, and has an enriched information content. It contains ghostly, silent traces of the "D" structure, of which it is a transformation.

Chomsky maintains that when a phrase is moved from one place to another in a sentence by a rule of transformation, the phrase leaves a tacit residue, or "trace" of itself, in the original place in the sentence, even in the "S," or surface, form. He argues that the sentence

Who do you want to choose?

for example, is ambiguous, because it is the "S" form of two different, more explicit, underlying "D" strings, namely

1. You want to choose who.
2. You want who to choose.

If it is the "S" form of string (1), an American speaker might run together the words "want to," saying, "Who do you wanna choose?" But if it is the "S" form of string (2), such an elision would be prohibited, since another word, "who," stands between them in the "D" string. Nor would an elision of the words be allowed in an expression such as

Who do you want to see Bill?

even in this "S" form, though the words "want to" are not separated by a third, intervening word. The reason for this is that the sentence is derived from the "D" structure

You want who to see Bill?

where, again, another word stands between "want" and "to."

Chomsky asserts that although the word "who" moves by transformations from its original place in the "D" structure, it leaves a silent trace in the "S" form, so that the trace effectively separates "want" and "to," even though it is only an inaudible, wraithlike surrogate:

Who do you want to choose (trace)?
Who do you want (trace) to see Bill?

In the second of these two sentences, the elision "wanna" is inadmissible. The trace which intervenes to make it inadmissible is imaginary in terms of sound, but real in terms of syntax. It means that, from the point of view of syntax, of structure alone, the sentence contains more useful information than might have been thought.

———————

Chomsky regards language as a highly efficient system for processing information, because, while speech itself may be disorderly and corrupted, there is regularity and order just beneath it. Grammar, which is part of competence, acts as a filter, screening out errors and incorrect arrangements of words, showing a speaker which sentence forms are admissible, and whether they are connected with certain other sentence forms by rules of transformation. Language is therefore protected from randomness at the source, giving it great stability and helping to keep it intelligible, even when it is disorderly at the surface level. This, after all, is the basic requirement of any information system, that its messages should vary unpredictably, but vary according to certain specific rules and conditions.

Grammar is an antichance device, keeping sentences regular and law-abiding. It is a systematic code applied at the message source. But there are millions of possible grammars, all different from one another, that could have been selected by the learner of the language. These other grammars, if chosen, would lead to error and confusion, because they would not coincide with grammars possessed by other speakers. The "freedom of choice" of the message source must be restricted in a special way so that the correct grammar and only the correct grammar is chosen, without very much in the way of conscious thought. This restriction is imposed by another kind of antichance device, one which is more general and which insures that the messages are coded in just the right way before they are sent. Chomsky calls this device universal grammar. As an innate predisposition, enabling a child to acquire competence in a language quickly and without methodical instruction, universal grammar leaves almost nothing to chance. It is the reason why children learn a language with fairly uniform ease and speed in spite of wide differences in intelligence. As the master coding principle, it is located at the message source, here in the brain and not out there in the world. It determines, of necessity rather than by accident, that the "basic relationships" underlying the structure of language will hold between one person and another when they converse.

A child listens to adult speech, but that speech is performance, not competence. It is overlaid with randomness and muddle. Moreover, the examples of grammatical rules the child hears are haphazard, not systematic, so that if learning a language were a matter of copying sentences others speak, or guessing at general principles from bits and pieces of data, the child would need to be very lucky or very clever, or both, to succeed at mastering a native tongue in such a brief space of time. It is clear, however, that luck is not necessary. The development of speech in young children does not vary markedly from one child to another. As for cleverness, it has been estimated that an IQ of only about 50 is sufficient for the acquisition of a first language.

Universal grammar, as Chomsky describes it, is not a grammar itself, but a theory of grammars in general, a set of hypotheses about them. And it is an observation worth repeating that the whole point of any theory, whether in linguistics or in physics, is that it does not merely account for the limited number of facts already known, but predicts the existence of additional facts which are still unknown. In short, a theory generates new information. It makes a lot of knowledge out of a little data. From the sparse and chaotic information given in the form of adult speech, children arrive at the grammar of their own language in a leap, as it were, rather than by a slow and painful process of learning and instruction, because a theory of grammar is in their heads as a gift of nature.

This in turn leads to an explanation of why language is inexhaustible in its capacity to generate new messages, to convey fresh meanings. The information a speaker can produce is very much richer than the information obtained by listening to others speak. The speaker's output is unpredictable, in the sense that it cannot be wholly accounted for externally, in terms of the input of experience, though it is essentially systematic and regular, obeying the rules of the game of language as all other speakers do.

Why this should be so is a question that has occupied philosophy in one form or another for centuries. It was tackled head-on in the eighteenth century by Immanuel Kant, who believed that knowledge begins with experience of the world, but is not all provided in that way. Some part of it is *a priori*, given in advance, supplied by a mental faculty which is not linked to a particular experience.

Kant described his thesis as a Copernican revolution, because he thought it was comparable to the discovery that when we see the sun change its position in the sky, it is not the sun which moves, but we ourselves. Chomsky, though his views are by no means accepted by all or even by most linguists today, may be said to have started his own Copernican revolution by proposing that knowledge of language arises in large part from within rather than from without, and it is this internal knowledge that we ought to spend our time investigating.

For Kant, there are three types of true statement. The first type is analytical and *a priori*, needing no help from experience. In the sentence "All bachelors are unmarried men," the predicate is already implied by the subject. Singleness and maleness are aspects of the definition of a bachelor. The truths expressed by this sort of sentence are universal and necessary. The second type of truth is synthetical; that is, the predicate is not contained logically in the subject, but adds something to it *a posteriori*, out of experience, by observing facts in the world and generalizing about them. However, this extra knowledge, imported from outside the mind, is not certain, but only probably true, since the material world is so full of variety and change. It is not fully predictable. The statement "All ducks quack" would be undone at once by the discovery of a single duck which purrs.

A third type of truth Kant called the synthetical *a priori*. Here the predicate adds new knowledge, but the knowledge does not come from outside, from the unreliable world of experience. It is contributed by the mind, and it is both universal and necessary, rather than local and accidental. "Matter is convertible into energy by the equation $E = mc^2$" is a sentence of this third kind.

The point is that in the first type of statement, the analytical *a priori*, no new *information* is provided. The predicate is redundant, because it is already present in the subject. In the second and third types, however, the information contained in the subject is enriched; in one case by uncertain, accidental knowledge from experience, in the other by certain knowledge from the pure understanding of the mind. Synthetical *a priori* truths are the product of abstract rules which organize the data of reality rather than simply letting reality impress itself on the mind as if on a film in a camera. Kant declares,

> We must not seek the universal laws of nature in nature by means of experience, but conversely must seek nature, as to its universal conformity to laws, in the conditions of the possibility of experience which lie in our sensibility and in our understanding.

Chomsky is in the tradition of Kant in that he asserts as a fundamental belief that knowledge of language, and probably other kinds of knowledge as well, are incomparably more extensive, systematic, and rich than the input of experience. There is a disproportion between the amount of information that the mind takes in and the amount of information that it gives out in the form of speech. That disproportion is not accounted for externally, in terms of behavior, but internally, in terms of principles which are not contingent, but certain; not learned, but innate; not *a posteriori*, but *a priori*.

———————

An explanation of these principles would be highly abstract and general. Indeed, Chomsky is looking for a "language-independent" theory of language, much as Lila Gatlin has made a start at developing an "organism-independent" theory of organisms, based on the theorems of information theory, which makes it possible to apply universal laws to information systems of all kinds and to investigate their structure. He writes,

> The more abstract the principles, the more deeply embedded in a particular theoretical structure and remote from the presented phenomena, the more interesting and significant is the study of language.

This point of view, controversial as it may be in linguistics, is familiar enough in physics, where some of the most illuminating results have come about through highly abstract concepts—imaginary spaces, complex numbers, noncommuting algebras—which are not models of physical reality, but mental constructs. Einstein, in his later period, was very much an advocate of this approach to truth and made it the basis of his scientific philosophy. He came to hold different opinions at different phases of his working life on the question of how far the constructs of the mind are linked to the evidence of the senses, but in his mature years he held firmly to the view that a formal theory does not describe the facts of experience, but is freely invented by the mind. It enables statements of facts to be derived from this mental invention. A fully unified theory of all the forces of nature, the prize Einstein sought unsuccessfully up to his death, would require laws of great generality and abstractness, and these laws would be simple, beautiful, and remote from actual experience. They would go beyond experience, by generating all the physical "facts" about the world, including those which cannot be observed. In a letter of November, 1930, Einstein wrote:

> I tell you straight out: physics is the attempt at the conceptual construction of the *real world*, and of its lawful structure. To be sure, it must present exactly the empirical relations between those sense experiences to which we are open, but only *in this way* is it chained to them . . . in short, I suffer under the (unsharp) separation of Reality of Experience and Reality of Being.

Chomsky's proposed theory of language, therefore, has a great deal in common with Shannon's theory of information. It deals with source rather than with output, and with the message system as a whole rather than with single messages. Its chief aim is to discover universal principles applying to language in general, and to make predictions about the structure of language based on these principles. This means we can expect the theory to be coherent, testable, and applicable to language generally, not just to this or that language in particular. Chomsky's work, like Shannon's, has its roots in mathematics, the most abstract of the sciences, the most distant from concrete meaning and the texture of experience here, now, in the real world. His point of departure is the theory of recursive functions: a recursive rule in language is one which can be used over and over again on the same finite number of elements to generate an infinite number of different sentences. For this reason, the relation between deep and surface structure can be seen as that of a function, in the special, mathematical sense of the word.

Shannon is interested in pattern, relation, order, the control of error, the relationship between randomness and nonrandomness. In Chomsky, too, these concepts appear and reappear. They characterize his approach. He shares with Shannon an inclination to separate form from meaning, and let the study of form reveal new truths about language. This is the basis of his unique place in the history of linguistics.

15

A Mirror of the Mind

A modern theory of language, by its very nature, is part of a more general theory of what the mind knows, and why it appears to know more than it is taught. The principles of transformational grammar, outlined in the previous chapter, are closely compatible with the ideas of modern psychology, which assumes that there are structures processing information at more than one level in the brain, some closer to conscious expression than others. Since the behavior of the mind at the surface may be a highly distorted and misleading version of its behavior at deeper and more abstract levels, psychiatrists must use their own rules to "transform" information at one level into information at another.

Chomsky insists that language is a "mirror of the mind." By that he means that any progress toward a fuller understanding of what really happens when human beings use language must bring us closer to a theory of unconscious human knowledge. Of all the modern practitioners, Chomsky is the most refreshing to read, the most intellectually satisfying, even when his ideas are so strongly stated as to lay him open to reasonable attack. This is because he makes it clear at the outset that if linguistics has any shallower goal than that of a deeper insight into the nature of mind, he would prefer to have nothing to do with it.

In one sense, Chomsky, though nearly always referred to as a revolutionary, is firmly in the tradition of linguistics as it was practiced in America more than half a century ago. At the heart of this tradition is the belief that a theory of language ought to be as scientific and precise as possible, shunning all vague or metaphysical notions. Thus linguists who preceded Chomsky concentrated on aspects of language that seemed to be scientifically manageable. When linguistics was established as an academic discipline in the United States in the 1920s, it chose to make a special study of phonology, the sound of words. Sounds could be treated as formal units, like the x's and y's of algebra. They are the "primary substance" of language, few in number, a finite set of objects that science could list and label and combine in certain ways according to certain rules. Phonology was highly abstract, making the study of language more exact and bringing it closer to mathematics and mathematical logic. As linguistics developed, it moved from the study of sounds to the study of the structure of words, or morphology, and thence to syntax, the structure of sentences. This was a very natural progression, and all three approaches shared one feature in common: they were context-free, regarding language as form and pattern, and keeping meaning at a distance.

Chomsky, too, aims at a theory of language which is scientific, in the sense that it makes predictions which can be tested for truth or falsehood. He studied at the University of Pennsylvania under the American structural linguist Zellig Harris, who not only deplored the intrusion of meaning into the science of language, but made every effort to shut it out completely by using mechanical methods of description that computers, which were not very intelligent at that time, were able to process. While Chomsky himself is fully aware of the importance of meaning, he also recognizes how elusive it is, how it is forever spilling out into new contexts, becoming entangled in questions of interpretation, use, and subjective, personal experience. The ground of linguistics is littered with failed attempts to capture meaning in a single theory. So Chomsky, too, decided to set aside those aspects of meaning that lie beyond syntax, and beyond language itself, in order to confine himself to his search for deep, general principles of structure.

Where he makes a clean break with the past, however, is in his belief that the study of the structure of language can lead to discoveries about the hidden structures of the mind. His predecessors had made no such claim. They were of the firm opinion that linguistics should restrict itself to what can be observed directly, namely surface behavior. In this respect these pre-Chomsky linguists were strikingly out of tune with the mainstream of ideas in other sciences, especially physics, which had made great advances in the exploration of nature by deriving new truths about the unobservable properties of the atomic domain from theories based on its observable properties.

Beneath the surface variety of the world's languages, Chomsky proposes, lie abstract principles and rules which are universal. And they are universal not because they happen to be the most reasonable and convenient, nor because they became established during the history of language by means of some consensus or tradition. All these factors are external to language, and they are accidental. The universals Chomsky considers of interest are those which are *necessarily* in the language, because they are programmed into the mind by the information in DNA. There are many types of universals, but the ones he chooses to study are quite formal, having to do with rules and the way in which rules determine the structure of sentences; and they provide us with valuable information about the formal properties of the mind.

A speaker's knowledge of the rules of grammar is not conscious, and this means it is extremely difficult to make rules explicit in a theory of language. Large aspects of English grammar, in the full sense of the term, are still *terra incognita* for the linguist. The reason why it is so hard to describe this unconscious system of rules is that they are not logical, but psychological. They are peculiar to the human mind. They are not usually self-evident; the discovery of a universal often comes as a surprise. We shall see later what a formidable task it is to make explicit other forms of unconscious knowledge, most notably memory, that process by which information is stored in the brain and transformed into conscious information when the need arises.

Grammars which are known unconsciously are called "psychologically real" grammars. If we could make them fully conscious, which is what a linguist aims to do, they would lead to a greater understanding of how it is that human beings acquire such elaborate forms of knowledge, and why they acquire just these special, peculiar forms, and not others. A grammar, which is a system for describing in exhaustive detail every properly formed sentence in a language, is a very sophisticated information device, admitting messages but screening out noise. But it is only one of an infinite number of possible grammars. It is selected because it is compatible with the innate and more general principles of universal grammar, which is a meta-theory of language in general, and because the other, myriad hypothetical grammars are incompatible.

Universal rules of the kind Chomsky describes arise because other, different rules are excluded by constraints which are genetic in origin. This leads to a number of interesting and highly controversial conclusions. It means that the unique information system known as language comes to humans almost whether they want it or not. It is as natural as the appearance of arms and legs, an accomplishment on which nobody is likely to congratulate us, since, in developing as they do, arms and legs merely fulfill the plan of biology. It is true that a child needs to immerse himself in language and practice speaking it. But for that matter, he also needs nourishment and the experience of walking and running if his body is to develop strongly and well.

If this hypothesis is correct, there is something paradoxical about linguistic knowledge. The fact that a human being will have legs whether he tries to grow them or not gives him a certain freedom, since he is independent of help from others to an important extent. He does not require advice or guidance on the rules of leg development. But, in another sense, he is quite restricted. He is not at liberty to grow wings or a tail, even if he wants to. The information in his genes specifies legs, and legs are what he will get. It is somewhat the same with language. Universal grammar sees to it that there are rule systems which are natural, and rule systems which are unnatural, and the latter are inaccessible, off-limits. Legs, like languages, are free to vary in relatively superficial ways. They come in many different shapes and sizes, some more pleasing to behold than others. But the ways in which they do not vary are of more significance from the point of view of biology than the ways in which they vary.

Constraints are an essential part of any process in which order is of value. A thermodynamic system cannot do anything useful if all its parts are free to arrange themselves in any way whatever. Its entropy will be a maximum and its energy inaccessible. To do work, the system's entropy must be reduced, and that means limiting the number of permitted arrangements of its parts. Similarly, information theory makes it clear that if symbols can be strung together at random, in any order, the messages they generate will not be intelligible, nor will they be protected against error. In biology as well, there are certain restrictions on the freedom of the message source, DNA. Indeed, living organisms share with Chomskyan language structures the property of not being at liberty to assume any and every form. Rules stored in the information system of DNA are responsible for the rich complexity of body and brain. They are the grammar of the genetic language. But these rules are bound by other rules at a higher logical level. They must generate legitimate forms of life, not monsters. It is possible to imagine the most bizarre creations of nature, of the sort which populate the pages of science fiction, but while these are permitted in principle by the laws of adaptability of classical evolution theory, they appear to be ungrammatical according to the rules stored in DNA. "Why are there no organisms with wheels?" asks the geneticist Richard Lewontin. Boyce Rensberger takes this question a stage further:

> More significantly, why are there no six-legged vertebrates? The answers to such questions, many evolutionists feel, might well be tied in with the problem of the origin of species.
>
> The classical Darwinian answer is that such things could well arise, but only if they improved an organism's ability to flourish in its habitat. The fact that certain conceivable organisms are unknown reflects either the selection bias of the environment, or simply the fact that the requisite mutations have never occurred.
>
> Most biologists today feel the answer must be more complex or something else entirely. One widely mentioned factor involves con-

straints inherent in the embryological development of an organism. There appear to be natural laws that govern the way cells assemble themselves into specialized tissues. No one knows what the laws are, but they appear to channel embryological development into certain patterns.

In Chomsky's theory, constraints play an all-important role, which is why it often seems to be a theory of what a speaker *cannot* do with language, rather than of what he can do. Universal grammar constrains rules in various ways, and these constraints are often quite unpredictable, so that one learns of them with a genuine sense of discovery. A striking example of such a constraint is given by Neil Smith and Deirdre Wilson, who point out that, while there must be thousands of possible ways of forming relative clauses, most languages adopt one or the other of only two main strategies. Certain languages, such as English and French, use this kind of relative clause construction:

> The man *that I saw* was your brother.
> I read the book *that you read.*

Other languages, Hebrew for instance, insert an extra pronoun. In translation the Hebrew sentences would look like this:

> The man *that I saw him* was your brother.
> I read the book *that you read it.*

The constraint on formation of relative clauses becomes really interesting, however, when it is found that English and French contain traces of the Hebrew strategy as well. Many regional dialects of French take the Hebrew form with the extra pronoun, as certain informal, conversational constructions used in English also do. Smith and Wilson give the following examples:

> That's the kind of answer *that,* (when you come to think about it,) *you find you've forgotten it.*

> This is the sort of book *that,* (having once read it,) *you feel you want to give it to all your friends.*

An elementary example of a universal is what Chomsky calls the structure dependence of language. Structure dependence means that language rules do not concern themselves with the order of words in a sentence, but with the structure of the whole sentence, even though there is no obvious need for them to do so. This is one reason why a theory of syntax is so complicated. For instance, one can transform the sentence

The tall, blond man with one black shoe is running

into

Is the tall, blond man with one black shoe running?

by applying an apparently simple rule that moves the word "is" up to the front of the sentence. Yet the rule is not as simple as it looks. What if the word "is" occurs more than once? Suppose the sentence reads

The tall, blond man, who is wearing one black shoe, is running.

Moving up the first "is" leads to an incorrect form:

Is the tall, blond man who wearing one black shoe is running?

The rule works by taking notice of sentence structure, not word order. It treats

The tall, blond man who is wearing one black shoe

as a single unit, leaving it intact, and moves up the first "is" that follows the unit. Such a rule is not logically necessary in a language. Nor is it the simplest one to learn. But structure dependence is a property of universal grammar, and therefore no rule of language can be indifferent to structure.

Other kinds of word relations are also forbidden for no apparent reason other than that they would violate principles which are peculiar to the human mind, and anchored in the human genes. A more recent and sophisticated example of this phenomenon is the embedded clause in an indirect sentence, where sometimes part of the clause can be missing, and the sentence still be correct. One can say, for example,

It is unclear what to do

where the subject of the embedded clause, "what to do," is absent. If the subject were present, the sentence would read

It is unclear what someone does.

If the subject were simply dropped to make the shortened form, the sentence would become

It is unclear what does

which does not mean the same thing. When all the possibilities are examined, it turns out that the only part of an embedded clause that can be missing is the subject of an infinitive. This kind of constraint appears very widely in the world's languages, much more widely than might be supposed, and the general principles which account for it are universal, as far as is known.

Universal grammar is the innate, antichance device in the brain which restricts syntax in this way. As his ideas developed, Chomsky found that the rules of transformation alone, as he originally proposed them, leave the learner of them too much freedom of choice, and this freedom needs to be constrained even more strictly. Rules of transformation in themselves, unlike universal grammar, are not innate. They are acquired easily, however, because the language learner is predisposed to select them by the meta-theory of universal grammar, which excludes all types of transformation rules except the correct ones.

Yet even if the meta-theory guides a child to select the right rule, how is he to acquire it rapidly if the rule itself is complex and difficult? For example, the rule which transforms an active sentence in deep structure into a passive sentence in surface structure, once thought the most basic and firmly established, became the greatest nuisance of all, because of its cumbersome, Rube Goldberg machinery. To convert the active sentence

The hunter shot the fox

into the passive sentence

The fox was shot by the hunter

involves the movement of two noun phrases, the insertion of an auxiliary verb, the insertion of the word "by," and the creation of a prepositional phrase out of thin air. All these changes were supposed to have been accomplished by a single transformation.

It is hardly likely that a child would be able to learn to use such an elaborate procedure spontaneously and without effort.

Chomsky's answer to this problem was to suggest new kinds of restriction on the choice of rules, ones which would make horrors like the old passive transformation inaccessible and simpler ones accessible. He proposed that transformations can move only one element of a sentence at a time. This meant that, in forming the passive, a child learns two simple rules instead of a single complicated one. The first rule says, "Move 'hunter' into the object context." The second rule would then say, "Move 'fox' into the subject context." Later, Chomsky replaced these two rules with a type of transformation so simple and general that it need say no more than, "Move 'hunter.' " Universal grammar supplies knowledge about context and the specific conditions so that the rest of the sentence falls quickly and easily into place.

This means that the innate constraints of universal grammar are increasingly central to Chomsky's theory. Language is learned easily and naturally because the learner is provided with remarkably little freedom of choice. The expanded role assigned to universal grammar implies that language is even less dependent on the conscious intellect than might be supposed. Ray Jackendoff, a linguist of the Chomskyan persuasion at Brandeis University, argues that only by discovering the universal principles constraining choice, reducing possibilities, can we hope to explain why language is natural rather than invented:

> What has happened is that people realized you couldn't just start inventing transformations right and left, because how could a child figure out how to do them? It became clear that a theory had to be found that gave the child a lot less room for maneuver, limiting his freedom of choice. The errors children make are by and large not very drastic, and they make pretty much the right choices. If a bizarre and crazy rule like the old passive transformation really existed, then it meant there were other wild, crazy transformations and other rules that sneak in with them. That violated the condition Chomsky began to emphasize in 1965, that language must above all be *learnable,* and a linguistic theory must account for this learnability.

The eventual goal of linguistics, Jackendoff believes, is to find a complete set of conditions on rules, restraining them from craziness, making them learnable. The analogy he likes to use is that of the theory of the movement of heavenly bodies. Grammar can be thought of as being like Kepler's laws for planetary motion, describing with beautiful precision what is happening and what constraints there are on the planet's orbit, constraints which keep it within certain bounds. But Kepler's laws do not tell us why the orbits are constrained in this fashion, any more than a grammar tells us why sentence structures are bound in the particular way they are. To explain boundary conditions on planetary orbits, we need a more general theory, the theory of gravity. To explain boundary conditions on language, we need a theory of what goes on in the brain when linguistic information is processed. Such a theory might be highly abstract and, when discovered, lead us to think of grammar in an entirely new way, much as the discovery of the laws of gravity led people to take a completely new view of the motion of the planets.

Einstein once stated as an axiom of modern quantum physics that "it is the theory which decides what we can observe." By that he meant that the mental constructs used to explain the behavior of matter at the subatomic level restrict the freedom of the scientist, so that he can obtain only certain kinds of information about matter and not others. Chomsky might amend Einstein's precept in the following way: "It is the theory—that is, universal grammar—which decides what kind of linguistic knowledge we can acquire." Experience cannot explain the rules of language. Internal principles in the mind, deep and abstract principles, are the only explanation we can have of why language is so special, so universal in certain of its aspects, and unique to human beings.

The question that exercises Chomsky so much, and that he asks so often, is whether there are other, uniquely human "grammars" in the brain, generating other very complex kinds of knowledge. Innate constraints would exclude many other possible grammars, restricting freedom of choice, as in the case of spoken language.

It may be that music is one of these other forms of knowledge. Some sketchy evidence for this is given by recent investigations into the mental strategies of musical child prodigies, who acquire musical competence almost as easily as a normal child acquires a competence for language. This research, which is itself still in infancy, suggests that extraordinarily gifted children possess an antichance device, a "meta-theory," which makes it easy for them to pick up the grammar of musical form. Such a device is innate in the brains of child prodigies, enabling them to make a lot of musical knowledge out of a little data. But the meta-theory is not innate, or at least not as strongly so, in normal children.

Howard Gardner, the Harvard psychologist who is connected with Project Zero, a program for learning about the growth of artistic ability in the young, concludes that musical prodigies have a special gift for mastering symbols more rapidly than others. Complex, rule-governed structures are more accessible to them. As Gardner puts it, "The patterns jump out." He compares this unusual predisposition of the mind with a genetic disease. "Certain people are susceptible to certain diseases because of their genetic inheritance," he says. "They are at risk for that disease." Children for whom the patterns jump out are susceptible to music. They catch it, provided they are exposed to it, as children in general catch language.

The conductor and composer Leonard Bernstein, in a series of lectures at Harvard University, has taken this idea much further. He speculates that abstract, inborn constraints, operating at an unconscious level of the mind, may exclude certain rules of musical structure and admit others, so that the human brain is led to accept a "correct" theory of music without much conscious thought. Even a listener who possesses no extraordinary gifts needs relatively little in the way of experience to acquire such a theory, because the constraints on his freedom render incorrect theories much less accessible. In effect, Bernstein is proposing the existence of a universal grammar of music, which makes some kinds of musical form more natural to the ear than others.

In the nineteenth century, it was thought that the music intervals of thirds and sixths were the most attractive, because they lie at the limits of the relationships that the ear can grasp. It was assumed that audiences enjoy making sense of sounds which are just irregular enough to be interesting, but which, nonetheless, conform to a basic system of constraints. The limits have been extended considerably since then. However, the public has shown that it is not comfortable with works which violate the old rules of structure too drastically, in particular those which break completely with the tonal system.

The tonal system is essentially a set of rules for generating sequences of musical notes, where one particular note serves as a point of stability, to which the composition refers and returns. In tonal music, all the notes are connected by virtue of their relationship to this one, primary note, called the tonic, or key note of the piece. It is the most probable note, in a statistical sense, as the letter e is the most probable letter in English text.

Tonal music is strictly organized, just as the grammar of a language is organized. It has its own rules for departing from randomness, and is very rich within those limits. The atonal or serial music of Arnold Schoenberg, while also rich in structure, violates those rules. Its sequences of notes are not random, but the probabilities with which certain notes will occur at certain places in the score are not the same as in tonal music. In some respects they are the classical rules turned upside down, enforcing dissonance where harmony had been enforced under the classical system of rules. Schoenberg himself thought it of the greatest importance that his work should be comprehensible, somewhat as a language in the throes of change strives to retain intelligibility. But his music was not as widely accepted by concertgoers as that of his pupil, Alban Berg, who brought tonal elements into serial music.

An interesting question is whether the reversed rules of atonal music violate innate principles determining which rule systems the mind accepts naturally, as a matter of course, and which it does not. Ray Jackendoff comments:

> Tonality is not simply man's response to physical facts about sound. Rather, like language, tonality in music provides evidence for a cognitive organization with a logic all its own. The mind is not simply following the physical path of least resistance . . . but is creating its own way of organizing pitch combinations into coherent patterns.

Another, more speculative kind of knowledge, which may be

based on innate principles, rather than being learned in its entirety from external experience, is the system of psychological archetypes proposed by C. G. Jung. Some Chomskyan linguists believe a study of archetypes and their structure, like the study of language, might lead to a better understanding of the formal properties of the mind. Evidence for the existence of archetypes is no better than circumstantial and there is probably no way of proving them as scientific facts. On the other hand, Jung does use them as the basis for an impressive and coherent theory of the psyche.

In his opinion, archetypes are essentially constraints, mental structures in the unconscious mind, which make it possible for messages, in the form of images, to be sent to the conscious mind. The nature of these messages is mythological and symbolic. Jung speaks of archetypes in very much the same way Chomsky speaks of universal grammar. They predispose the mind to special kinds of universal knowledge, insuring that the themes of world myths, like some of the constructions in languages, are universal, appearing and reappearing over long periods of time across cultures which have little or no contact with each other.

Archetypes, as Jung describes them, supply possibilities, conditions, for the actual production of ideas and fantasies. They are not in the mind as a result of training or instruction, but are a biological endowment, specified by DNA. An archetype cannot be known directly, but only through the appearance of the archetypal image, which arises spontaneously. Because mythic information has a universal base, outside time, it is not dependent on particular experiences and is not tied directly to intelligence. It plays a role in artistic and literary activity. The rational intellect may dismiss myths and images as nonsense, and try to suppress them, but they always return in one form or another. However, the form is constrained. It is not free to be just any form. Myths, like dreams, have their own peculiar logic and structure. And this structure reflects the structure of the mind.

Jung also proposed that the set of natural numbers is an archetype of order, represented in the conscious mind, helping it to put the "chaos of appearances" into some sort of regular pattern.

If he is right, the number system is one more form of *a priori* knowledge with extraordinary power to organize the randomness of experience. Like language, it is acquired easily, because other, different kinds of number systems are less accessible. Not for nothing have they been called the "natural" numbers.

———————

There is a paradox in Chomsky's view of language. On the one hand, a grammar of the type he describes is highly restricted by universal, necessary principles. An infinite number of word sequences are excluded by means of such built-in restrictions. On the other hand, Chomsky's importance as a linguist lies in the fact that he regards the limitless abundance of language as its most important property, one that any theory of language must account for, or be discarded. This paradox is resolved in his theory because, while it forbids so many possible grammars, the actual grammar selected is able to generate a limitless abundance of properly formed sentences.

Chomsky believes that the intrinsic, formal devices of language should be studied independently of their actual use, because this approach is simpler, more revealing, and makes it easier to test predictions about the structure of language. He regards linguistic creativity as being based on "a system of rules and forms." It is true that Chomsky provides a place for rules which interpret the meaning of a sentence according to the way it is being used in a particular context in the "real world." But for him syntax, as pure framework and pattern, is unconnected with meaning or sound or context. It is more or less mindless. Syntax generates grammatical sequences of words, whether or not they are appropriate; at a later stage of processing, the rules of interpretation reject those which make no sense. Syntax as thus defined is divorced from use and from experience. Universal grammar, the linchpin of Chomskyan linguistics, resembles, as we have noted, theories of modern science, whose essential power is to carry the mind beyond experience, so that new information arises not from the world, but from abstractions in the mind.

However, there is a danger that in placing so much emphasis on innate, *a priori* organizing principles, other important structural aspects of language will be missed. Chomsky's critics, who are numerous, question whether relegating experience to such small importance does justice to the true richness of language, to its "rules and forms" in a much wider sense. They wonder if he is not underestimating the complexity of language, and therefore underestimating the complexity of the mind. It might be thought that the essential structure of language is all inherent, supplied by syntax, and unrelated to the function of language as an act of communication with other people. Chomsky's view is that language need not be communication in this sense. It may have arisen in evolution for that purpose, but now language principles are wired into the brain whether they are used for communication or not. They can play a purely private role, as an unspoken medium for clarifying one's thoughts or for writing poems nobody else will read.

However, recent investigations of language, not as text or isolated sentences but as connected discourse, show that many of its underlying patterns are dictated by the social purposes to which words are put. And these patterns are as essential to language as syntax, even though they are not syntactic in the strict sense of the word. For example, linguists are discovering that telephone conversations, which may seem formless and haphazard on the surface, are really systematic, full of hidden structure and unexpected regularities. The rules of conversational structure are very different from the rules of dialogue in television soap opera, which has also been subjected to linguistic analysis. But both types are an aspect of the complexity of language, of its nonrandomness.

The plays of Harold Pinter are yet another example, except that here language is used in such a way that nearly all meaning is outside the sentences themselves. They must be interpreted by a special set of rules, because in Pinter words are spoken, not for the purpose of referring to ideas or things but to coerce people, to determine how a character stands toward another character in a relationship. The "meaning" of the words is the effect they have on other parties to the conversation, how they change the way each person regards the other. The literal sense of the words is of little importance, because the structure of sentences reflects the structure of a relationship rather than the formal rules of syntax.

Chomsky, we remember, makes an important distinction between competence, which is regular and orderly, and performance, such as conversation, which he sees as entropic, "noisy," full of errors. For this reason it is supposed to contain less useful information. Yet performance may not be as random as it appears. One feature of performance that Chomsky dismisses as irrelevant to a linguistic theory is the use of interjections, such as "er," "ah," and "um," which appear so frequently in conversations. At first sight the distribution of these interjections appears to be quite disorderly, having nothing to do with either the structure or the content of the sentence in which they occur. On closer examination, however, they turn out to be an essential part of both. They are messages, not noise. One who is especially persuasive on this point is Robin Lakoff, of the Berkeley Linguistics Department, which harbors distinguished dissidents and breakaways from the Chomsky camp, a continent's breadth away at MIT. Dr. Lakoff gave me the following sentences as examples:

1. I understand that, uh, Kissinger is a vegetarian.

2. I understand that Kissinger is, uh, a vegetarian.

In the first sentence, the "uh," coming before Kissinger, expresses some hesitancy about the statement as a whole, and implies that the speaker does not take full responsibility for it. In the second sentence, the "uh" means that the speaker is sure Kissinger is something, but unsure whether he is a vegetarian. Interjections of this sort are a conversational device, and the rules for using them parallel rules of syntax. In syntax, the same word, moved to a different place in the sentence, changes the meaning of the sentence. Saying "John hit the ball" is not the same as saying "The ball hit John." In the Kissinger sentences, changing the position of "uh" has a similar effect on meaning. Like other conversational devices, it changes the message of a sentence rather than simply increasing its entropy by adding noise.

Clearly, syntax is far from being the only organizing principle of language. Performance has its own rules, some of which may be universal. The order of words in a spoken sentence is determined only in part by formal mechanisms which are under the control of universal grammar. It is also affected by more concrete and specific factors, which have to do with the state of mind of the speaker, his intentions, the context in which he is speaking, the impression he wants to make on other people.

Language, then, is much richer in structure of various kinds, much more elaborately organized, than linguists once supposed. It was Chomsky's achievement to show that even formal, syntactic structure is not what it seems on the surface, but is derived from other, hidden structures at a different level of information-processing in the brain. At this level, more distant from the actual sounds of speech, messages are coded in an explicit form. The receiver of the message must reverse the process, using the rules of transformation to go from the often misleading surface down to the more abstract, but less confusing, messages beneath.

But this is also true of organizing principles underlying performance, principles which are not syntax in Chomsky's sense, yet are part of the structure of language. The intentions of the speaker may be unclear at the surface, which is often a distorted version of patterns of thought or emotion at a deeper level. To explore these deeper patterns is to learn as much about the nature of the mind as about the nature of language. This carries linguistics far beyond the boundaries Chomsky set for himself.

If language is truly a mirror of the mind, it must reflect not just the algorithms of syntax but the mind as a whole, the complete set of rules by which a human being, in Lakoff's words, "gives form and sense to his universe, where without them there would be none." Thus linguistics becomes deeply entangled with psychology, for both are studying the relationship between randomness and information. Each science is as complex as the other, which may explain why neither has yet surrendered all its secrets to inquisitive and ingenious probing; not by a very long way.

PART FOUR

How the Brain Puts It All Together

16

The Brain as Cat on a Hot Tin Roof and Other Fallacies

Shannon was keenly interested in computers, not as mere calculating machines, but as information systems which might increasingly imitate human intelligence. He had been impressed with the prophetic quality of Samuel Butler's satirical novel, *Erewhon*, published in 1871, in which simpler machines were depicted as evolving into more complex ones in a kind of parody of Darwinian natural selection. In the early 1950s, computers were relative idiots, and were so cumbersome that, it was estimated, to build one containing as many vacuum tubes as there are nerve cells in the human brain, a room as big as the Empire State Building would be needed to house it and the power source would have to be as large as Niagara Falls. But even at that time, Shannon foresaw the great improvements in design which would enable computers to use logic, translate languages, and play games.

However, unlike many of his contemporaries, Shannon believed that science could learn more about the human brain by studying the ways in which it differs from the computer than by looking for resemblances between the two, even though the resemblances seemed very striking at the time. This approach is very much in harmony with present-day thinking. As the brain becomes better understood, its special ways of generating knowledge are seen as being quite dissimilar to those of computers in many important respects.

Computers are good at swift, accurate computation and at storing great masses of information. The brain, on the other hand, is not as efficient a number cruncher and its memory is often highly fallible; a basic inexactness is built into its design. The brain's strong point is its flexibility. It is unsurpassed at making shrewd guesses and at grasping the total meaning of information presented to it.

The primary components of the brain are remarkably similar in certain respects to those of the computer, but quite different in other respects. These components, called nerve cells, or neurons, number between ten and perhaps as many as fifty billion in the human brain. A neuron sends a message to another neuron by means of electrochemical pulses, which may come a few at a time or in bursts of up to a thousand a second. Whether or not the second neuron acts on the message depends on whether the pulses are sufficiently numerous to trigger a response. Like binary digits (the 0's and 1's of Shannon's code), a neuron can be in only one of two possible states; it can answer "yes" or it can answer "no," fire off a signal or refrain from firing.

No one neuron is the same as another. Each has its own particular threshold, below which it will not fire and above which it will fire. A neuron switches itself on only when a stimulus is strong enough to break through the threshold. If the stimulus is too weak, the neuron will not act, in which case the stimulus might just as well not be there at all. To make matters even more complicated, the pulses sent out by a nerve cell in action do not vary in strength according to the intensity of the stimulus, as in a power engineering device. What happens is that when the stimulus becomes stronger, the size of each pulse remains the same but the number of pulses per second increases.

Consequently there is an inherent uncertainty in this system of message transmission. For example, when something cold touches the skin, neurons flash information about that event to the brain, and the brain responds, but it is not true to say that the stimulus directly produces the response. The relation is not nearly as straightforward and linear as that, because it is the neuron which acts, not the stimulus.

Nerve cells do not simply pass on information. They convert it from one form to another. One neuron makes contact with others by means of threadlike fibers in a complex communications network, but the connecting links do not work by simple cause and effect. It is not simply one cell tied to another cell by a cable, like two people talking to each other on the telephone. Rather, the signal must cross a tiny gap, about a millionth of an inch wide, called a synapse. The effect of the synapse is to introduce a further element of uncertainty into a fundamentally uncertain system.

For all its minute size, the synapse is of great importance. There are probably more than a thousand billion synapses in the brain, and each one is a kind of coding station, where signals arrive in the form of bursts of electrical pulses, so many a second, and are translated into chemical signals in the form of very small, separate packets. Only if a sufficient number of packets accumulates is a critical threshold reached and information sent across the synaptic gap. The nerve cell on the other side of the gap computes the frequency of the arriving packets and, if the frequency is high enough, fires off a signal of its own. This is the means of transmission along the basic communications channels of the brain. The code of the message is changed from electrical to chemical and then back again to electrical as it moves from one nerve cell to another. Such a procedure allows plenty of room for chance to enter, and shows how misleading it is to compare the essential processes of the brain with those of a computer.

Even when a signal is sent across a synapse to another nerve cell, it is not necessarily an order to fire. The signal may inhibit the neuron and make it less likely to fire. In fact, this happens very often. When a neuron receives an inhibiting signal it is not so ready to switch itself on when a later signal crosses the synapse, giving an order to fire.

Like language, the brain is both stable and unpredictable. It is highly redundant, as Shannon argued it must be, in order to obtain overall reliability using unreliable components. The role played by one neuron in processing a certain type of information may be duplicated by perhaps tens of thousands of similar cells. Some connections between neurons are "many-to-one," as if several different words in a language had the same meaning, improving reliability. Other connections, however, are "one-to-many," as if one word had several different meanings, leading to ambiguity.

As we have seen, whether a neuron fires or does not fire depends not on a single event, but on the total effect of many events, some more uncertain than others. Indeed, packets of chemicals may cross the synapse spontaneously, not as signals but as chance happenings, like interference in a radio receiver, as part of the meaningless and unpredictable background noise of the brain. In *The Conscious Brain*, the English biochemist Steven Rose describes three types of events which may trigger the release of the chemical packets across the synapse to a receiving neuron. Only one of these three events is certain and predictable: a message arriving from somewhere else in the central nervous system or from the outside world. A second sort of trigger, the spontaneous firing of a neuron due to its own internal changes, may be the effect of a predictable cause, but on the other hand it may also be random. A third kind, the release of chemical packets across the synaptic gap for no particular reason, is completely random. So the mechanism for passing information along these myriad coding stations of the brain is a mixture of the predictable and the unpredictable, a property shared by many information systems which occur in nature. A lack of certainty is programmed into the brain. Rose writes:

> At the synapses between cells lies the choice point which converts the nervous system from a certain, predictable and dull one into an uncertain, probabilistic and hence interesting one ... It is not too strong to say that the evolution of humanity followed the evolution of the synapse.

The pioneers of communication theory, cybernetics, and intelligent machines came to recognize that they were dealing with a new set of concepts and a new vocabulary unlike any that science had previously known. Von Neumann, especially, stressed that words such as force, energy, work, power, were being superseded in importance by different words, like codes, signals, messages, information. This change of emphasis is particularly true in the modern approach to the brain.

Freud's writings on the brain still speak the old language of energy and power. His approach is reminiscent of the early days of thermodynamics, when new laws of nature evolved out of the study of steam engines and when the chief purpose of such investigations was to obtain more work for less fuel. The Freudian lexicon, full of such terms as drives, repressions, discharges, sources, and sinks, belongs to the nineteenth-century world of steam power and the mystique of railways. The brain was seen as an engine waiting to have its boilers stoked.

Norbert Wiener made it clear at an early stage, however, that there is a critical distinction between power engineering and communication engineering, and this distinction must be grasped if we are to begin to understand how the nervous system works. A television transmitter, Wiener said, may need large amounts of power to do what it is supposed to do, but it is first and chiefly a device for sending messages. A dentist's drill, on the other hand, may use only a tiny fraction of the power needed to drive the transmitter, but the prime consideration in designing the drill is the energy it consumes. Wiener, no shrinking violet where his own reputation was concerned, claimed credit in his memoirs for first alerting the scientific world to the importance of this distinction, and for showing that control devices, like the ones used for aiming antiaircraft guns at German planes, were as much a part of communications science as the telephone or the radio, even though their function might be to move an object as heavy as a large gun.

The design of the brain, contrary to Freud's assumptions, is that of a communications device. Like the television transmitter, it is a very hungry consumer of power. The brain weighs only about 2 percent of the total mass of the human body, but it uses up to 20 percent of the body's supply of energy. Yet it is pointless to approach the study of the brain in terms of its general metabolic activity. It is a system for coding and organizing information, and can best be understood within that framework of ideas.

Two American psychiatrists, Robert McCarley and Allan Hobson, have presented a detailed case for supposing that Freud's essential view of the psyche was based on quite erroneous assumptions about the actual biology, chemistry, and physics of the brain. It is as if a scientist were trying to explain the working principles of a radio set by comparing it with a diesel engine. Freud devised a model of the central nervous system in his *Project for a Scientific Psychology*, written in 1895 but not published until 1954. From it he derived many of his later theories of the mind; implicit in much of his work is the belief that the brain may ultimately be explained in terms of its physical structure, although he was well aware that contemporary scientific knowledge of the structure of the brain was in a very primitive state. Freud's ideas about the function of nerve cells in the brain, McCarley and Hobson conclude, were "simply and fundamentally wrong."

Freud was correct in regarding the cells as separate units connected in certain not very straightforward ways, but he went astray in assuming that they were docile receptacles for energy coming from outside the brain itself, passing on the energy, in greater or lesser amounts, to other cells. As a result, Freud thought, nervous energy, all generated externally, coursed about in the central nervous system until it could be discharged through bodily action. Impulses and wishes not released in action were repressed, often surfacing to consciousness in dreams. High levels of nervous energy, bottled up like steam in a railway engine, were unpleasurable to the conscious brain, which was strongly inclined to the pleasurable process of discharge, to what Freud called the "nirvana principle." Having no independent energy of its own, the brain was at the mercy of sense impressions from the environment or impulses from instinctual drives such as hunger or aggression, which were all the more powerful because they were not avoidable, as are sense impressions. A person could not shut them out by closing his eyes or walking away, as he could shut out an overpowering experience in the real world. A burst of energy from instinctual drives might affect memory cells so strongly as to produce hallucinations, unless some of it could be siphoned off by the ego. McCarley and Hobson call this scheme of Freud's the "cat on a hot tin roof" model, because it portrays the conscious brain dancing frenziedly under the impact of rushes of energy from down below, in the chamber of the instincts:

> Freud held tenaciously to the ideas of neurons as sources and sinks
> of energy ultimately derived from outside the brain; he on no occa-

sion postulated that neurons had their own metabolic energy or that they formed self-regulatory networks. This assumption was of critical importance for Freud's neural model, and it led him to place the cause of dreaming outside the brain, since the ultimate sources of energy were also necessarily extracerebral. Dreams originated from somatic or external stimuli. This assumption further committed Freud to a reactive, essentially passive brain and to a model of the psyche that shared these characteristics.

A picture of the brain as deterministic, with every cause leading directly to a specific result, and instincts asserting themselves as imperious forces demanding release, is at odds with what is known today. One especially important difference between energy and information is that the first is subject to the laws of conservation, while the second is not: information can be created or destroyed. By taking nerve cells to be sources and sinks of energy, Freud had to exclude the possibility that events in the nervous system could be simply neutralized or canceled. In his system, nervous energy was siphoned off, discharged, or repressed. Messages do not behave in this way at all. They can be stopped, switched off, with no price to pay in the form of pent-up forces lurking morbidly in the psyche. The brain, far from just reacting to gusts of energy bombarding it from the instincts or from the outside world, maintains its own information system in a more or less stable balance, and to a large extent drives itself.

Normally, at any one time more neurons are switched off in the brain than are switched on, so there is no need for safety valves to blow off superfluous heads of steam. The brain does not passively accept what it is given. It selects and structures the messages it needs, shutting down unwanted circuits. As many as 80 percent of the neurons in the human brain may act to suppress activity rather than to excite it. Selectiveness is the hallmark of the brain; it excludes certain types of information when such information is not needed, and admits other types which have meaning or novelty or usefulness at a given time and under particular circumstances.

Selective mechanisms amplify some messages, while "turning down the volume" on those which are unimportant, overfamiliar, repetitive. Putting on a wristwatch in the morning creates a clear impression on the senses, but this impression soon recedes, so that the watch is not noticed unless we look at it. Sounds which are of no significance recede into the background, so that it is possible to read a book with perfect concentration on a crowded bus, unless a strange or unusually loud noise occurs, in which case the brain will pay attention to it. Sailors on night watch during the Second World War were able to drowse while listening to routine signals traffic coming in over Morse code on their headphones, but as soon as the normal pattern of signals changed, they would become alert. It is thought that models of familiar or unimportant messages are stored somewhere in the brain, at an unconscious level, and that when the messages change, or new, significant messages arrive, the mismatch between the incoming information and the models triggers attention for that information.

In a wide range of activity, the brain chooses the information it needs. In visual perception, the nervous system attunes itself to certain aspects of a scene rather than to others, so that each act of perception is unique to the person and to the moment. Seeing is not like holding a camera up to the world, merely registering an image, but a restless searching and scanning. Hearing is a complex process of disentangling sounds we need to hear from sounds we need to ignore. Memory is not a tape recorder, storing information at the flick of a switch. It, too, is selective. In part, memory is a way of reorganizing information so as to make it special to the individual who remembers; this process is so variable and idiosyncratic as to confound the formal models psychologists are forever trying to build.

The rise of the doctrine of the selective brain spells trouble for any hypothesis based on the idea of mind as helpless victim. This doctrine is not at all compatible with the tenets of behaviorism, which assumes that mental processes are uniform, predictable, and easily controlled from without. Behaviorism holds that the mind is best motivated externally, rather as some thinkers, before Newton, imagined that physical objects in space move only when they are pushed, and stop when they cease to be pushed. There is a wealth of evidence to show that this is not the case. One of the best-known examples is the failure of political propaganda to coerce or win over large audiences to a particular point of view, even with the resources of the modern media behind it. The sociologist Wilbur Schramm has described the consternation created by the collapse of the bullet theory of communication in the 1950s. The bullet theory assumed that an audience was passive, waiting for the media to shoot a propaganda message into it, and would roll over in a state of docile surrender when hit, as long as the bullet was sufficiently powerful. Accordingly, researchers did not bother to study the audience. Instead, they analyzed the content of the messages, assuming that content was the secret of a successful propaganda bullet. However, the researchers were due for a surprise. The audience obstinately declined to fall under the spell of the messages. Sometimes they reacted in ways that were opposite to the propagandist's intentions, or enjoyed the bombardment without allowing it to change their opinions in the slightest. In the end, researchers had to change their whole approach, and

> were able to demonstrate dramatically that the audience was far from passive; that it actually went out seeking what it wanted from the mass media, interpreted what it found there to fit its own needs and predispositions, and seldom changed its mind as a result of mass persuasion. This development from the bullet theory to the study of an Obstinate Audience to the concept of an Active Audience is one of the most interesting and important chapters in modern social science.

In artificial intelligence research, scientists are learning some lessons from the fact that the brain processes information in ways which are peculiarly, even perversely human, rather than mechanical in the old sense. For example, they have made the paradoxical discovery that forgetting serves a very important function, and is a by-product of learning. Computers are now being programmed to forget selectively, as the brain does, rather than store every item of information in its memory. Linked up to news agency teletype machines, these computers monitor detailed stories about world events. But instead of retaining all the facts in every story, they single out only salient information of a specific kind and discard the rest. By doing so they can make generalizations about past stories and draw inferences from new stories on the basis of these generalizations. Reading an item about a terrorist attack in Italy, the computer might make an inference, from the location of the attack alone, that the victim of the attack was a businessman; or, if the terrorist incident took place in Northern Ireland, that the victim was a British policeman or soldier. Information which is not relevant to the task of generalizing is simply forgotten.

Other programs have been written imitating the brain's ability to ignore certain types of information if the information is of relatively minor importance. This is done by means of what are called "programming demons," which lie dormant in the computer unless triggered by a particular message, in which case the demon prompts the computer to change its normal procedure. Thus the machine can recognize unexpected events which do not normally occur in a given context, and act accordingly. If a program describes a man walking from his house to a grocery store, the surprise appearance of a truck bearing down on him as he is crossing the road would awaken a demon and cause the man to jump back onto the sidewalk, abandoning for the moment his plan to reach the store. Presented with this story, a computer would "understand" why the man jumped back.

In a similar program, an imaginary third world country is required to devise a plan to acquire foreign-aid money. The government of the country then considers possible sources of aid, such as the United Nations or the World Bank. However, if the plan includes threatening one of the superpowers with war unless aid is forthcoming, a programming demon steps in and warns that such a war would certainly result in the defeat of the smaller country. And if, during negotiations, one country becomes offended, the demon of cordial relations rises from electronic slumber to calm down ruffled feelings.

The aim of such a program is to give computers some of the flexibility of the brain. This may entail imperfections if computers are regarded as machines which should never forget and never ignore information. To make computers even less computerlike, researchers are now looking for ways of making them less literal-minded. This problem was highlighted by a machine at Yale University, which was set to monitor a news ticker and select only stories about earthquakes, condensing such stories to essential details. The machine nonplused its operators one day by reporting simply, "There was an earthquake in America today," omitting to mention where the earthquake had taken place and how severe it was. The answer to the mystery was that the computer had failed to recognize the metaphorical use of a verb in a story which began, "The death of the Pope shook America today."

Some thought is also being given to the problem of making computers capable of subjective interpretation. Human beings are able to organize random material into patterns even where none exists in an objective sense, for example in Rorschach tests. This patterning is done unconsciously by mental structures in the brain. Computers, on the other hand, cannot recognize order in apparently random collections of dots or shapes, and reject most of these items as being entirely structureless.

It is true, as Shannon said, that we are able to understand the brain better by studying the ways in which it is unlike a computer. It is also true that the more ingeniously scientists try to devise programs to build aspects of the brain's peculiar mental strategies into the software of their machines, the more glaring and remarkable the dissimilarities seem.

17

The Strategies of Seeing

The brain is a sophisticate, not an innocent, in its dealings with the world. It acquires an elaborately expressive language on the basis of rather inferior data. It remembers complex mental experiences better than it remembers simple ones, and even in an activity as routine and basic as visual perception, the brain has ingenious ways of going to work on information reaching the eye, so that it sees the world not passively, by accepting an imprint of it, but actively, according to its own rules. For that reason, it sometimes makes mistakes. The brain's visual system, like its memory, is partly uncertain, sometimes deceived, making do with incomplete knowledge. But it is dependable in special, nonsimple ways which meet the unique needs of human life.

Error, and how to control it, was one of the main themes of information theory. Shannon took it for granted that error will always be with us, because noise in communications systems is as natural as entropy is in thermodynamic systems. The unmixed will always have a tendency to become mixed. Shannon's solution was a code which corrected random changes in the messages caused by noise. He established as a universal principle, contrary to what we might expect, that reliable information is possible in an unreliable world.

The code works by adding redundancy. This means that some sameness is mixed in with change. Change is the essence of information. A message source must be free to vary its messages, to send different sequences of symbols. There is no point in sending the same sequence over and over again. But redundancy insures that a pattern of probabilities remains constant across all the messages. That is something the receiver can depend on. A measure of consistency is introduced into a system which, by its very nature, needs to be partly inconsistent, to surprise with the unexpected.

The same general principle is at work when we look at the ever changing flux of impressions, of "messages" reaching the eye. Nearly always we are able to make sense of them, to experience them as consistent. Many psychologists believe this is possible because the brain unconsciously selects stable, reliable elements from the bombardment of sense impressions. In perception this is, as Shannon said of his code, "the crux of the matter."

John Ruskin's famous advice to painters to cultivate what he called "the innocent eye," to see the world pure and straightforward, just as it is, looks dubious, if not untenable, considering what we know today about vision. Sir Ernst Gombrich, the British art historian, has declared in a commentary on naturalism in art that the innocent eye does not exist. It is a fiction. To look at a scene simply as an image of light and color on the retina, emptying it of meaning, stripping it of all extraneous mental activity, cannot be done, because all seeing is interpretation. The painter must see a meadow, not naïvely as pure light and shade, but as pigments in a context. A patch of color on a canvas is never absolute, right or wrong, on its own solitary merits, but always exists in a complex relationship with all the other patches of color on the same canvas. On its own, it may not be an exact match with the color of that small region of the actual meadow that it represents. Only when the picture is finished, and the entire system of color relations is established, will it correspond to reality in a satisfactory way.

The artist, Gombrich says, must hold all these relations in his mind at once while he paints, just as chess players retain a mental grasp of the relation of one piece to another on the chessboard, and composers of relations among notes in the musical score. Matching art to reality is the work of the "inquiring mind that knows how to probe the ambiguities of vision." For Gombrich, naturalism, in the sense of a form of art in which every stroke of the brush is uniquely determined by what is given to the senses, is a phantom. Even if a painter were to succeed in reproducing a scene on canvas exactly as he saw it, not everyone would see the painting in that way.

Perception is still one of the vexed questions of psychology. Does the brain have a theory of perception, as it seems to have a theory of language? On this issue, researchers tend to be divided along Chomskyan and anti-Chomskyan lines, some at the extreme edges, others somewhere in no man's land, being shelled by both sides. Behind one set of barricades are those who believe the brain constructs its own version of reality, relying on very little in the way of information coming to the senses. Behind the other set are workers who insist that experience provides all the information we need, and the brain makes a selection from that wealth of data. The differences in ideology are often great. But it is proof of the universal nature of information concepts that perceptual psychologists and linguists use similar arguments to explain two very dissimilar functions of the brain, vision and language.

Typical of the one extreme is Richard Gregory, the English neuropsychologist of whose work Chomsky explicitly approves. Gregory holds that the brain does not perceive the world exclusively from the data of the senses at a given moment, but uses the data to build and test hypotheses, as scientists do with the often sparse ration of facts at their disposal. When the eye looks at an ambiguous figure, such as the famous Necker cube, which seems to turn itself inside-out and then outside-in again while we are watching it, it is as if the brain were testing first one and then another hypothesis, trying to establish a correct theory on the basis of insufficient evidence. The eye never does determine which is the correct hypothesis, but keeps switching from one to the other. Indeed, Gregory thinks the perceptual system of the brain, so active in testing possible answers to a puzzle set by what the eye sees, is more "intellectually honest" than the supposedly rational parts of the cerebral cortex. Faced with an ambiguous object or drawing, it will not fasten on one interpretation and stick to it, unlike the rational mind, which will often espouse a particular dogma in politics or religion and refuse to relinquish it, no matter how impressive the countervailing evidence may be.

At the opposite end of the ideological spectrum are the ideas of the perceptual psychologist James J. Gibson, whose influence has grown steadily over the past few years and shows no sign of diminishing. Gibson, who died in 1979, argued that all the information needed for perception is outside the brain, in the world itself. His work has inspired research in fields not obviously related to his own, and his theories turn up in books on art, aesthetics, and language, as well as in technical papers on the mechanics of vision. He gives the environment a great deal more credit for keeping us informed than representatives of the Gregory school do.

It is hard to think of a doctrine more unlike Eastern mystical thought, which regards the visible world as an illusion. "Ask not what's inside your head; ask what your head's inside of" is a typical slogan of the Gibsonian movement in psychology. His band of admirers and followers swelled in his later years, and his ideas were taken up by those struggling to discover coherent theories of elusive mental processes like memory and imagination.

Gibson's theory of perception is based on the normal experience of ordinary people in the everyday world. It is far from exotic. Early in his career, he made a special study of how motorists judge speed and distance, and during the Second World War he did research into the perceptual problems of pilots landing planes on the decks of aircraft carriers. In neither of these activities is it very helpful to indulge in philosophical speculation about the nature of reality. If a plane careens over the side of a flight deck, or a motorist hits the back of a truck, philosophy is not likely to be of much assistance. Gibson held that all the information needed for perception is in the world, not in the head. To put the argument a little less glibly, all the information is present in the structure of the light as it is reflected from objects and events in space. The objects and events give the light its specific organization as it reaches the eye. An observer is immersed, drenched, in this information, and the perceptual system of the brain is attuned to pick up certain aspects of it, either by means of innate neural circuits or by the fine discrimination which comes with experience.

The visible world may never be known in its entirety. An octopus can detect horizontal and vertical lines but not diagonal ones. Humans are not aware of ultraviolet light. Yet, while this visual information may be incomplete, it is not, in the ordinary course of things, incorrect. It is direct, in the sense that while memory, inference, and imagination may accompany perception, they are not essential to it. The information does not need to be enriched by the brain, because it is already rich when it arrives at the eye.

The information in the light, Gibson maintains, specifies the relationship of things one to another. It keeps us informed about what is changing and what is unchanging in a scene we are looking at, and whether, when movement takes place, it is the world that moves or we ourselves. The information is immensely subtle, an inexhaustible store of data that can never be wholly perceived even in a lifetime of trying, but it is not in general misleading. As the observer goes about the world, he learns to detect many of these subtleties. It is not a question of the brain making sense of a swirl of sensations, patches of disorganized color on the retina, but of paying attention to invariant properties in the fine structure of the light.

Light never stays the same from one moment to the next. It dims or brightens, changes its frequency. The observer, too, is never wholly at rest. He moves around things, seeing them from different angles. Cars and people recede into the distance, throwing smaller images onto the retina of the eye. Shapes loom up as we walk toward them. Seen through a train window, closer objects appear to move faster than those far away. Yet the viewer imposes a certain stability on all this shrinking and swelling, on these gross distortions and deformations, by paying attention to the stable features of change and ignoring the rest.

The process is something like recognizing the melody of a song even when it is transposed into a different key. The relationships between notes are unchanged, even though the notes themselves are not in the same places on the keyboard. Such relationships are known as "higher order variables," and are attended to by people because they are interesting and significant. They are what the viewer or listener wants and needs to know.

For Gibson, invariants in the structure of light reaching the eye correspond to the stable features of the real world: the surfaces and edges of objects, to which the brain pays such alert attention, the texture of the ground that grows more dense with distance. In spite of the fact that the image of an object on the retina may shrink in size as it recedes, the image is invariant with respect to the texture of its surroundings. A house standing on a checkerboard of fields looks smaller as a viewer walks away from it, but so do the fields immediately surrounding the house. The house still occupies the same number of units of space, but those units all shrink together as they become more distant. In other words, the relationship between the house and its own space remains the same.

We recognize the face of a friend, whether it is smiling or sad, whether seen in bright sunshine or by the light of the moon. The face may be glimpsed in profile through the window of a passing bus, or observed close up from the front. Much about the face may change, but something essential stays the same. Through all these variations, invariants have been preserved, and these are what we notice. Shapes can be deceptive when seen from strange perspectives. A cup does not look very cuplike when seen from above. A penny turned sideways is not easily recognized as a penny. However, as the viewer's eye explores the penny and the cup from various angles, he is able to detect and isolate their invariant properties: the roundness, flatness, and hardness of the penny, the hollowness and rigidity of the cup.

Mathematicians deal with this process of invariants being preserved under transformations by means of a very powerful, formal system called group theory, which has proved of great usefulness in making intelligible the structure of matter at the atomic level. Group theory is concerned with patterns and relations, with the essential sameness of things concealed beneath their surface differences, in much the same way that Chomsky's work in linguistics is concerned with universals, elements of language that are invariant, even though languages differ from one another in relatively superficial ways.

Group theory is highly abstract and general. It enables scientists to make sense of the hidden world of the atomic microcosm because of its peculiar power to generate information about the *structure* of events, even if the events themselves cannot be known. In mathematics and physics it unifies disparate things by revealing their common, underlying form. Appearances are stripped away, specifics are ignored, so that only the essentials, the abstract, invariant relations, the sameness in the midst of change, make themselves known.

James R. Newman, in one of his essays on mathematics, likened the workings of group theory to an archeologist at the site of a lost city, stripping away the surfaces of hills to reach the buried masonry beneath, digging into the rubble of houses to uncover ornaments and vessels, tunneling into tombs to find sarcophagi and at last unwrapping the mummies within.

Group theory is even more abstract than algebra. In algebra, the x's and y's do not have fixed values, but at least the operations of addition and subtraction we perform on them are known for sure. In group theory not even that is explicit. A group consists of a class or collection of elements, which may be as specific as numbers or squares or atoms or as vague as an undefined "object of thought." Or the elements may be a class of operations performed on something.

Suppose the class of elements in question is the set of all whole numbers. One of these numbers, added to itself, results in another number, which is usually different. Yet this second number, obtained by the operation of addition, is still a member of the class of all whole numbers. The first number has been transformed by the operation. But while it is different in one sense, it is the same in another sense. Four added to four is eight. Clearly, eight is not the same as four, but it has kept the invariant feature of being a whole number. It retains the group property.

For a class of elements to be a group, in the mathematical sense of the term, certain conditions must be satisfied. One of these conditions is the rule that if the elements A and B are members of the class in question, then combining A and B by some operation, say addition or multiplication, results in an element which is also a member of the class. Another is the rule that there must be an "identity" element in the class, such that, when it is combined with another element A, of the same class, the result is again A, unchanged by the operation. In simple arithmetic, four added to zero is still four, and four multiplied by one is still four. Here the identity elements would be zero and one respectively. A further rule states that there must exist an element which, when combined with any other element, results in the identity. Only if all these conditions are met can the class of elements be called a group.

A group may also consist of a class of operations performed on something, one after another in succession. In this case, any two operations must lead to a result which could have been obtained by just a single operation. These operations might be to move certain objects, transforming them into different positions or deforming them into new shapes. A well-known example is the class of operations that rotates a simple square on its own axis. In the diagram below, the corners of the squares are numbered to show the changes brought about by rotation:

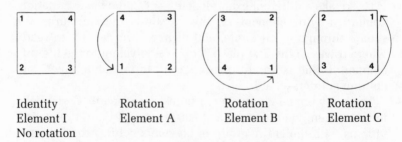

Identity   Rotation   Rotation   Rotation
Element I   Element A   Element B   Element C
No rotation

In this class of four rotations, the elements are I, A, B, and C. The first is not a rotation at all, but an operation which leaves the square exactly as it was, unchanged. In the second rotation, A, the top left-hand corner becomes the bottom left-hand corner, and so on. Adding two of the rotations together—performing them one after another—leaves the square in a position which could have been reached by means of just a single rotation element. We can add identity elements to each other any number of times and the result will still be an identity element, leaving the square unchanged. Adding two A elements together transforms the square into the position it would be in if a single B rotation element had been used. A and B combined is equivalent to C. The results of combining various rotation elements can be expressed by means of an array, of the kind bus lines use to show the distances in miles between major cities on their route:

COLUMNS

	I	A	B	C
I	I	A	B	C
A	A	B	C	I
B	B	C	I	A
C	C	I	A	B

ROWS

Here it is easy to see what happens when rotation elements are combined. At the point where horizontal row A intersects with vertical column B is the letter C. So the array shows in the simplest possible fashion that the result of combining A and B is C. To take a different example, element C, the largest rotation, combined with element A, the smallest rotation, turns the square through a full circle, 360 degrees, and leaves it exactly where it was in the first place. This is equivalent to the Identity element, I; that is, to no rotation at all. In the table, row C and column A intersect at I.

The array possesses one very interesting property. Certain elements, when combined with themselves again and again, provide us with the entire group of elements, while others do not. Single elements which yield the whole group in this way are called "generators," an important term. An example of a generator is the rotation element A:

A combined with A gives B.
B or (A combined with A) combined with A gives C.
C or (A combined with (A combined with A)) combined with A gives I.

I or (A combined with (A combined with (A combined with A))) combined with A gives A.

Thus simply raising A to the power of four generates all four members of the group. But not all elements have this property. B combined with itself yields only two members of the group, one after the other in an endless succession:

B combined with B gives I.
I or (B combined with B) combined with B gives B again.
B combined with B gives I again.
I or (B combined with B) combined with B gives B again.

And so on forever.

———————

Two American psychologists, Robert Shaw and Buford Wilson, both of whom concur with the broad lines of Gibson's theory of perceptual invariants, whereby the brain pays attention to the unchanging features of sensory impressions, have made the intriguing proposal that the perspectives of solid objects, the various viewpoints from which they may be seen by an observer, form a group. Shaw and Wilson suggest that, for many objects, a few perspectives only are enough to provide us with sufficient information to specify the whole shape of the object, because some of these perspectives may be generators of the complete group of perspectives. It is not necessary to experience all of them to perceive what the object actually is. This is a fresh and exciting approach, which dispenses with the need for the brain to make guesses about what the world is "really" like. It also suggests that conceptual thought, like perception, may use some of the same group generator principles, since, in abstract mental processes, the brain does tend to complete incomplete information.

The notion of a group generator, Shaw and Wilson believe, may lead to new insights into how human beings perceive the world as well as how they know it. They are careful to point out, however, that this is neither a physical nor a psychological model in the accepted sense of those words, but rather an "ecological" model, shedding light on the way people interact with the world around them. Mental and physical mesh in a systematic fashion. As Shaw and another collaborator, Michael McIntyre, put it, "Ideas are not in the mind, nor objects in the world, but . . . both are in the meeting of mind and matter."

The world is not constructed inside the head. On the other hand, the brain is by no means a passive nonparticipant, merely registering and taking copies of every message which reaches it from outside. We may forget particular instances, and yet retain the abstract system of relations that generates the complete group, including the forgotten parts, by means of partial information. The perception of the shape of objects depends, not on examining an object in exhaustive detail, but on a set of properly ordered perspectives of it; in other words, on its generator set. The human face may be transformed by the lines and strains of age, but enough of the structure of the face remains invariant to make it easily recognizable, rather as the exaggerated, incomplete features of a politician in a newspaper cartoon make recognition simpler, not more difficult, for the average newspaper reader.

Shaw and Wilson see the group generator model as a mathematically explicit principle which could be important in teaching higher forms of knowledge, such as science, philosophy, mathematics, art, history, and law. In learning these subjects, the brain might acquire, half automatically, an abstract structure of relations from suitably chosen examples—"core concepts"—which would generate more complete knowledge. Expert judgments, the two psychologists conclude, "are a by-product of generative systems of knowledge rather than of inert banks of factual information." A student would be likely to reveal these tacit knowledge structures through a tendency to reject irrelevant information, while mistakenly assuming that new, relevant information is not new at all, but something already experienced. This would be a result of being able to generate a whole from its parts, as long as they are the right parts.

Shaw and Wilson comment:

One important insight that emerges from a study of such cases is that for generative concepts there are no truly novel instances. There are only those instances that are actual, because they belong to a generator set, and those that are potential, because they lie dormant among the remaining totality of instances. Consequently, the only difference between actual versus potential instances is whether the instance has been made manifest by application of the generator principle. Once done so, a newborn instance bears no marks of its recent birth to denote that it is new rather than old.

The organism is linked to the world directly, and evolution has designed this linkage to be a snug fit, the brain being tuned to acquire accurate knowledge of the particular environment the organism inhabits. "A perceiver is a *self-tuning* system," Gibson has said. Such an approach has a tonic effect, because it compels psychologists to pay attention to the richness and unlimited subtlety of the information in the environment, and it is a cautionary reminder that human beings are equipped to master the actual world, their ecological niche, not to sit still in a laboratory while psychologists flash lights at them or read them lists of nonsense syllables.

But to say that evolution fashioned our perceptual system for the single, utilitarian purpose of finding our way around in the world, with accuracy and objectivity as the sole criteria, leaves psychologists open to the same criticism Chomsky has lodged against theories of language as an exclusively public act of communication. Perception may have arisen in evolution to solve the problem of navigating the environment, but it need not have that purpose now. It is clear that, at the very least, perception has its own rules of aesthetic preference, which are hardly a strategy for survival in the Darwinian sense. Certainly there is no simple relationship between what enters the eye and what we experience as seeing. Shaw and McIntyre, who reject the idea of perception as a preconscious process of constructing visual experience out of random bits of data, concede that

> There does seem to be evidence that perceptual modulation of physical information might create new information which has psychological significance.

Perception is a personal act never undertaken innocently. The eye does not just let impressions fall on it while it holds still, observing. It is highly active. Watching a scene, the eye jumps, jerks, and dances around it. While in motion, the eye sees nothing. Only when it rests for a fraction of a second between jumps does it send a message back to the brain, a packet of information. On the basis of these separate bursts of data, the brain decides where the eye will jump next. Eye movements do not follow the outline of the object, making a copy of it, but concentrate on salient features, those of interest to the viewer. Different viewers make different movements and even the same viewers do not make the same movements every time they look at the same object. There is a continual cybernetic feedback between what the eye sees and the movements it makes.

Even when the eye appears to be quite still, staring fixedly at one spot, it makes tiny, quick movements, several times a second, slightly shifting the image on the retina. And it is these abrupt shifts, not the scene itself, which produces a response in the nerve cells of the brain. There is no question of the eye perceiving everything in a scene all at once. At an advanced level of processing in the visual system of the brain, only about a thousand neurons may fire when the eyes are watching quite a complex object. Important features of the scene are grasped and nonessentials discarded, and as information is processed farther back in the brain, the cells respond with more and more discrimination. Action, purpose, choice, and control are of the essence in any cybernetic system, and the brain's way of seeing what it sees is no exception.

The less simple the relationship between the information presented to the senses and what the brain does with that information, the more likely it is that strategies of knowing are not uniform, but differ from one person to another. An act of perception is personal and unique. So is an act of learning or remembering. Even experts who acquire the same body of knowledge from a uniform system of training, and who read the same textbooks, use that knowledge in different, idiosyncratic ways to solve the same problem.

Not only is perception, by its nature, nonuniform, there is evidence that people who are more creative than others tend to explore the world of shapes and objects from more unusual visual perspectives. Some American schoolchildren were asked to sketch as many objects as they could manage in ten minutes, using a circle as the starting point of each drawing. Certain children drew objects as if seen from uncommon angles—from underneath, from inside, at a distance, or very close up; or they were depicted as being in unexpected relationships with other objects. Other children kept to the standard perspectives from which things are normally expected to be seen. Twelve years later, many of those who had taken the test were given a questionnaire, asking whether they had written plays or books, poems or songs, undertaken research in science, invented new gadgets, started their own businesses. A clear connection was found between the childhood tendency to see things from unusual perspectives and original, creative activity in later life.

In perception, as in language, an antichance device is needed. The group-generator theory of perception provides this when it decrees that not just any element enables the whole to be generated from partial information, but only a properly ordered set of elements linked to each other by statistical rules; in other words, by redundancy. In Gibson's scheme, the brain searches for invariants amid the varying impressions which reach our eyes. This, too, is an information process.

The flaw at the heart of many scientific "explanations" of how the mind works is the premise, not always obvious at first sight, that there can be direct, transparent ways of knowing the world. This idea is often coupled with a belief that experience is imprinted on a docile brain. Experience is changeable, which is only to be expected, because without change there is no information. Without redundancy, however, there is noise and error. Shannon may have had something like this in mind when he referred to the possibility that the human being is "an ideal decoder."

18

The Bottom and Top of Memory

It is generally agreed that there must exist a "syntax" of memory. Information is easier to remember when it is in an orderly state, rich in pattern and structure, highly interconnected, containing a good deal of redundancy. Disorderly information that lacks structure is easy to forget.

This is not a modern discovery by any means. It is very ancient, going back to classical times, when the Greek poet Simonides of Ceos, in the fifth century B.C., showed that an effective strategy in remembering is to establish relationships between things which might otherwise seem unrelated. Simonides had been giving a recital of a poem in praise of Castor and Pollux, the heavenly twins, at a banquet arranged by a nobleman of Thessaly. The nobleman was less than delighted with the poem because it flattered Castor and Pollux too extravagantly and did not flatter him enough. Irritated, he cut the poet's fee in half. Later in the evening Simonides was summoned out of the hall by a messenger, who brought the news that two young men, presumably the twins themselves, were waiting to see him. While Simonides was out, looking in vain for the visitors, the gods caused the roof of the hall to collapse. The nobleman and his guests were killed, crushed so thoroughly that their next of kin could not identify the remains.

Simonides, however, could give names to the dead because

he remembered the place at which each guest had sat at the banqueting table. In his mind's eye he proceeded from one face to the next in a connected sequence. From this experience he decided that order and structure are the secret of a good memory. He developed a system for remembering lists of words or ideas by imagining them arranged in succession in some familiar setting, such as a house. The items to be remembered were envisioned as occupying places in specific parts of the rooms in the house, "so that the order of the places will preserve the order of the things." Relationship and pattern were the key to the device. This basic idea reappeared in various manifestations after classical times. Frances Yates, in her excellent and much quoted book, *The Art of Memory*, suggests that one approach to understanding Dante's *Inferno* might be to regard it as an ingenious system for memorizing hell and its punishments by placing each kind of sinner in a precise region of the cosmic architecture, creating a highly ordered structure in which the spheres of hell are the spheres of heaven in reverse.

In the Renaissance, fantastic memory machines were devised, such as Giulio Camillo's wooden memory theater, which was divided into seven levels, each representing a stage in the evolution of the world from the beginning of creation to the peaks of human wisdom and learning. The levels are ascended by seven gangways, symbolizing the seven known planets. Camillo's theater was a device for organizing knowledge about the universe, and it made use of the important psychological fact that new information is remembered better if it is embedded in a wider context of information already known from personal experience.

In more recent times, Mark Twain, when giving a speech in a strange town, would walk through a park beforehand, imagining the ideas for his speech as being seated on a bench, hung from this or that tree, attached to a fountain or a bandstand. Twain was then able to talk for two hours at a time, without using notes, by strolling through the park in his imagination, "seeing" his ideas in their correct sequence.

In remembering, the brain does not like randomness. It looks for ways to lower the entropy of a collection of items by reducing the number of ways in which they can be arranged. It cuts down the value of W in Shannon's equation, $S = k \log W$, and therefore reduces the entropy, S. Indeed, it tries to arrange the items in a unique sequence. If the items display no obvious relationships, no discernible pattern, the brain will invent relationships, imposing some arbitrary order on the disorderliness of the material. A list of items in which each item is independent of all the others is just noise. Memory has no taste for noise; it needs a message. Clearly, there are analogies here with language, which does not allow letters and words to follow one another in just any order, and with perception, which seeks out invariants among the varying sense impressions reaching the eye.

Given several words to remember, most people succeed much better at the task if they organize the words into some sort of structure, perhaps by categories and classes. Good learners will concoct a pattern of their own devising to give coherence to a random word list, often making the most unlikely connections between one word and the next. As a result, the words become more predictable, as in a message which contains redundancy.

One frequently used method of remembering strings of unrelated words is to give them a narrative structure, in which one event leads to the next in a series of often outlandish scenes. The secret of survival in the well-known party game in which players try to remember ten words or pay a forfeit is to string the words together into a story, the more ridiculous the better. For example, in one such game the list

RESISTANCE

NAUSEA

WINDOW

GALOSHES

PIRATE

SHOELACE

PEPPER POT

BUS STOP

SHIRTTAIL

MARMALADE

was constructed into this spontaneous mental screenplay: A Second World War resistance fighter, living in Paris, is reading

Sartre's *La Nausée*. He hears raindrops on the window, puts on his galoshes and sallies forth into the Boulevard St. Germain, which is flooded to such a depth that a pirate ship sails by with a cargo of hijacked shoelaces and pepper pots. Floating toward a bus stop which protrudes above the surface of the water, he moors himself to it by his shirttail and fends off the pangs of hunger by consuming a jar of marmalade.

The story is easily stored, and with it the list of words. Players of these memory games often remark on the oddly dreamlike quality of the scenes concocted out of random words, raising the interesting question of a possible relationship between memory and dreams.

We have already seen how, in printed text, redundancy makes certain sequences of letters and words more predictable than others. In fact, greater redundancy is virtually equivalent to greater predictability. The two types of redundancy, D_1 and D_2, the first context-free, the second context-sensitive, help to reduce the unexpectedness of a message and give structure and pattern to what would otherwise be highly unpredictable sequences of symbols. Shannon experimented with these different kinds of redundancy. He generated nonsense sentences from words chosen at random. Then he introduced the condition that words should appear, on the average, with the same frequency they do in sensible English prose. His sentences were still highly random, but they contained a context-free type of redundancy; they were not as random as they could possibly be. The result was a sentence such as this:

> REPRESENTING AND SPEEDILY IS AN GOOD APT OR COME CAN DIFFERENT NATURAL HERE HE THE A IN CAME THE TO OF TO EXPERT GRAY TO FURNISHES THE LINE MESSAGE HAD BE THESE.

When context-free redundancy was held steady and context-sensitive redundancy was increased, so that the likelihood of a certain word appearing was affected by the word immediately preceding it, a more respectable, though still hardly comprehensible, sentence emerged:

THE HEAD AND IN FRONTAL ATTACK ON A ENGLISH WRITER
THAT THE CHARACTER OF THIS POINT IS THEREFORE ANOTHER
METHOD FOR THE LETTERS THAT THE TIME OF WHO EVER TOLD
THE PROBLEM FOR AN UNEXPECTED.

Shannon was interested in discovering the amount of redundancy in English prose and how this might affect the reliability of the text. Psychologists have now become interested in the effect of redundancy on memory. They have found that people are apt to remember sentences better the more context-sensitive redundancy the sentences contain, and are poor at remembering sequences which contain little or no redundancy. It became clear that most people can sense a distinct change that occurs when unorganized strings of words acquire structure. Some sort of barrier is crossed, with powerful effects on the effectiveness of memory.

The psychologist John Bransford believes that a major goal of theories of learning and memory should be to describe explicitly the nature of the organized structures which underlie our feelings of comprehension, of mastery over the material. Interestingly, this sense of structure which seems to have such an important effect on remembering is not confined to the surface of sentences. Memory seems to penetrate beneath the surface down to the more abstract level of the "deep," or conceptual, structures underlying the surface form.

The classic pair of Chomsky sentences

John is eager to please

John is easy to please

have similar surface forms, but the underlying conceptual structures which contain the intention of the speaker are quite unlike, as we saw earlier. These two sentences, and others like them, were read aloud to college students in a memory test. Sometime later, the students were asked to recall the sentences, and were given only the first word of each as a cue. It turned out that even though the cue word was "John" for each of the Chomsky sentences, the students were better at remembering "John is eager to please" than "John is easy to please." Bransford suggests that a reason for this odd result is that, in the deep structure of the first sentence, John plays a role in two events: he is eager, and he pleases. In the deep structure of the second sentence, he plays a role in only one event: it is easy for someone to please John.

Clearly, the brain does not simply store sequences of words as it hears or reads them. Even though all the sentences in a list may contain the same number of words, they are not all remembered equally well, because their conceptual structures may vary in complexity. As Bransford points out, people rarely remember written or spoken material word for word. When asked to reproduce it, they resort to paraphrase, which suggests that they were able to store the meaning of the material rather than making a verbatim copy of each sentence in the mind. We forget the surface structure, but retain the abstract relationships contained in the deep structure. In psychological tests, people tend to think they recognize as familiar sentences they have never heard before. The reason appears to be that while these new sentences have a surface structure which is different from sentences already given, they have the same deep structure relationships.

Dependence on structure, Chomsky declares, is one of the universal properties of language. It is something that will always be found in the rules of any human language. In a way not fully understood, memory also depends on the structuring of information, the making of patterns, and is at its most fallible when pattern does not exist. People can remember random, unconnected lists of words, but not easily, and not for long. If the list has no obvious structure, successful memorizers will organize it into a structure of their own invention. But memory theorists have learned to beware of glib answers to fundamental questions about how this elusive mental process accomplishes what it does. In one specific act of memory, the brain may organize the material in a hierarchy, grouping items into classes and grouping these classes into larger classes, like the families, species, and genera of zoology. Yet this method of recall cannot be regarded as universal. Another person, under different circumstances, might organize the material into loops, or circles, or linear arrays. There will be structure, but the structure will vary according to the material, the way the material is experienced, and to what use the person doing the remembering intends to put the knowledge once it is stored. The "syntax" of memory—the formal patterns imposed on information in order to retain it in the mind—is related to meaning and use, just as in language, and this relation may be different for different individuals, an alarming prospect with which scientists, understandably, are reluctant to come to grips.*

———————

The American psychologist James J. Jenkins is one who has faced, more squarely than most, the idiosyncratic nature of memory and all the awkward problems that creates for anyone trying to devise a comprehensive theory of remembering and learning, a theory which, like theories of mechanics, will be good for all times and all places—and all individuals. Jenkins' papers are extremely readable, and tend to have breezy titles such as "Remember That Old Theory of Memory? Well, Forget It!" He himself held to an "old" theory of memory in the 1950s, based on the premise that complex mental behaviors are built out of simple components, as machines are, and that these behaviors function automatically as long as the machine runs. In the early 1960s, Jenkins abandoned this assumption and with it the hope that knowing the inner workings of such a machine would yield a full understanding of memory. He came to accept that remembering takes place in a psychological and physical context which not only varies in itself but is embedded in a

———————

* Specialists in children's heart diseases use highly individualistic ways of storing and retrieving the same body of knowledge. Paul Johnson, a psychologist who spent five years studying these physicians, found that, unlike medical students or hospital interns, who arrive at a diagnosis by a slow, thorough process of logical deduction, experts short-cut these chains of reasoning and move rapidly to a judgment by what appears to be a magical leap of insight but is more likely a result of special ways of storing information in memory. The novice tries to remember all the information he has been taught, and derives conclusions from it in a formal way. The expert knows as much as the novice, but he recollects a much smaller class of ideas, and these are ideas which are more likely to be correct.

This reduced set of items is organized in memory in very strategic ways, so that it can be summoned quickly. If it proves to be incorrect, the next most likely set is recalled. Such a type of thinking is called heuristic, and it seems to be common among specialists in many fields. But while pre-experts tend to approach problems in much the same way, by standard methods of deduction, experts are vastly less uniform and predictable in their methods. Enormous wider and wider set of contexts, so that expecting hard-and-fast laws for memory that apply in all circumstances is rather like believing in a Laplacean superintelligence which is able to know the state of every molecule in the universe.

The old approach to memory was "bottom-up." It assumed that a scientist could describe what happens by starting with the basic organizing principles in the brain and working up to the behavior of the person in the act of remembering, much as the "old" view of language assumed that sentences could be explained fully by examining their internal structure and the literal meaning of each word. After several years of exciting and successful work on word associations, which seemed to confirm the mechanistic theory, Jenkins decided that the bottom-up approach, starting with the cogs and wheels of some hypothetical memory machine in the brain, was wrong, even though it was enjoying more and more popularity at the time.

A better way, he thought, was "top-down," beginning with a person's total experience of the information to be remembered. And if memory is to be understood correctly, that experience should be as natural as possible, just as it is in the real world. Laws of memory, Jenkins argued, are like the "law" of the stock market, which tells investors to buy low and sell high. That is impeccable as an abstract principle, but it is perfectly useless to the novice investor who tries to apply it. What is low? What is high? The novice cannot know just by looking at the share price on a single day. Only when the price is set in the context of information about prices over the previous twelve months is the

---

individual differences appear. One cardiologist, who prefers to play it safe, might retrieve from his memory the whole domain of possibilities for a certain set of symptoms (though not nearly as many as the pre-expert), and gradually narrow them down as he moves along with his diagnosis. Another, no less skilled but more of a gambler, may propose only one or two possibilities, proceeding with them until one is disproved and then jumping to the second. He generates a better set of initial guesses than the first doctor, and knows at once when a guess is disproved by a critical piece of evidence. His strategy is based on the way he has organized the information in memory, and the exact nature of this organization is peculiar to him. "This tells us, among other things, that memory is a lot more flexible than we might want to suppose," Johnson comments. "You can make a large mistake in thinking that content is represented in memory in the same way as is represented in text books. Information is stored in memory according to the way in which the individual person knows it is going to be used. It is stored according to the demands of the tasks with which he is familiar."

glimmer of an answer possible. The wider the context, the better the answer. But, as we have already seen, a context has no fixed boundaries. It spreads out in widening circles like the context of a conversation. Whether someone will be able to remember information depends on what *meaning* the whole experience has for him, as well as what is expected of him when he recollects it. This is the formidable challenge set for psychologists by the top-down approach to an understanding of memory.

Making memory stand still so it can be defined once and for all, therefore, seems to be out of the question. What memory *is* depends on context, and contexts change. The existence of fixed and final laws of memory, Jenkins believes, is another myth which needs to be exploded. An analysis of memory is worth something only for a specific and limited purpose. "*All* analyses eventually 'sheer away' from the event into more extensive contexts," Jenkins says. "This means that being a psychologist is going to be much more difficult than we used to think."

Memory is not a lower mental function, working automatically and independently. To explain memory a scientist would have to understand all the higher mental functions simultaneously, because in an act of memory we construct and reconstruct experience, using any or all of these mental functions —perception, comprehension, inference, belief, language— whether unconsciously or in full awareness. Here Jenkins agrees with William James that memory is no different from perception, imagination, comparison, or reasoning, apart from the fact that, in remembering, we attribute these mental constructions to the past.

Remembering does not happen as a matter of course whenever a person is exposed to information. It does not even happen automatically if the person wants and intends to commit the information to memory. Jenkins proposes that, if memory is to work well, the rememberer must pick up those aspects of the events or material to be remembered that make possible a well-defined personal experience. For this he needs to be attuned in some way to what is put in front of him, just as in Gibson's theory of perception the brain is assumed to be attuned to certain features of the light reaching the eye. It is the quality of the experience that counts, and that is never quite the same for each person. Questions such as how long a time was taken in studying the material and how much effort was spent in trying to store it in memory are of surprisingly little importance.

Of greater importance is the particular way in which an individual "processes" the information, endows it with syntax and meaning, places it in a personal context. Hermann Ebbinghaus, the nineteenth-century founder of scientific memory research, who used nonsense syllables in his memory tests to insure that the pure act of recall was not tainted by meaning, found that people forget up to 80 percent of what they learn within twenty-four hours. After that the loss is less rapid. This swift loss of information from the conscious mind became known as "the curve of forgetting." Yet the Ebbinghaus curve is not a universal law. It does not apply when unsophisticated people come fresh to memory tests, nor when the information to be remembered takes the form of stories rather than nonsense syllables carefully drained of context. The answer to this apparent paradox, Jenkins suggests, is that the inexperienced, naïve person is intrigued by the nonsense syllables and tries to make sense of them, attaches images to them, notices interesting properties of the list as a whole. Because he enriches them in this way, extending their artificially cramped context, he is able to remember as many as 75 percent of them a day later, throwing the Ebbinghaus curve into reverse.

This good retention does not last, however, as the subject loses his naïveté. After a score of tests have been taken, one after the other, he realizes that all he has to do to satisfy the psychologist is to repeat the lists immediately after hearing them. If he gets them right, he is allowed to go home. He progressively simplifies his mental behavior to suit the demands of the task. As a result, he is able to remember almost none of the lists a day later and the Ebbinghaus curve once again applies. Contrary to what might be expected, the mental behavior of a person fresh to the experience of a test is more complex than that of a sophisticate, not less so, and that is why the information stays in his memory.

———

Clearly, meaning is an important ingredient in remembering. Indeed, people show a marked ability to abstract quite elaborate meanings from fragments of unconnected material, and they do so without any special effort. What is more interesting, they tend to remember the meanings while forgetting the exact form of the fragments. John Bransford and Jeffrey Franks, in a famous experiment to test abstract memory for ideas, compiled lists of sentences of varying length, some very simple, others less simple, and still others quite complex. At the highest level of complexity was a sentence like:

> The rock which rolled down the mountain crushed the tiny hut at the edge of the woods.

This same idea was broken down into parts and represented by four shorter and simpler sentences:

> The rock rolled down the mountain.
> The rock crushed the hut.
> The hut was tiny.
> The hut was at the edge of the woods.

Students who took the test were given only some of these shorter fragments. They were not given any of the long sentences which expressed the complete set of ideas, so that they were exposed to no more than bits and pieces of the full meaning of the complex sentences. Nor were the students allowed to spend time thinking about the material they did experience. As soon as they heard a fragment, they were asked a question, to distract their attention. At the end of this stage of the test, the complete list of sentences was read out, and the students were asked to say how familiar each sentence sounded to them, from a rating of plus five for sentences they were sure they had already heard, to a rating of minus five for those they were equally certain they had not heard.

The results boded no good for the theory that memory is literal-minded and passive. In general, a top rating was given to the sentences which combined all the ideas, even though the students had never heard these sentences before. Other, shorter sentences were rated more familiar the more complex they were, regardless of whether the students had actually heard them or not. The shortest, simplest sentences scored very poorly for recognition. Actual familiarity turned out to have almost nothing to do with how the students responded. All that mattered was that a sentence was or was not compatible with the complete, most complex idea which the students had abstracted from the short fragments. This abstract idea had not been experienced directly by the students; they had never heard it. It was, in fact, a mental construction. But it behaved as if it were a memory. As in the case of language, the abstraction was able to generate new forms, which seemed familiar but were really artifacts created in the conscious mind.

Out of disconnected elements, a complete meaning is constructed, and that is what a person remembers. That does not imply that memory necessarily preserves the original meaning intact. The brain goes to work on information while it is being stored in memory, interpreting, drawing inferences, making assumptions, fitting it into a context of past experience and knowledge already acquired. When the information is recollected, the elaborations added by the brain may behave like a memory, so that people have the mistaken impression that the extra information is part of the original message.

Once placed in memory, the two kinds of information are not easily disentangled. The students in the test were *certain* that they had heard the full, most complex sentences expressing the complete idea, when in reality they had constructed them out of fragments of the meaning contained in the shorter fragments. The various strands of meaning were so thoroughly fused together that they could not be unraveled. This knitting of parts into one whole experience appears to be a one-way process, not reversible without conscious effort, and not always then.

James Jenkins points out that this notion of fusion, which has a history all its own in the study of the mind, may be one reason why psychology has been notably unsuccessful in breaking down aesthetic and mystical experience into its component parts. He says:

> Any study of knowledge structure brings you face to face with fusion, things you know that you have no idea how you know. There's no specific memory. There is only the residual of the result. Most adults have the multiplication table stored away in their heads. They know the results of multiplying eight by five or seven by nine. But they

don't have any notion of where these results come from, except for
the general belief that they learned it at school. People take bits and
pieces and construct an event which they remember, but they forget
the bits and pieces. Studies of witnesses describing what they think
they remember about an accident suggest that the brain can construct
the event under the influence of the questions it is being asked.

People tend to interpret new information in the context of
their previous knowledge, and the two elements, old and new,
become fused in memory. We construct meanings and remember
our constructions. There is evidence, too, to suggest that we
reconstruct information when retrieving it from memory. Only
the gist of the information is stored. The details are added at the
time of recollection, on the basis of what we expect to have been
true. Reconstruction may seriously distort the original information, but the rememberer may be quite unaware of the distortion.
If the material given to us is consistent with our knowledge and
expectations, it is more likely to be recalled correctly, but if it is
inconsistent, then there are likely to be systematic distortions.
The past is unconsciously adjusted to suit what the rememberer
knows and expects in the present. There is a linguistic parallel
to this phenomenon in the patterns of unconscious expectation
that speakers use when they converse with other speakers.
When the expectations are not met, conversation can break
down.

All this hardly speaks well for a theory of memory as an automatic machine. Bransford has described how the reconstruction of memory may enable someone to make untrue replies to
questions and still pass a lie-detector test, or give false evidence
at a trial in full innocence if the leading questions of a cross-
examining attorney alter his expectations and produce unconscious changes in his memory. Later information can affect
memory in other ways. Bransford suggests that our social re-
flexes and prejudices can warp our recollections about individuals, so that if we hear bad things about them today, we tend to
reconstruct our memory of them to suit the new information,
reinforcing the new opinion and making it extremely resistant
to change.

Why is memory so intrinsically personal, so idiosyncratic in its ways of organizing information, so sensitive to context and meaning? Why is it tangled up with other activities of the mind, and so difficult to disentangle? Even emotional states and moods seem to affect remembering. A certain state of mind—intense happiness or sadness, mild intoxication, lack of sleep—may serve as a special context for recollection, so that if a person is exposed to information while in a specific state or mood, that information is more likely to be remembered when the person returns to the same state. If he was intoxicated when he heard the information, he can be expected to recollect it more readily when intoxicated.

Memory is not autonomous, as some linguists believe syntax to be autonomous. Would it were that simple. Indeed, it appears to be no simpler than language, which has also escaped capture in the net of an all-inclusive scientific theory. Memory does not store information infallibly and reproduce it impeccably merely by organizing it according to uniform, highly constrained sets of rules.

At first sight, it seems incredibly inefficient of evolution not to have developed an autonomous mechanism of that sort, one unaffected by context, use, and personal meaning. On further consideration, however, such a type of memory has only surface conveniences. Human beings are not designed to function uniformly. Their success as a species arises in part from their lack of specialization. Mechanical accuracy is not what we are best at, and it is not what people, generally speaking, want to be best at. The brain is not a device for processing information in a one-dimensional, linear fashion only. Unlike a computer, which is subject to very little "noise" in the form of electrical interference, and which works by performing a long chain of simple operations at high speed, the brain is both noisy and slow, but it uses its colossal number of components to pass information along many different channels at the same time. The brain is probable rather than certain in its actions, arriving at many answers, some more nearly correct than others, and these answers are modified continually by feedback of new information.

Unlike the parts of a computer, nerve cells are highly individual. No two cells are exactly the same, nor do they respond to the same incoming information in the same way. The system is extremely redundant, yet extraordinarily diverse. This enables the brain to make sense of the world on its own terms and for its own purposes. It stores common knowledge, but also knowledge of a highly idiosyncratic kind. When people explore the world, they use their brains in ways which are very similar, but they also need to establish a very personal relationship with certain parts of the world. For that reason, memory needs to be partly idiosyncratic.

James Jenkins believes that we remember experiences which have a personal meaning for us, even if the meaning is a pure construction of the mind:

> I think we will eventually conclude that the mind remembers what the mind does, not what the world does. That is, experience is the mind at work, not the world impinging on a passive organism—and experience is what will be remembered.

So the brain constructs and reconstructs information, creating a highly personal mental artifact and calling it a memory. If people remember best when they enrich information in their own way and remember least when they simplify experience, draining it of meaning, each act of memory must be special, even unique, to each person.

Memory appears to be constrained by a structure, a "syntax," perhaps at quite a low level, but it is free to be variable, deviant, even erratic at a higher level. Certain definite rules govern its basic mechanism, but in the context of actual use, memory is less strongly constrained, more unpredictable. The psychologist Robert Verbrugge compares memory with the action of a horse moving cross-country at a gallop. The horse coordinates its limbs in a very regular, rhythmic fashion and such coordination appears to be organized at an elementary level in the spine. And yet if the horse encounters a rock in its path, or a hedge, its locomotion system shows tremendous adaptability in adjusting the basic regularity of its gallop to unpredictable irregularities of the terrain. Actions of the body and of the mind have a great deal of underlying syntax, whose rules are basic and apply in general. But these actions are also free to be less regular at the surface, where universal principles must be made to apply to specific conditions, concrete instances, unique circumstances.

Whatever is retained in the brain as a memory is abstract. To be expressed, it must be converted into a different code, transformed into a structure closer to consciousness. That is why memory's precise, concrete manifestation on any given occasion is apt to be so variable, whether it is for language, or for how to ride a bicycle. We have a mechanism for producing perfect grammatical sentences, but the sentences we actually speak are often imperfect: this is the difference Chomsky makes between competence and performance. The basic constraints are regular, but the surface details are extremely nonuniform. In the same way, memory has great flexibility, but at a price. It also means that we are likely to remember incorrectly.

Like the information system of language, memory can be explained in part by the abstract rules which underlie it, but only in part. The rules provide a basic competence, but they do not fully determine performance. The passage from the abstractions of structure to the rich products of the mind in its encounters with the world is never simple, seldom direct, and always reflects the uniqueness of the event, the richness of context and meaning, and the peculiarities of the human psyche in action, because that, for better or worse, is the way we are.

19

The Information of Dreams

The brain's unique capacity for making patterns out of seemingly patternless material may not be confined to the waking life. Even in sleep, the search for structure goes on. The forces of antichance are at work in dreams, the nightly theater-in-the-brain that never closes.

At first sight, dreams may seem to be highly random, entropic and out of control. But as they are examined in greater depth and breadth by modern psychologists, dreams yield evidence of hidden form, of a relatedness between one dream experience and another, so that underneath the apparent chaos can be found regularity and system.

Indeed, dreaming displays some of the characteristics of a theory-making device, fitting known facts into a context, connecting them in a pattern of relations, reducing entropy. But a theory does more than that. It generates new facts, not known at the time the theory is formulated, and these new facts are also part of the pattern. A theory is an ordering process, and the order not only connects the known to the known; it also connects the unknown to the known. Universal grammar works in this way to systematize the rules of a language; rules not given in experience are given by the theory. Memory, too, tries to create order out of disorder (though it does so idiosyncratically), and to construct a coherent meaning out of what the mind experiences.

The old idea that dreams are repressions in disguise, intruding on a literal-minded, passive brain, does not sit easily with present-day thinking. It is more natural to see them as events, "messages," generated by the brain in the normal course of its affairs.

C. G. Jung had an extraordinary range of knowledge and a sense of the many-sidedness of mental life, its struggle to unify the various strands of being. He argued that dreams are not simply old images thrown up by memory, but are new information, which has never before reached the frontiers of consciousness. "Every dream is an organ of information and control," he wrote.

For Jung, the unconscious is not a library of archives from the past history of the individual, but an active source of ideas for the future. Dream symbols, he writes,

> are the essential message carriers from the instinctive to the rational parts of the human mind, and their interpretation enriches the poverty of consciousness, so that it learns to understand again the forgotten language of the instincts.

Unlike Freud, Jung did not believe that a dream is a mask for a meaning already known but deceitfully withheld from the conscious mind. In his view, dreams were communication, ideas expressed not always straightforwardly, but in the best way possible within the limits of the medium. Dreaming, in Jung's psychology, is a constructive process.

It follows, then, that if a dream is a message, if it is information and not noise, it ought to serve some useful function. Information, by definition, is something new, something which adds to the information already in the mind of the receiver. This is also Jung's conclusion. After studying some 80,000 dreams, he came to believe that all dreams are relevant, in greater or lesser degree, to the life of the dreamer. They fit into the psychic scheme as a whole.

Some central source in our psychic being, Jung proposed, invents and organizes dream images. He called this center the "self." The function of the self is to guide and integrate the whole of psychic life, conscious and unconscious, and the medium by which this process of guidance and integration is accomplished is dreaming. Of course, this does not happen all at once, in one dream or a few. The self works slowly, by means of numerous dreams spanning weeks or months. One by one, a person's dreams may seem nonsensical and capricious. Seen as an extended series, however, they begin to conform to a pattern. They reveal a structure. The pattern is not smooth and regular, but full of stops and starts, containing themes which appear, vanish, then reappear.

Dreams are not usually logical, ethical, or even pleasant to experience. Much of what happens seems to be ludicrous and meaningless. Often dreams are in outrageously bad taste. They do not follow well-defined laws. In the long run, however, Jung maintained, dreams convey information which tends to balance the unbalanced state of the dreamer's conscious mind. If the dreamer is too narrowly absorbed in his work, a dream may remind him of the need to open himself to a wider range of experiences. If he leads a balanced and harmonious psychological life, a dream may reflect and reinforce existing tendencies, but it will always retain its own independence. Looked at in isolation, a single dream may seem random and unconnected. In their totality, however, dreams arrange themselves into a kind of plan:

> They seem to hang together and in the deepest sense to be subordinated to a common goal, so that a long dream series no longer appears as a senseless string of incoherent and isolated happenings, but resembles the successive steps in a planned and orderly process of development.

Dreams convey information by means of symbolic images, which contain a wider range of possible meanings than can be expressed by literal facts. They are set in a broader context of knowledge and experience. To understand a dream, the dreamer must examine it from every aspect, Jung thought, just as, in the perception of the material, waking world, an observer takes an unfamiliar object in his hands and turns it over, so that it reveals all the details of its structure. Indeed, Jung speaks of dreams at times almost as some present-day psychologists speak of the act of perception, in which the perceiver is "in tune" with the information around him, and picks up significant aspects of it. Jung insists that the information in a dream cannot be interpreted apart from the dreamer—an insight he credits to Freud—or at too many removes from the dream. His practice was to "walk around" the dream picture rather than explore paths of association which lead randomly away from it, always keeping the dream as the center of his study. The dreamer is linked unbreakably to the dream, which is as normal and natural to him as the information processes of his own genes.

Allan Hobson and Robert McCarley, the two Harvard psychologists who made a detailed criticism of Freud's steam-engine model of the brain, refer to the brain as a "dream state generator." According to this view, the active brain generates its own information for dreams in giant nerve cells in an important region of the brain called the pontine. This information, they contend, is partly random and partly specific. The two psychologists challenge the Freudian hypothesis, accepted throughout most of this century, that dreams are censored versions of unconscious wishes set free in sleep by memories left over from the waking day. Freud's explanation of the biological, and therefore evolutionary, function of dreams is that since these wishes are unacceptable to the sleeper, and threaten to disrupt his consciousness, the brain distorts and degrades them in the seemingly crazy episodes of a dream sequence. The reason why the dreamer usually forgets his dreams is that they are repressions in disguise. Freud also believed that dreams have the secondary purpose of protecting sleep against the troublesome interruptions of the unconscious, rather than playing the primary role of shaping the conscious life of the individual. This followed logically from his mistaken notion that the brain is a power-engineering device, accumulating nervous energy which is either bottled up or discharged. Dreams, for Freud, were a safety valve, discharging the bothersome head of steam. They were totally egoistic. They had to be, since sleep itself was narcissistic, reenacting the self-centered existence of an embryo inside the mother's body.

Hobson and McCarley do not deny that some sort of defensive

distortion of dream messages may take place, but they reject the proposal that such transformations are paramount in shaping the formal content of dreams. They argue that dreams arise from basic physiological processes, not from disguised wishes. When a sleeper dreams, his eyes, under closed lids, make rapid movements up and down and from side to side. Giant nerve cells in a region of the brain stem called the pons are forty times as active during dreams as they are in the waking state. They are thought to initiate these rapid eye movements, and also to cause the special patterns of brain activity associated with them.

Hobson and McCarley propose that these giant cells trigger dream images in two ways. One way is by the direct internal activation of the visual centers of the brain, without any external stimulus whatever. The other way is by the rapid movement of the eyes. When we are awake, eye movements are under the control of centers of the brain more highly evolved than the relatively primitive pons. When the eye is given the command to move, messages about this movement are sent to other parts of the brain, which act to correct and structure our perception, so that, for example, we perceive the world as staying still even though our eyes are in jerky motion. In dreaming sleep, nerve cells in the pons send specific information about eye movements to the brain's higher centers. But this information may be sheer nonsense to brain systems which, under normal waking circumstances, initiate eye movement. The brain would then have to try to make a reasonable story out of incoherent data.

Hobson and McCarley think this is a plausible hypothesis, though they do not insist on it as a final and complete explanation of what goes on when we dream. The brain copes as best it can by comparing the information from eye movements with information stored away in memory. It pulls out pictures from its files, so to speak, trying to match the outlandish data coming from a pair of eyes twitching wildly in the dark. "What we are saying," the two psychologists declare, "is that the absurdity of dreams may be the nervous system's failure to completely and logically integrate its own information." The weird aberrations of dreams, the flitting from one scene to another, the erratic behavior of time, the shuffled sequences of scenes, may be due to the random yet specific nature of the signals which generate the dream state.

This explanation of dreams differs from Jung's in fundamental respects. Yet the two theories also agree in some important ways. They both begin from the premise that dreaming is an information process. They reject the notion that dreams are designed to censor awkward and disturbing messages by putting them through a psychological shredder and take exactly the opposite view. In Jung's version, dreams are useful information. They are of central importance to normal development because they help to develop an integrated relationship between the conscious mind and information in the unconscious psyche, enabling the latter to become conscious. For Hobson and McCarley, too, the task of the brain in dreams is not to degrade information but to make sense of it, to organize disorganized data which are generated internally and in bursts of great intensity, activating many different systems of the brain.

—————

Like sentences in Chomsky's theory of language, dreams do not wear meaning on their sleeve. They communicate obliquely, so that the surface form of the message is often the reverse of the underlying message in the dream's deep structure. But if dreaming is a process hard to interpret correctly, it clearly has a useful function, one which is beneficial to the individual, whether biologically or psychologically or both. Indeed, the modern view is not that dreams protect sleep by degrading unwelcome information. Quite the reverse. It is sleep that protects the information process of dreaming. Evolution has seen to it that dream experiences are intense and uninterrupted.

In the dream state, the body is paralyzed, frozen into immobility by a mechanism that shuts down neurons which control movement in the spinal cord. Messages telling the muscles to move are blocked, making it impossible for the dreamer to act out his dreams. Not only is physical movement suppressed (except for rapid eye movement), but information coming to the senses is also damped, and damped to coincide with bursts of activity in the eyes. Apparently it is more important, biologically, for the dream to proceed undisturbed than for the sleeper to have the use of his legs to run away in case of danger. The extent to which the body is paralyzed varies with the intensity of the internally generated messages and the degree to which information from the outside world is suppressed.

Rapid-eye-movement sleep seems to be indispensable, for reasons not fully understood. If someone is deprived of this kind of sleep for one night, he will have more of it the following night. There is also some evidence that during dreaming sleep, knowledge acquired during the day is reorganized and consolidated. Rapid-eye-movement sleep increases after a person has been studying, and artificially reducing such sleep impairs the ability to remember what has been learned.

Certainly the brain is not passive when we dream. In certain respects, it works twice as hard as in the waking state, and is extremely alert to its own internally generated information. There is a parallel here in hypnosis, in which the brain is also extremely active and pays keen attention to what is going on. The brain is susceptible to orders and instructions given by the hypnotist, but the person's observable behavior does not tell the whole story of his mental state. Ernest Hilgard, a leading authority on the psychology of hypnotism, has proposed the existence of what he calls—speaking metaphorically—a "hidden observer," which functions at the intellectual level but does not share what it knows with the conscious mind during hypnosis.

To illustrate this thesis, a student was hypnotized and told he would be totally deaf to all sounds until the hypnotist touched him on the right shoulder. Large wooden blocks were banged together close to the student's ear, and a starter's pistol was fired. He showed no response whatever. Then he was told: "Perhaps there is some part of you that is hearing my voice and processing the information. If there is, I should like the index finger of your right hand to rise as a sign that this is the case." At once the student lifted his finger. Still under hypnosis, he asked the hypnotist to restore his hearing and tell him what he had done to make his finger move in a way which was not spontaneous. He knew it had moved for a reason, but did not know the reason. Evidently there existed, at some level of awareness, a listener able to hear and understand the voice of the hypnotist, while the student, to all outward appearances, was deaf to the loudest sounds. In later experiments the hidden observer proved to be superior, in many ways, to the conscious individual inside whom it was hidden: more mature, more realistic and logical, and *in possession of more information*. One student remarked that he could let his imagination run free in a hypnotic trance, and indulge in some pleasing fictions, "but somewhere the hidden observer knows what's really going on."

Dreams are not chaotic, nor are they irrelevant. They supply new context and thus enrich knowledge. By doing so they serve an educational function for the dreamer, because they lead him across a dimly lit landscape of riddling images, from information he knows to information he does not know yet in his conscious, waking life.

Dreams use information as a means of control, helping to put the waking life in order, providing stability, balancing the unbalanced. This is much the same function that some scholars assign to myth, the function of keeping our mental life on course, which is almost the literal definition of the word "cybernetics." In an analogous way, codes keep messages "on course" in information theory, preserving their original structure, safeguarding their order against the disturbing effects of randomness and maintaining their meaning, which is the value they have for both the sender and the receiver of the message.

20

The Left and Right of Knowing

The human brain is designed in a curious way. To the naked, untutored eye, it is virtually symmetrical, each hemisphere a duplicate of the other. Functionally, however, the two hemispheres are very different. The brain's various styles of coding information, its multiple ways of making sense of the world, are skewed either to left or to right. In some important respects, each half of the brain generates knowledge according to its own special set of rules.

Asymmetry is not the safest strategy for evolution to adopt. It does provide greater versatility: dissimilar functions placed far apart in the brain can work together in complementary fashion without interfering with each other. This means we can perform two or more different tasks simultaneously. But such a strategy is also risky, because there is less in reserve in case of mishap. If a portion of the left brain containing a special function, such as speech, is damaged in adult life, no counterpart exists in the right brain to take its place.

Human beings are not the only members of the animal kingdom with asymmetric brains. In cats, rats, and many other species, inequalities have been found between the left and right hemispheres. It is clear, however, that asymmetry is of a more elaborate kind in humans than in other species. This point is an important one.

A creature which never thinks abstractly, never makes plans or forms images of reality in its head, is best served by a symmetrical brain. Moving about in search of prey, or running away from predators, such a creature needs to know, at every instant, the exact state of its immediate environment. Accurate perception and quick, precise action are of the highest importance. The creature needs to be equally adept at turning left or right, equally accurate in seeing and hearing with both eyes and ears, because there is no telling from which side prey or predator may appear.

In humans, as in cats or rats, the systems of the brain that control movements in space are bilateral. When tracking, chasing, or escaping, there is very little bias toward left or right. In fact, it seems that in evolution, anatomical symmetry is selected for in mobile animals, while for animals which are stationary such selection is often relaxed. The larval forms of certain deep-sea creatures, for example, are symmetric, because they move about in the water, while in the adult of the species, lying immobile on the ocean floor, this symmetry is broken.

For human beings, movement in space is an important function, but not the one which defines us as a unique species. The distinguishing characteristic of *Homo sapiens sapiens* is not agility or quickness in response, but a highly developed capacity for abstract thought, reasoning, imagination, language, and a concept of the future. Humans are not so directly at the mercy of their surroundings as other animals. They do not always act as soon as they perceive, which leaves them free to think "useless thoughts," to process information without needing to use it straightaway, so that a bias to left or right is not a disadvantage. Our brain has been freed from the tyranny of the moment.

The basic inequalities of styles in the brain are well known. One hemisphere, usually the left, is good at handling things in sequence. It specializes in numbers and analytical thought and plays the dominant role in speech. The other hemisphere is better at dealing with space, shapes, pictures. It makes multiple and simultaneous connections among items of information, rather than treating them sequentially. The right side tends to use a "top-down" strategy, processing information as a whole, perceiving its full meaning, rather than approaching it "bottom-up," using the parts to construct the whole, which is often more than the sum of its parts. In the case of language, the right hemisphere thinks in terms of entire sentences, rather than single words, and is sensitive to the way sentences fit into paragraphs. The coding device for recognizing faces, for example, is right-brain, and it is different from the code for recognizing objects, which is in the left brain. One may identify a house as "the one with the peculiar roof," but usually a face is not "that man over there with the crooked nose" but "the man who reminds me of my Uncle Arthur." The face has a meaning as a whole, and is set in a personal context of experience.*

A person experiences information arriving from the world, and the two sides of the brain work on the information in dissimilar ways. This leads to great variability from one individual to another. One hemisphere may be more strongly developed, or both sides combine in a special way for a given task. The two hemispheres are not wholly independent, neither are they fully fused together, and the interplay between them changes continually. Activity shifts in the brain from one side to another from moment to moment, and which side is more active at a given time depends to a large extent on who the person is, what he knows, and how easily the information presented to him can be placed in the context of his previous experiences.

In the normal brain, the two hemispheres are not separate, but are connected by an enormous bundle of fibers called the corpus callosum, containing more than 200 million nerve cells. This great cable of tissue enables each side of the brain to communicate with the other side, although the exact nature of the communication is not known. At birth, there is virtually no

---

* When pictures of faces are shown to people upside down, they are much harder to recognize than pictures of houses. The psychologist Robert K. Yin says:

> Objectively measured, the differences between one face and another are minute. We code these differences very much as if we possess a special device for doing it. The rules of this code are probably simpler than those of the speech code, and not the same as the rules of the code for recognizing other objects. The rules are not wholly innate. Some sort of mechanism is there at birth, and it develops early. But there is a stage, usually between the ages of six and eight, when young people are not necessarily good at recognizing faces. They can be thrown off completely by a thin disguise. When a man grows a mustache, or a child's mother puts on a pair of goggles at the beach for snorkeling, the faces may become completely strange for children of these ages.

> What is more, the face code appears to be free-running. It will function even if there are no people to look at. This explains what happens when we imagine we can see faces in the fire. The code translates images into faces, even if they are the wrong images.

information traffic between the two hemispheres, because the corpus callosum takes about two years to begin working, and is not fully formed until about the age of ten. This delay in establishing a mature connection may enable the two sides of the brain to develop independently in their own special fashion in early life. Even when the link is complete, there is no reason to assume that all information is shared by both sides, or that the bridge spanning the two halves provides a perfect unity for the entire brain.

Possibly the exchange of messages within the brain is only partial. Some research points tentatively to this conclusion. In one famous experiment, a man's left brain was put to sleep with a drug, sodium amytal. The man was asked to explore, by touch and with his left hand, which is under the control of the right brain, an ordinary teaspoon. Later, when the anesthetic had worn off, he was unable to name the object he had touched, and declared his total ignorance of it. Yet when shown a collection of objects, he selected the spoon by pointing to it. The memory of the spoon was in the right hemisphere, which is virtually speechless. It was coded there in a form which was untranslatable into the language of the left, speaking hemisphere, even though the information link between the two sides of the man's brain was intact. Presumably, only some kinds of information and not others are able to cross from one side to the other. If this is correct, the presence of ciphers to which the conscious brain does not possess the key may help to explain why the life of an individual is in some respects a never ending quest to know the self in all its aspects and dimensions.

Joseph Bogen has compiled a list of terms used by psychologists who, over many years, have been groping toward a definition of left-brain and right-brain styles of knowing. This list makes extremely interesting reading for those who are familiar with the concepts of information theory. The terms Bogen uses to distinguish each hemisphere reverberate with echoes of ideas already examined in this book. Here is a slightly truncated version of Bogen's list:

Left Brain	Right Brain
Intellect	Intuition
Convergent	Divergent

Intellectual	Sensuous
Deductive	Imaginative
Active	Receptive
Discrete	Continuous
Abstract	Concrete
Realistic	Impulsive
Propositional	Imaginative
Transformational	Associative
Lineal	Nonlineal
Historical	Timeless
Explicit	Tacit
Objective	Subjective

At the risk of generalizing about conclusions which are already general, one can say that the left-hand column suggests the presence of constraints more than the right-hand column does. Linguistically, it is more Chomskyan than the other, referring to what speakers of language cannot do rather than what they can do. There is less uncertainty, a sense of fewer possibilities, on the left side. The categories suggest that information is coded in ways which are more strictly organized, more formal, stable, and free from error. They refer to modes of thought in which structure is of great importance, but structure of the kind in which one component is fitted to another, by a single connection, leaving no room for ambiguity or for multiple relationships. Convergent implies the idea of meaning shrinking into the confines of the well-formed, grammatical sentence, rather than carrying many interpretations. Deductive describes an analytical type of reasoning, sentences in which the predicate is already contained, logically, in the subject: "All bachelors are unmarried men." The propositional style of language is of the true-or-false variety, a declaration. Lineal events are more rigidly ordered than nonlineal events; their redundancy is greater. And the explicit is more firmly committed to present reality than is the tacit. Is it any surprise, then, that the left hemisphere is the primary seat of language?

Sequential forms of order, in which specific items succeed one another discretely, are products typical of the left hemisphere. Such sequences, as the psychologist Marcel Kinsbourne has pointed out, are constructed by excluding possibilities. At each step in the chain, one item is selected from among other, possible items. By exclusion, one abstracts something from a context. By inclusion, that something is fitted into a context.

Speech is the most clearly asymmetric of all the brain's activities. The right hemisphere has no preference as marked as that of the left for spoken language. The single generalization many psychologists permit themselves on the subject of asymmetry is that in most people, the left side is primarily engaged in the production of spoken language, while the right is almost speechless. It may be that the ability to make radical changes in the structure of information, to convert it from one code to another by means of formal and highly constrained rules, marks the essential difference between the two hemispheres. And this is because the speech code is one of the most, if not the most powerful, complex, and intricate in the entire brain. The device which analyzes the internal phonetic structure of words must be enormously ingenious.

The spoken word, though it may seem simple, is really immensely intricate. The sounds of speech are not like the letters of the alphabet, each one separate and distinct. If that were the case, conversation would be painfully slow and cumbersome. For example, when a person says the word "bag," the sounds are not divided up neatly into consonant, vowel, and consonant. They overlap in a very complex fashion, and one which is peculiarly human, since it is practiced by infants in their early babbling, but not by apes.

This method of speeding up spoken language by the overlapping of phonetic segments, so that an entire syllable is produced in a single stream of sound, is a remarkable illustration of the power of codes to make rapid yet reliable communication possible. Disentangling a code of such necessary complexity, being aware of the separate segments merged into one complex sound, must call for a mental device of a more abstract and nonrepresentational kind than any which exist in the nonverbal part of the brain.

The psychologist A. M. Liberman proposes that this special information coding device is the possession of the left hemisphere. It is what that side of the brain is supremely good at doing.

It is well known that the right brain is poor at comprehending consonants and does not do well at syntax, which is the left brain's special province. How far this is a result of sheer absence of function, and how far it is an effect of the left brain inhibiting the right across the corpus callosum, is still not clear. There is little doubt, however, that the right lacks the transformational skills, the ability to convert one structure into another by means of rules, which Chomskyan linguistics considers of central importance. Even in split-brain patients, where there is no chance of the left hemisphere interfering with the right, the right displays a significant limitation. While it can understand the meaning of word pairs like "ache" and "lake," recognizing them to be different, it is unable to preserve the sameness amid the change; it does not know that the words rhyme.

Yet the right brain is not a linguistic idiot. It has its own codes, its own rules, and these are worth examining. It does have some comprehension of spoken language, and is good at detecting pitch, intonation, stress, cadence, loudness and softness. It knows whether a sentence is asking a question, giving an order, expressing a condition, or making a statement. It can construct imaginary "situations" into which these various different non-verbal items of information might fit and make sense. On hearing the sound "bee," the left hemisphere will be dominant if it is clear that the speaker is talking about the letter b. However, if the speaker says, "I was stung by a bee," the right brain will be more accurate in identifying the meaning of the sound.

There is evidence that the right brain, for all its linguistic limitations, may be an active partner in the sophisticated use of language. We have seen that if language is regarded simply as structure, as form, then speech becomes too innocent. Meaning converges into the sentence instead of diverging out into wider contexts. The right hemisphere corrects this tendency to constrain meaning. It makes the brain as a whole less literal-minded. It probably plays a role in the understanding of poetry, where words have many shades and levels of meaning beyond mere reference and dictionary definition. It pays attention to the meaning of sound and tempo, not merely to the content of words.

Left hemisphere activity on its own, the psychologist Howard Gardner has said, "is like reading the script of a play instead of going to see it." It is the right hemisphere that knows what words connote, what associations they have, rather than merely attending to what they denote, what they refer to. It can recognize the ridiculous and inappropriate, and be aware that words and sentences are embedded in a wide matrix of relationships. One way of describing the right hemisphere is to say that it is more worldly than the left.

Gardner is one of a relatively small number of workers who have examined the activity of the right brain when it responds to language which has more than a single explicit interpretation. With Suzanne Hamby he has investigated the behavior of the "minor" hemisphere when it is presented with stories, jokes, and figures of speech. Both normal and brain-damaged people were subjects in the tests. The results were highly enlightening. Those with injured right and functional left brains had a perfect command of syntax and phonetics. Their mastery of the facts of stories and jokes was good enough, though not as good as for normal subjects. They tended to remember passages word for word, instead of paraphrasing them as people usually do. Most strikingly, it turned out that when answering questions about the stories, they were extremely literal-minded; too serious about certain events, and generally poor at entering into the fictional realm of a story on the story's own terms.

One patient with right-brain damage refused to accept the statement that a little girl was riding on a fire engine. "Only authorized people are allowed to do that," he protested. Another echoed his complaint: "No kid would sneak on a fire engine; they can ring the bells in a firehouse, but not ride on engines." A third, asked to recall a story which had been read to him, left out of his account the fact that a shop stood on a side street in a town. He omitted this fact, not because he had forgotten it, but because he did not think it was correct. "It doesn't make sense to be on a deserted street," he objected. "That's why I didn't say it."

These patients with impaired right brains were uncertain as to what was important in the stories and what was incidental. They seemed unable to guess future events in the narrative, even when these events were quite predictable. While they sometimes changed plausible features of a story, bizarre details were often accepted without question. They could not appreciate the pattern of connections among key points of a story, and intruded themselves into the events when retelling the plot or answering questions about it. Instead of treating a fictional narrative as something with a separate existence of its own, they failed to respect its integrity, tinkering with details which did not conform to their notion of the truth. They were sensitive to emotions, but misinterpreted them, thinking, for example, that a character in a story was frightened when she was manifestly being portrayed as sad. However, the patients were able to conjure up logical reasons for supposing the character was frightened, even if these reasons were irrelevant to the story itself. Many of their comments were feasible and even appropriate when applied very narrowly, to a single incident. Only when the wider context and the general setting of a story were taken into account did the comments stand out as bizarre and out of tune with the clear, overall intention of the author. These patients had a good grasp of syntax and spelling, and of the meaning of individual words and phrases, but did not deal well with information about context. They could not assimilate the "basic scaffolding" of a fictional plot and so were unable to judge whether this or that detail was important or insignificant in the light of the story as a whole. People with right hemisphere defects seemed to

> lack anchorage with respect to the external world: they were uncertain of their own status in relation to diverse social environments or literary creations, and thus, they cannot appropriately distance themselves . . . It is as if the left hemisphere is a highly efficient, but narrowly programmed linguistic computer; the right hemisphere constitutes the ideal audience for a humorous silent film, but only the two hemispheres together can appreciate all four of the Marx brothers.

In those few cases where severe brain damage makes it necessary to remove the right hemisphere altogether, the patient is still able to speak with perfect grammatical propriety, but much of his conversation is on a remarkably "innocent" level. Jocular remarks are taken seriously. Language becomes extremely direct. Asked "Would you pass the salt?" he is apt to reply, "Yes, I will pass the salt."* One man, a patient of Dr. George Austin, a neurologist at the University of Pennsylvania, was asked to identify a collection of familiar objects. He described a cushion as "cloth or leather to maintain irregularities of the body," and a toy cat as a "token for commercial use." Dr. Austin asked another patient, "How do you feel?" The man replied, "With me [sic] hands."

In addition to its worldliness, its power to confer a sense of the appropriate, the right brain is also receptive to metaphor. When that hemisphere is defective, people often see nothing odd about a ridiculously literal-minded interpretation of a figurative expression. It is as if, on reading a phrase from a Dylan Thomas poem, "The dead oak walks for love," they should show no surprise at seeing it illustrated by a picture of an oak tree striding down the road to keep an assignation with another oak tree. Gardner presented each of his subjects with the printed metaphorical sentence, "A heavy heart can really make a difference," followed by two drawings, one of a man staggering along under the weight of a heart-shaped object, the other depicting someone crying. They were asked to point to the picture most compatible with the sentence. A large number of those with impaired right brains chose the literal illustration.

We might now attempt to rewrite Bogen's list of typical right-brain and left-brain coding styles in the light of these rather tentative discoveries:

Left	Right
Literal	Metaphorical
Innocent	Sophisticated

* Interestingly, this sentence, "Would you pass the salt?" has been used in linguistics to illustrate the argument that such use of language, while strictly correct syntactically, is not the product of formal rules of syntax alone, but in a wider sense is dictated by the social need not to make a request sound like an order: "Pass the salt." The sentence has an indirect form not just for linguistic reasons of syntax and sense, but for pragmatic social reasons. In normal conversation, no one would be expected to take it literally.

Denoting	Connoting
Contrasting	Comparing
Banal	Rich
Bottom-up	Top-down
Verbal	Nonverbal
Inappropriate	Appropriate
Exclusion	Inclusion

A quick, impressionistic conclusion to draw from this list is that the column on the right suggests information strategies which contribute to context. But context may be of more than one kind. If it is predictable and familiar, it is redundant. If novel and unexpected, it is information. In information theory, the influence of context is of great importance. Players who took part in Shannon's word games were quite successful at guessing the next letters or words in a sentence once they knew the first few letters of the sentence. What they knew formed a context for what they did not know.

If the context of a message is familiar, it reduces the surprise value of that message when it is received, and surprise is virtually equivalent to information. As we have seen, the structure of English text is such that the letter q, for example, is always followed by the letter u, so that in the context of q, u is completely predictable and adds no information. Certain sequences of words also provide a familiar context for the words which follow. Shannon's players needed to be given only eight letters of context in order to guess the complete word sequence "The room was not very bright." A familiar context, being redundant, improves the reliability and the readability of a passage of prose, because it reduces the uncertainty of the reader as to what he should expect. In James Joyce, almost every word comes as a surprise because there is no familiar context preceding it. In *Finnegans Wake*, the reader must supply context from his own knowledge or his knowledge of Joyce commentators to make sense of the sentences as they appear on the page. Some of this context will be composed of mental concepts.

There is some interesting evidence to show that the right hemisphere of the brain does supply context for information stored in the left hemisphere, and that often such context is in the form of concepts which render apparently chaotic sequences of ideas or words intelligible or orderly. Context of this sort may help to unscramble sentences which otherwise would seem nearly random. For example, the sentence

Despite the danger the anger reprogrammed the bus sandwich

possesses an abstract grammatical structure, which is regular, but it looks semantically like nonsense, pure noise. Its entropy is high, because many of the words come as a complete surprise. The word "sandwich," following "bus," is highly unpredictable. In Shannon's sense, it conveys a large amount of information. But it is not useful information, because it appears to violate the rules of meaning. The choice of words seems entirely random, with nouns and verbs unrelated to one another.

However, Robert Hoffman and a colleague, Richard Honeck, show that this sentence can be made meaningful by placing it in a familiar context. Imagine a traffic jam in a mass-transit system that is under the control of a computer. To clear the jam, an enraged controller hastily pushes buttons on his console. The sentence, formerly semantic gibberish, at once begins to make sense.

Hoffman and Honeck believe that the limitless creativeness of language, to which Chomsky has drawn attention, is not due solely to the use of rules of syntax (a typically left-brain skill), used again and again on a finite number of words to generate an unbounded variety of sentences. Creativity, they suggest, may also stem from the brain's ability to generate concepts.

It was once thought that there were quite strict limits to the capacity of human beings to form concepts. That belief is no longer held so strongly. The process is probably less constrained than might be expected. A speaker may be able to produce an infinite number of semantic relationships within a language. In other words, he can supply an endless amount of context. Then, "nonsense" can be made intelligible, not just by means of rules of syntax, but through the use of inference, worldly knowledge, and the power to form metaphors. Chomsky regards "computational" forms of knowledge, the sort which generate new sentences by means of rules of syntax, as being unique to humans.

It is a left-brain aptitude. Conceptual knowledge, on the other hand, he thinks is shared by other animals.

Another kind of context supplied by the right brain comes from its superior grasp of metaphor. Metaphors are devices which make connections between things which have no obvious relation to one another, just as the concept of the furious traffic controller made connections between a program, a bus, and a sandwich. Metaphors synthesize disparate ideas. They allude, match, compare. They include and integrate possibilities, whereas the sequential style of organizing information typical of the left brain excludes possibilities. Metaphors are divergent, not convergent.

But metaphors not only place the familiar in a context of the strange. They also place the strange in a context of the familiar. When a novelist describes "a sky of hot nude pearl," he is making the sky more exotic by linking it to the pearl, and the pearl less exotic by connecting it to the sky, which is something people see every day.

Teachers use metaphors when introducing students to a new field of knowledge, because they form a bridge between information which the students already possess and which is familiar to them, and new information which they are required to learn. Children, for instance, are able to absorb a large amount of new material quickly if the material displays a pattern of relations, a structure. Robert Verbrugge has used metaphors to help children who are studying botany for the first time. He describes tree trunks as "straws for thirsty leaves and branches," thereby giving a fresh perspective on a tree as something which sucks water out of the ground, as a person sucks soda through a straw, by making a connection between the unfamiliar behavior of the tree and a very familiar experience.

Verbrugge was attracted to the study of metaphor after noting that many of the sentences Chomsky rejected as not being part of the English language were figurative, and essentially metaphoric. Chomsky's grammar permits a sentence like "Sincerity frightens John," but excludes a sentence like "John frightens sincerity." The constraints of the grammar insure that the word "frighten" can be predicated only of a person. Verbrugge points out that a timid person, reluctant to show that he is sincere when in the presence of an overbearing person called John, can indeed speak of his sincerity being frightened. This is a figurative use of language, since the speaker is personifying one of his own qualities, but that should be no reason for thinking it deviant or affected. Metaphors appear constantly in ordinary conversations. They are an essential part of everyday speech, not mere decoration, because they often contain multiple connections among ideas and therefore communicate a great deal of complex information in a brief phrase. Metaphors are an effective encoding device.

Is the supplying of concepts and context, then, a special function of the right brain? Eran Zaidel, a University of California psychologist, thinks it is. He has noted the distinction made between computational and conceptual knowledge, and has come to the conclusion that the right hemisphere possesses the second kind but not the first. He surmises that the right brain may be the one which assimilates novel information and embeds it in a context of the familiar. Zaidel suggests that the right hemisphere is the seat of a particular type of intelligence, "crystallized" intelligence, or knowledge resulting from experience; a sort of worldly wisdom. Crystallized intelligence does not decline with age, but goes on developing as one grows older. Zaidel says:

> When a skill or task is new, sometimes the right hemisphere is superior, and this superiority shifts to the left hemisphere when the skill becomes entrenched, better acquired; more conscious, perhaps.
>
> The right does seem to be the one which specializes in processing new information. That's speculation, but it does capture in a single generalization the results of a collection of studies that are available in the literature.
>
> When you present a new symbol to someone, and he has to learn new associations between visual symbols and linguistic material, the right brain is dominant in the beginning. But as he becomes more familiar with the system, the action moves over to the left brain. Now why that is, is not clear. Perhaps because the right hemisphere provides the context for the new information, through its rich associative network.

Human experience is endlessly rich because the ways of organizing it are endlessly variable. The rules of syntax generate an unbounded number of new sentences from a finite number of words, and at this the left brain excels. But meaning is produced in similar abundance, by a profusion of concepts, a process in which the right brain plays an essential role. There are examples of prose writing by schizophrenics that demonstrate the two extremes of this spectrum. One type consists chiefly of propositions; it is all form and framework. The second type is incoherent, but crammed with concrete images, sensuous nouns, and personal experiences. It is brimful with meaning.

The rhetorician W. Ross Winterowd has used passages from schizophrenic compositions to contrast worst-case examples of the two styles. This one is left-brain and propositional:

> The subterfuge and the mistaken planned substitutions for that demanded American action can produce nothing but the general results of negative contention and the impractical results of misplacement, of mistaken purpose and unrighteous position, the impractical serviceabilities of unnecessary contradictions. For answers to this dilemma, consult Webster.

And this one is right-brain, displaying some of the features of Dr. Bogen's list for that hemisphere:

> I hope to be home soon very soon. I fancy chocolate eclairs. Doenuts [sic]. I want some Doenuts. I do want some golden syrup, a tin of golden syrup or treacle, jam . . . See the Committee about me coming hom for Easter my twenty-fourth birthday. I hope all is well at home, how is Father getting on. Never mind there is hope, heaven will come, time heals all wounds.

The English essays of normal students, Winterowd adds, are "only a shade less schizoid" than these two samples. In the first, "we have the ghost of coherence without the substance of tangible content; in the other, the cup of meaning runneth over."

In the integrated brain, these two polar styles coexist and collaborate to a greater or lesser extent. The left brain prefers a tightly organized sequential pattern of relations, excluding possibilities, singling things out, fitting parts together step by step, contrasting rather than comparing. The right brain contributes pattern, too, but it appears to be a pattern of meaning, a network of semantic connections that form a worldly context into which the structures of the left brain can fit and find their place. It can show that information does not always mean what it appears to mean, and make semantic sense out of semantic noise.

The right brain is more conceptual than computational, but it does not specialize in chaos. It seeks out order and supplies order. Memory, as we have seen, needs not only an abstract structure, a "syntax," but also a personal context of meaning, where the strange becomes familiar and the familiar strange. All this is entirely compatible with the fundamental principles of Shannon's theory, that there is no information without uncertainty, and no information worth having without redundancy, under whichever of its various manifestations redundancy may choose to appear.

21

The Second-Theorem Society

Simple systems, by definition, contain little information. In thermodynamics, the word "entropy" has no meaning when it is applied to one or two objects. Shannon's entropy, his measure of the amount of information, has a statistical form, and statistics deals with mass behavior, not with individual instances. The codes envisaged in Shannon's second theorem insure that the reliability of the message system as a whole is high, even though the reliability of transmission of individual symbols may be poor. Thus information theory has to do with a system in its totality. It takes into account possibilities, and a choice from among possibilities, and the freer the choice, the larger the amount of information will be. Shannon's equation makes that clear. The theory is not interested in what must happen, because information is the resolving of uncertainty, and unless uncertainty exists first, there can be no information. It is a theory of the nonsimple and the noncertain.

In "postclassical" thermodynamics, the view is taking hold that simplicity is not the most natural state of matter. At the quantum level, of course, matter is extremely complex, and grows more so the deeper scientists probe into its secret depths. But this is also true, in a different way, of the physics which deals with nature on a scale larger than the atom. When a thermodynamic system is at or near equilibrium, the laws of physics are universal and, being universal, lead us to expect great uniformity in nature. Sameness, simplicity, would be the hallmark of the world. There would be no indication that time is passing. But Ilya Prigogine has pointed out that the world is not like that at all. It is full of rich structures which change in interesting ways. It is innovative and nonuniform. There is more one can say about the world now than at any time in the past. And this one-way direction of time, rather than the timelessness of classical physics, is fundamental. "We must go beyond the temptation to define the eternal as truth and the temporal as illusion," Prigogine says. What is more, irreversible, entropy-producing processes "play a fundamental, *constructive* role in the physical world; they are at the bases of important coherent processes that appear with particular clarity on the biological level."

As soon as we have a system out of equilibrium, an organized system consisting of many parts, of which a living organism is a typical example, the simple laws of cause and effect let us down. They are too simple to be of much use. When a billiard ball hits another billiard ball, energy is transferred from one to the other, and the balls move along a determined path. But when a cause produces an effect in an organized system, matters become a great deal more complicated. The cause does not produce action by contact, as in the case of the billiard balls. It triggers action in something which is not one simple object, but a pattern of relations. The action is intrinsic, linked only in an indirect way to the stimulus which set it off. The physicist Ernest Hutten writes:

> ... the behaviour of an organised system, the action of an organism, or human activity cannot be explained in terms of causal energy transmission alone ... information rather than causality describes processes in, or between organised systems. The most general model of a natural process on which scientific explanation may be based is no longer the movement of a particle under the action of a force, but the storage (or organisation) and the transmission of information within a system. This is the genetic model.

The new departure made by modern information theory was that it broke away from classical ideas about communication. It abandoned determinism, and with it simplicity. Information theory did not regard a message as a separate, independent object, but as part of an organized system, related to the other parts, even if those existed only as possibilities.

———————

A code is really a set of statistical rules, a form of stored information. It restricts the amount of choice allowed to the message source in special ways, by introducing redundancy, making some possibilities in the system more probable than others. But the whole point of a successful code is to retain an optimum amount of freedom, a wide variety of possible messages, consistent with the need to make and keep the messages intelligible. Shannon's second theorem assures us that this can be done.

Such a code does not make an information system simpler, by any means. It increases rather than diminishes complexity, because complexity is not just a question of the number of parts in a system, but also has to do with their relatedness. Without redundancy, complexity cannot persist, because there would be no way to control error. As we have seen, nature's use of the principles of Shannon's second theorem in the information system of the genes may have enabled evolution to accelerate away from simplicity. Vertebrates, Lila Gatlin thinks, were the creatures who first crossed over from "pre-Shannon" codes to second-theorem codes. They vaulted the barrier that von Neumann proposed as a dividing line between simpler systems and those in which complexity becomes explosive. Vertebrates became less simple even when they did not travel to more complicated and challenging environments. Jumping the complexity barrier led to new chemistry, to new structures; not just structures of the body alone, but also of the brain. Indeed, one of the most notable innovations of vertebrates, as they evolved, was the larger brain. And only at a certain level of biological and neurological complexity, Chomsky believes, can a system of knowledge as fantastically complex as a human language appear.

Von Neumann stressed two of the "critical and paradoxical" characteristics of complex as opposed to simple systems. First, such a system can do things that a simpler system cannot do. Second, more information is needed to describe a complex system; qualitatively, as well as quantitatively, more information. A complete description of a simple automaton, von Neumann said, would be simpler than the automaton itself. A complete description of a very complicated automaton, on the other hand, would be more complicated than the automaton. In fact, the automaton would be its own simplest description.

It is on this very problem of the adequacy of description that old ways of explaining the highly elaborate structures of nature and human knowledge broke down, pointing the way to new methods and radically different approaches. Information theory has stimulated the search for such methods, as von Neumann expected.

In linguistics, a vast wealth of facts was amassed by observing the surface of utterances, but this superabundance of data still did not make a complete description of the grammar of a language possible. If anything, it was an obstacle to full understanding. Only with the arrival of Chomsky and his successors did a new way of looking at language arise, one which began to do justice to the complexity of language by investigating rules which operate beneath the surface of an utterance. If a complete description of English, for example, were ever achieved, it would not be a catalogue of observables. Rather, in Chomsky's scheme, it would include: phrase structure rules, which determine what can be a constituent of the language, and the basic order of constituents; transformation rules, which convert deep structure to surface structure; and the lexicon, which gives information about the environment in which words are placed in a sentence, the rules that are triggered by certain words in certain environments and exceptions to the rules.

However, even using this new approach, which recognizes fully that appearances do not tell the whole story, our knowledge of language is still minute. Huge tracts lie undiscovered. It is not uncommon for a linguist to spend a lifetime studying a single construction. The nature of the English gerund, for example, remains an utter mystery. A sentence like "John's smoking bothers me" bothers linguists acutely. On the surface, "John's smoking" appears to contain a possessive and a verb, yet in reality it contains neither. The ambiguity is unresolved, in spite of years of patient effort.

Biologists are similarly baffled, despite the immense abundance of recorded facts at their disposal. They have not succeeded in describing the living system, because they do not understand the many different kinds of internal rules in DNA, the algorithms by which genes are expressed. Biologists know the alphabet, but not the grammar, of the genes: they can describe the surface, but not the principles which lie beneath the surface. Until these principles are known, there will be neither a theory of biology nor a theory of evolution, in the full sense of the word. Biologists share with linguists a sense of frustration at the slow progress of their investigations.

There is another kind of organized system for which an external description would be unmanageably more elaborate than the system itself: a human society. A society, like a language, is rule-governed, and its surface properties may be a misleading guide to an understanding of its internal structure. It is complex by its very nature, and remains complex by reason of its inner rules and principles.

In a modern, democratic society, certain types of action are excluded by the rules. There are constraints on the freedom of its members. But within the limits of such constraints, a great profusion of choice is permitted, leading to innovation and change. Sameness persists amid the change, insuring that the society remains "intelligible," despite the randomizing forces of chance which are always present in all organized systems, whether natural or artificial. We could call this a "second-theorem" society.

F. A. Hayek, the economist, has argued that in a free society, order exists without having been created deliberately. Such a society shares with language the property of being partly spontaneous, partly uninvented. The Greeks in their political theory distinguished between *kosmos*, a spontaneous form of order, and *taxis*, a made order. In a *taxis*, all the rules are known to the members of the society, because they were created deliberately and can be written down. In a *kosmos*, on the other hand, the rules may not be explicit; they are often used without full awareness. This is precisely why rules of a language are so difficult to identify and describe: they are hidden in the unconscious mind.

A skater observes the rules of skating without being able to state them explicitly in words, just as a bicyclist pedals along not worrying about whether he knows the rules for keeping the machine upright. If he thought about them hard enough, he would probably fall off. So it is for the members of a spontaneous society. They do not need to make a list of the rules, or to have conscious knowledge of them. But while individuals cannot describe all the rules which generate their behavior, the rules themselves, if they could be made explicit, would describe the society.

In life, mind, and society, Hayek believes, structures have a complexity which could arise only through spontaneous ordering forces. A person can know, *at most*, the rules observed by part of the structure, but not all the parts and never all the circumstances affecting each part. The actions of individuals are guided, not by strict commands from on high, but by rules, as information stored inside the system. The rules define general principles, while leaving the details open. This enables an extremely complex society to maintain itself in a steady state. The rules of a *kosmos* are general and abstract and may be satisfied by many different kinds of action, according to circumstances. Authority does not lay down strict, exact commands, containing no uncertainty. And the reason authority does not do so is that authority cannot have perfect information on which to base the commands. General rules allow individuals the freedom to exercise some personal judgment, using special information accessible to them but not to authority.

An interesting, though controversial, distinction has been made between what are called primary and secondary rules of society. Herbert Hart, former Oxford professor of jurisprudence, defines primary rules as those which require people to act or refrain from acting in a certain way, whether they like it or not. These rules are coercive and strictly enforced. They concern physical behavior, especially crimes. Secondary rules, on the other hand, are rules to change rules. They provide ways in which parliaments or legislatures can modify or repeal the primary rules, or agree on new ones. Secondary rules confer powers on private individuals to make new wills or contracts, transfer property, get married or divorced. By means of such rules, individuals generate their own rights and obligations instead of simply obeying a set of permanent, coercive laws. They act according to their own special circumstances and their own special information.

Primary rules are highly deterministic and lead to a static or decaying society, unable to adapt to changing conditions or to new information unless laws are ignored or defied. A union of primary and secondary rules, on the other hand, avoids getting bogged down in this way. It makes for a dynamic, evolving society.

Human society has "emergent" properties. It evolves in unpredictable ways. Like a *kosmos*, its order is intrinsic, generated from within. The rules do not freeze it into immobility, but are dynamic, a source of innovation and renewal. Cause and effect as a model of human activity will not suffice, because as soon as we talk about relationships between rules, and the actions generated by those rules, the argument has moved to a higher logical level. It involves not information alone, but "information about information."

As Hayek puts it:

> Man is as much a rule-following animal as a purpose-seeking one. And he is successful not because he knows why he ought to observe the rules which he does observe, or is even capable of stating these rules in words, but because his thinking and acting are governed by rules which have by a process of selection been evolved in the society in which he lives . . .

Most of the rules which govern human actions come into existence for the very reason that no one person can possibly know all the myriad facts to which a society constantly adapts, in the sense that an engineer can know all about the workings of a machine. There are necessary limits to such knowledge. An individual does not need to know everything in order to engage in a very wide range of highly complex activity, any more than a business needs to depend on some mental superman at the apex of its corporate pyramid. The leader draws on the special skills of the people around him, just as the ordinary citizen relies on the expertise of bus drivers, telephone operators, motor mechanics, and a whole host of services based on arcane technical wisdom of which he has scarcely a glimmering of an understanding. A healthy, evolving society needs as much variety of knowledge as possible, and this variety must be maintained constantly. Uniformity would be fatal, because it would lead to enormous redundancy.

There are constraints on the rules governing a society, but the constraints make possible extremely rich structures of knowledge and action. It is Hayek's opinion that "it has always been the recognition of the limits of the possible which has enabled man to make full use of his powers." Chomsky has surmised that such constraints, analogous to those of universal grammar, may prevent human beings from selecting certain types of social order, and lead them to acquire other types, which are more natural to them. In an interview with the French linguist Mitsou Ronat, Chomsky outlines this idea:

If we succeed in finding our place within our society, that is perhaps because these societies have a structure that we are prepared to seek out. With a little imagination we could devise an artificial society in which no one would ever find his place . . .

Ronat:
Then you can compare the failure of artificial languages with the failure of Utopian societies?

Chomsky:
Perhaps. One cannot learn an artificial language constructed to violate universal grammar as readily as one learns a natural language, simply by being immersed in it. At most, one might conceive of such a language as a game . . . In the same way we can imagine a society in which no one could survive as a social being because it does not correspond to biologically determined perceptions and human social needs. For historical reasons, existing societies might have such properties, leading to various forms of pathology.

One reason for the failure of artificial languages as a universal means of communication is just this: that they underestimate the complexity of the language faculty itself. Few of these invented tongues, which began to be devised in the seventeenth century, have stood the test of time. Some seven hundred schemes for manmade languages have been launched at one time or another, including one consisting of strings of letters and numbers, a system based on musical notes, and a host of twentieth-century artifacts optimistically designed to be a Tower of Babel in reverse. Among these ingenious systems are Idiom Neutral, Novial, Ido, Interlingua, Interglossa, Ro, Occidental, and Monling, which uses nothing but monosyllables. Only Esperanto, which appeared in 1887, had a reasonable run of success. The others fell into disuse because they made the mistake of assuming that human language is simple, and each fell into this trap in one of two different ways. The early artificial languages, intended for the use of scholarly men, were too logical. The later ones, designed to be learned quickly by the masses, as their authors fondly hoped, were not complex enough in syntax and word use. Natural languages, by contrast, are complex and at the same time not always logical.

———————

It is a very plausible idea that the structure of a society, like a language, reflects, at least in part, the structure of the human brain. That would account not only for the complexity of social organizations, but also for the fact that they are complex in ways that might surprise a "logical" mind. Spontaneous products of the mind—language, myth, dreams—have a special logic and a peculiar structure of their own that we do not yet understand in any complete sense. Since the structure of language is such that universals are seldom predictable on the basis of logical reasoning, these universals usually come as a surprise when they are discovered. Possibly the same will turn out to be true of human societies if they are studied from this perspective.

If the ideas of information theory are thought of as trivializing nature and the mental activities of human beings, then they have been seriously misinterpreted. Rather, they suggest that systems of all kinds evolve toward more complex states, and that this is the natural order of things. We should not expect them to behave in any other way. Information theory, which is a universal body of principles applying quite generally to messages of all kinds, leads to the idea of complexity. It compels us to adjust our theories of evolution, language, and mind, so as to make them less simple, less one-sided. Randomness will not do as an explanation for the emergence of highly evolved biological species, any more than it will serve as the basis for a satisfactory theory of how human beings acquire a highly evolved faculty such as speech. Antichance enters into the process in a more sophisticated, more intrinsic way than was once assumed.

The information machine *par excellence* of our era, the computer, has not made life more uniform, as social prophets once predicted. Exactly the reverse has happened. The computer has turned out to be a device for generating differences and choice. It increases social complexity rather than reducing it. Computers are designed to deal with different choices because of the ease and speed with which they can decide among a myriad of distinct alternatives. The Model T Ford was mass-produced successfully because of the uniformity of the product. Today, a single make of American car has great variety, a wide range of accessories and options, extras, colors, and materials, aimed at a market of owners who dislike uniformity. The computer is used to select from among these various components and feed each one down the assembly line. Wherever goods and services are provided, the computer can be used to extend the range of individual choice. This is exactly the way in which we would expect an information machine to function.

It is certain that if a system, of whatever kind, reflects the structure of the mind, then it must be a very complex system indeed. Human beings attained their place on a high rung of the evolutionary ladder by not specializing too narrowly in particular modes of consciousness, by preferring a risky versatility to a less adventurous, safer way of life in which choice is limited. A successful society is similarly unspecialized. It protects the variety of talents, temperaments, and skills of its members, so that the society, too, can evolve in new and unexpected ways, retaining its complexity. It is predictable in some ways and unpredictable in others. It contains uncertainty, as all systems must if they are to reorganize old parts into new wholes.

Information theory teaches that without structure, without a code, a system is useless. It is perfectly free, but the freedom is indistinguishable from noise. There is no intelligibility, and no protection against error. It is unable to become complex. The system is useless, as a thermodynamic system is useless at equilibrium. Structure is natural to the world, natural to human beings. But if there is too much structure, the creative impulse is cramped and the patterns become stale, resistant to change. If there is too little, then art, literature, music, fashion, politics, slip into disorder and meaningless noise. Entropy rules. Structure and freedom, like entropy and redundancy, are not warring opposites but complementary forces.

Information technology is the physical embodiment of an abstract set of ideas. As information hardware plays an increasingly pervasive role in the day-to-day affairs of modern life, the ideas underlying the machines become better known, closer to ordinary experience, and more widely understood. People are not frightened of computers in a free society, and they are beginning to recognize that the principles by which computers work can shed some small light on how nature works, and, in an elementary and limited way, on how the mind works.

The new information machines make people aware of variety. More than that, the machines are agents of variety; they can both stimulate and satisfy a demand for it. If this should lead us to a theory of variety, that would be a social idea which is quite new. Such a theory would be a way of escaping the stale alternatives of traditional capitalism and traditional socialism, because it would pose an altogether different question: How much variety do we want in a society, and how much control? Asking that question at once shifts the center of intellectual gravity. The argument ceases to be over this or that doctrine or political theology and moves to a different ground. It considers instead the range of possible choices which should be made available to the members of the society. It begins with that consideration. Which choices should be restricted and which extended? Which made difficult and which made easy? This is a second-theorem approach to the design of institutions that elevates choice to a high place on the social agenda, but recognizes that choices must be constrained, made unequal, in ways that answer to the systemic needs of the society, just as redundancy answers to the systemic requirements of an information source. This is a very different point of departure from the simple slogans of the two extreme ends of the ideological spectrum: freedom for the sake of freedom, versus control for the sake of control. Carried to the limit, the first results in equilibrium, or chaos, and the second binds the system so tightly that it cannot move: it can transmit only one message. In the one case there is too much change, in the other too little.

The lesson of information theory is that choice and constraint can coexist as partners, enabling a system, be it a living organism, a language, or a society, to follow the arrow not of entropy but of history. This is the arrow which distinguishes past from future. by moving away from the simple, the uniform and the random, and toward the genuinely new, the endlessly complex products of nature and of mind.

AFTERWORD

Aristotle and DNA

Information theory, though very modern in its mathematical form, deals with ideas which reach far back into the history of thought. This is hardly surprising, in view of the fact that the theory itself—"information" itself—is a principle in nature generally. Any scientific system which includes in its range of interest such universal concepts as uncertainty and choice, structure and possibility, order and disorder, cannot help but be embedded in a rich philosophical context.

Often, when scientists are having some success in formulating a theory of living organisms, they tend to mention Aristotle's name with more than usual respect. Darwin's famous remark, "Linnaeus and Cuvier have been my two gods, but they were mere schoolboys compared to old Aristotle," is echoed today by many molecular biologists who search in the microworld of the cell for clues to the mechanisms of a process Darwin saw only in large-scale terms. They call attention to the almost shocking relevance of some of Aristotle's ideas to their own "revolutionary" discoveries.

There is a good reason for the new attention that biologists and others are giving to such an ancient source. Aristotle broke away from a materialist and mechanical explanation of nature, rather as modern physics has superseded the classical mechanics of Newton. He defined physics very broadly as the study of things that change, come into being, and pass away, and these include plants and animals as well as earth, air, fire, and water. In his universe, change leads to genuine novelty, not by accident, but because things possess a kind of concept, or plan, which they endeavor to realize, each in its own way. A chicken fulfills the plan implicit in the egg, an oak tree the "concept" contained in the acorn. This, for Aristotle, is a more satisfying explanation of the physical world than one which supposes it to be composed of particles colliding at random like billiard balls.

Using the term a little loosely, we can say that Aristotle saw the principle of information at work in nature, specifying the forms which matter takes, so that things are literally "informed" by an idea and strive to fulfill it. Nature builds according to the data which instructs matter to change in a particular way. As a modern commentator, John Herman Randall, puts it:

> Aristotle's viewpoint and approach are, as we often say, biological, rather than "merely" mechanical. They spring out of the experience of the biologist that Aristotle was. He takes biological examples, living processes, as revealing most fully and clearly what natural processes are like. He analyzes the behavior of eggs, not of billiard balls. He seems to have spent much time with the chickens, while the seventeenth-century founders of modern dynamics seem to have spent their lives, like Pascal, at the billiard and the gaming table.

The message of Aristotle is still surprisingly fresh and provocative, even across the span of so many centuries. In some respects the advances, not only of biology, but also of modern physics and logic, have not diminished the importance of what he had to say, but revealed the depth of his sophistication, and this on the basis of writings which are little more than lecture notes.

Plato, too, had an "information" theory of a kind, but it was a very different one. He taught that there are perfect, unchanging forms in an eternal domain beyond the reach of human senses, to which objects in the physical world bear only a certain resemblance. In other words, form exists independently of substance, and since the idea of a chair or table persists whether or not particular chairs or tables come into being or are destroyed, form does not alter, but goes on being the same forever. Plato did not deny that physical objects exist in the everyday world, but he believed that their existence depended on the forms, in whose true being they took part, but only in a limited, imperfect, secondhand sort of way.

For Plato, the reality of the forms was paramount. He put metaphysics at the heart of his theory of being, and gave an answer to the eternal question, framed by Leibniz and later by Heidegger—why is there something rather than nothing?—by proposing the existence of a superworld; static, extrinsic, ideal, where all is certain and finished in a timeless, transcendental realm.

Aristotle's "information theory" went off in quite another direction. He refused to separate form from substance. He took a more intrinsic view of being, accepting the reality of the form, or idea, but making it implicit in matter, so that things in the world of experience exist independently of our experience, in their own right, and not as shadows cast by sublime entities. Like Plato, Aristotle assumed that worldly things are neither perfect nor complete, but he saw reality as a process in which these things may become less imperfect.

Change is the essence of his system, and, along with change, time, movement, and becoming. For him, the physical world is above all dynamic. Matter is possibility, the potential for becoming, in time, something other and different. Change is a process of realizing this potential, of making the possible actual. Things, substances, do not aspire to be like their eternal, Platonic ideas. Rather, they make the implicit explicit and the potential actual, and this is accomplished by movement. The forms are in nature, not outside it, and they are dynamic and real. The "ideal" or concept of a house is both the end result and the reason why the house comes into being in the first place, although the concept is not fully realized until all the bricks and materials have been put into place. In the same way, the form of a human being is a possibility not made actual until that individual reaches maturity, but the form in the beginning is a force, moving the plan toward completion.

Form is an active, inherent principle of change, and takes part in the becoming of things. Matter is not dead stuff, but a means of transformation, without which change would be impossible. Having a certain form, matter may be free to assume other and different forms. Having no form at all, it contains within itself unlimited possibilities to receive or become any and every kind of form.

Aristotle proposed four types of cause responsible for bringing about change in the world.

Cause number one is matter, without which nothing would happen at all.

Cause number two is the form implicit in the thing which changes. The form is its meaning, determining what kind of thing it is, "what can be said" about it.

Cause number three is the efficient cause, an active agent of change, a mover, a force or power which brings about what matter only makes possible.

Cause number four is the end or purpose which a thing naturally tends to approach when it changes. This is the most controversial of all types of cause suggested by Aristotle, because it seems to imply that nature is directed toward some predestined goal, a notion science looks upon with horror. However, the common-sense view is that nothing so drastic need be inferred. Things behave in ways which are natural to them, Aristotle believed. Heavy objects fall to the ground, while light ones float in the air. Certain actions lead to predictable results. The sun warms the earth rather than freezes it, and animals go about their business in a manifestly purposeful, goal-seeking way. Indeed, Aristotle attached great importance to questions not given high priority in science until our own day. He talks about possibilities and the actualizing of possibilities: "The end and aim of all becoming is the development of potentiality to actuality, the incorporation of form in matter."

Information is in essence a theory about making the possible actual. It sets an event which does happen in the context of other and different events which only might have happened, so that potential and actual are related. A message sent conveys more or less information depending on how many or how few are the other messages from which it was selected. Aristotle talked about possibilities, but he also appreciated the importance of limits on the number of possibilities imposed by the forms. A form constrains matter, even while enabling it to realize its potential, and does not leave it free to be anything and everything.

Even more surprising, Aristotle gives a hint of the peculiar asymmetric relationship between energy and information, a relationship which was brought to light in modern science only when the full implications of Maxwell's demon were understood in the twentieth century. The demon needs enormous quantities of information about the particles in the dark chamber of gas in order to reduce the entropy of the gas by even a small amount. In other words, it is relatively easy, though not costless, to convert orderly energy into information, but difficult and expensive to transform matter into a more orderly state by the use of information. Aristotle showed that he had a general grasp of this inequality. He hints at the resistance of matter to form. Speaking of monstrosities in the animal kingdom, he says:

> A monstrosity, of course, belongs to the class of "things contrary to nature," although it is contrary not to nature in her entirety but only to nature in the generality of cases . . . Why, even in those instances of the phenomena we are considering, what occurs is contrary to this particular order, certainly, but it never happens in a merely random fashion; and therefore it seems less of a monstrosity because even that which is contrary to nature is, in a way, in accordance with nature, that is whenever the "formal" nature has not gained control over the "material" nature.

Plan, purpose, and information were among the *active* forces Aristotle saw at work in nature, which is unintelligible unless they are taken into account. These are concepts which have been confronted by science only in the present period. Today the frontiers of discovery in biology are inside the cell, where a coded model of a biological goal—a "potential" waiting to be actualized—contains the information needed to specify the substance of the organism. It is the form of the matter, by which its goal is fulfilled, and matter enables form to realize its plan.

More than one molecular biologist has remarked on the connection between Aristotle's conception of meaning unfolding in matter and the present-day idea of DNA as stored information. B. G. Goodwin, of the University of Sussex, who sees the genes as a source of biochemical "hypotheses," which are tested against the "facts" of the environment, notes that Aristotle thought along similar lines. Goodwin writes:

> Aristotle thought that from substance alone one cannot make deductions about form; that knowing the composition of something is not sufficient to determine its structure.
>
> One must add to substance a principle of organisation, which for Aristotle was a form or idea, immanent in the process whereby order of a characteristic type emerges from disorder or lower order, as the embryo from the egg. Plato considered such ideas to be transcendental and autonomous, but for Aristotle, the forms were also sources of energy in matter striving to organise it in some perfect order which was the final goal, the telos, of the process.

Unlike the Victorians, who were burdened by the legacy and imposing successes of two centuries of Newtonian mechanics, Aristotle was relatively unencumbered by the dogmas of his time. He made some errors, but he had a surprisingly clear idea of what anyone interested in the essential nature of living things ought to be studying; not this organ or that limb, but the totality of the form, the plan, the *information*, which gives rise to the organism over the course of time. He says,

> A given germ does not give rise to any chance living being, nor spring from any chance one; but each germ springs from a definite parent and gives rise to a definite progeny. And thus it is the germ that is the ruling influence and fabricator of the offspring.

This is a view which leads naturally to the assumption that nature is a unity; that, in the words of modern biology, the code of life is universal. Aristotle thought nature beautiful in all her manifestations, no matter how grotesque some might appear at first sight, because in each there is a plan, and the realization of that plan is the essential beauty of the creature.

Max Delbrück, professor of biology at the California Institute of Technology, and a Nobel Prize winner, has argued, with a mixture of playfulness and serious intent, that if the Nobel committee were able to award the prize for biology posthumously, they should consider giving it to Aristotle for the discovery of the principle of DNA. Delbrück notes that Aristotle thinks it remarkable, and a fundamental aspect of nature, that life unfolds according to certain rules. What is planted in the mother is not a miniature man, a homunculus, but a form principle. He goes on to make the ingenious suggestion that Aristotle's doctrine of the unmoved mover, the principle of change which is itself unchanging, perfectly describes DNA, because DNA acts, creates form in development, and does not change in the process.

Interestingly, the doctrine of the unmoved mover originated in Aristotle's studies of biology, and was incorporated afterward into his theory of physics. Still later, it was brought into astronomy and cosmological theology. The modern hostility to Aristotle, in Delbrück's view, stems from three hundred years of homage to Newton's system; in particular, to Newton's second law of motion, which says that to every action there is an equal and opposite reaction. If a body impinges on another body, changing its motion, the first body will undergo an equal change in the contrary direction. In other words, a mover is at all times and in all places moved by the act of moving. Any doctrine which contradicted this axiom was regarded as an outmoded relic from a muddleheaded past not yet blessed by the light of scientific reason.

The priority given to different aspects of Aristotle's work arose in part from a freak of transmission. They were stored for more than a hundred years in an underground cellar or cave, transported to Asia Minor and then back to Athens again. They were purchased and published in Rome, where they were catalogued and edited, only to be scattered and lost after Roman civilization collapsed. Arab scholars studied and interpreted the works, but all through the Dark Ages they remained almost unknown in the West. Only when cultural contact was established with Arab thinkers, partly as a result of the Crusades, was Aristotle revived in the Occident, and then he was taken up by the theologians and his ideas applied mainly to religion and logic. His biological insights were pushed into the background.

It is this accident of history, Delbrück argues, that is responsible for the "total barrier of understanding" which has existed to this day between scientists and theologians, "Catholic, Protestant and LSD mystic alike."

The unity of knowledge, which seemed so natural to the mind of Aristotle, is a goal to which occasional homage is paid by workers across the whole range of scholarly endeavor, but in practice it does not exist. Mathematicians and physicists, biologists and linguists, each live to a greater or lesser degree in their own separate worlds, speaking separate languages. They hold, as Delbrück sees it, "very different notions of reality and truth." If Aristotle was a philosopher preeminently able to look at all nature and human affairs as an undivided process full of beauty, which is above all intelligible to human beings, can it be a coincidence that he was also, alone among classical thinkers, a man who arrived at the first glimmerings of a theory of information?

Notes

Part One. Establishing the Theory of Information

Chapter 1. The Second Law and the Yellow Peril

16 Shannon's papers on information theory
Claude E. Shannon, 1948. "A Mathematical Theory of Information."
Bell System Technical Journal 27:379–423, 623–656.

17 Shannon's warning
Claude E. Shannon, 1956. "The Bandwagon." Institute of Electrical and
Electronics Engineers (IEEE) *Transactions on Information Theory* IT–
2(3):3.

19 "Great scientific theories"
Francis Bello, 1953. "The Information Theory." *Fortune* 48(6):136–158.

20 "There is a significant body of work"
Robert Fano, conversation with the author.

20 Pierce's remarks about Shannon
J. R. Pierce, 1973. "The Early Days of Information Theory." IEEE *Transactions on Information Theory* IT–19(1):3–8.

21 "He would let a piece of work sit"
Edward Moore, conversation with the author.

22 "mathematical carpentry"
Julian Bigelow, 1981. Letter to the author, October 26.

22 the founder of cybernetics
In deciding to call the science "cybernetics," Wiener acknowledged the
work of James Clerk Maxwell, who published a paper on governors, a

type of feedback mechanism (J. C. Maxwell, 1868. London, *Proceedings of the Royal Society* 16:270–283). The word "governor" is derived from a Latin corruption of the Greek word for "steersman." Mentioned in Norbert Wiener, 1948. *Cybernetics, or Control and Communication in the Animal and the Machine.* Cambridge, Mass., MIT Press.

23 Some details of Wiener's life and temperament are drawn from the following:
Norbert Wiener, 1964. *Ex-Prodigy: My Childhood and Youth.* Cambridge, Mass., MIT Press.
Norbert Wiener, 1966. *I Am a Mathematician: The Later Life of a Prodigy.* Cambridge, Mass., and London, MIT Press.
N. Levinson et al., 1966. "Norbert Wiener 1894–1964." American Mathematical Society *Bulletin* 72(1):1–145.

24 a "pose"
Norman Levinson, 1966. "Wiener's Life." Am. Math. Soc. *Bulletin* 72(1):30.

24 Hardy's refusal to take part in the First World War
Norbert Wiener, 1949. "Godfrey Harold Hardy." Am. Math. Soc. *Bulletin* 72(1):72–77.

26 "seemed to be in harmony"
Norbert Wiener, 1966. *I Am a Mathematician.*

27 The discovery of the relationship between Brownian motion and communication was not original to Wiener.

29 undermined in the 1920s
In 1928 R. V. L. Hartley published a paper ("Transmission of Information." *Bell Syst. Tech. J.* 7:535–563) in which he defined communication as the selection of a sequence of symbols, each selection eliminating other symbols which might have been chosen but were not. One could hope to find in the number of sequences not chosen a quantitative measure of information. Hartley stressed the need to base such a measure on physical factors alone, ignoring psychological questions of how a message is interpreted. Selection of each symbol is therefore regarded as perfectly arbitrary and not limited by the need to transmit meaningful sequences, so that the sequences could just as well have been generated by a chance device, such as a roulette wheel. Random processes in communication were investigated by S. O. Rice, 1944–45 ("Mathematical Analysis of Random Noise." *Bell Syst. Tech. J.* 23:282–332, 24:46–156). Shannon acknowledged fully the value of the work of Hartley and Harry Nyquist, and said of the Yellow Peril that it contains

the "first clear-cut formulation of communication as a statistical problem." Leo Szilard and John von Neumann applied the information concept to physics before Shannon's papers appeared. Others who made important contributions include Karl Pearson and R. A. Fisher in mathematical statistics, and A. N. Kolmogorov, A. A. Markov, and J. Willard Gibbs in mathematical physics and probability; these may also be considered precursors of Shannon.

30 "We took Wiener around, tongue in cheek"
Edward Poitras, conversation with the author.

31 "Wiener never became so directly practical"
Julian Bigelow, 1981. Letter to the author, October 26.

31 "a new interpretation of man"
Norbert Wiener, 1966. *I Am a Mathematician*, p. 325.

Chapter 2. The Noise of Heat

32 "no one knows what entropy is"
Shannon does not remember von Neumann's giving him such advice. However, Myron Tribus has a clear recollection of hearing Shannon tell him this story during a conversation in Shannon's office at MIT on April 2, 1961.

33 "operates as the hinge between matter and mind"
Olivier Costa de Beauregard, 1968. "Epilogue." In Robert Wallis, ed., *Time, Fourth Dimension of the Mind*. Betty B. and Denis B. Montgomery, trans. New York, Harcourt, Brace.

35 Carnot's memoir
Sadi Carnot, 1824. *Reflections on the Motive Power of Fire*. E. Mendoza, ed. R. H. Thurston, trans., 1960. New York, Dover.

38 Boltzmann's dismissal of Schopenauer
In Brian McGuinness, ed., 1974. *Ludwig Boltzmann, Theoretical Physics and Philosophical Problems: Selected Writings*, p. 185.

38 "only half of our experience"
Theoretical Physics and Philosophical Problems, p. 96.

41 Boltzmann to the Imperial Academy
Theoretical Physics and Philosophical Problems, p. 20.

41 "Economists are fond of saying"
Nicholas Georgescu-Roegen, 1975. "Bio-Economic Aspects of Entropy." In Libor Kubat and Jiří Zeman, eds., *Entropy and Information in Science and Philosophy*. Amsterdam and New York, Elsevier, p. 131.

Chapter 3. The Demon Deposed

44 "missing information"
Warren Weaver, 1949. In Claude E. Shannon and Warren Weaver, *The Mathematical Theory of Communication*, Urbana, University of Illinois Press, p. 3, note.

49 Leo Szilard's memoir
Spencer B. Weart and Gertrude Weiss Szilard, eds., 1978. *Leo Szilard: His Version of the Facts. Selected Recollections and Correspondence.* Cambridge, Mass., MIT Press.

50 A twenty-year-old man who smokes forty cigarettes
J. R. Lucas, 1970. *The Concept of Probability.* Oxford, Clarendon Press.

51 "Statistics belongs, like chronology"
Oswald Spengler, 1932. *The Decline of the West.* New York, Knopf, p. 421.

51 smells of its human origins
Percy Williams Bridgman, 1941. *The Nature of Thermodynamics.* Cambridge, Mass., Harvard University Press, p. 3. Bridgman said of thermodynamic laws in general, as opposed to other laws of physics, that "there is something more palpably verbal about them—they smell more of their human origins."

51 Henry Adams, Freud's death wish, and thermodynamics
Stephen G. Brush, 1978. *The Temperature of History: Phases of Science and Culture in the Nineteenth Century.* New York, Burt Franklin.

52 "the final touch of utter and impenetrable obscurity"
Dorothy L. Sayers (1932), 1968. *Have His Carcase.* New York, Avon Books, p. 236.

52 "It's God's work"
J. R. Pierce, conversation with the author.

Chapter 4. A Nest of Subtleties and Traps

53 A major encyclopedia article
Max Black, 1967. "Probability." In Paul Edwards, ed., *The Encyclopedia of Philosophy.* London, Crowell Collier and Macmillan, p. 464.

54 a modern writer on mathematics
James R. Newman, 1956. In James R. Newman, ed., *The World of Mathematics.* New York, Simon and Schuster, p. 1448.

56 Cardano's ups and downs
Jean Stoner, trans., 1930. *The Book of My Life (De Vita Propria Liber)*, by *Jerome Cardan*. New York, Dutton.

58 Jainan logic
Leonid E. Maĭstrov, 1974. *Probability Theory, A Historical Sketch.* Samuel Kotz, trans. and ed. New York, Academic Press.

58 One of the most attractive explanations
Ian Hacking, 1975. *The Emergence of Probability.* New York, Cambridge University Press.

59 Paracelsus
Henry M. Pachter, 1951. *Magic Into Science: The Story of Paracelsus.* New York, Henry Schuman.
Richard von Mises, 1939. *Probability, Statistics and Truth.* J. Neyman, D. Sholl, and E. Rabinowitsch, trans. New York, Macmillan.
Richard von Mises, 1964. *Mathematical Theory of Probability and Statistics.* Hilda Geiringer, ed. New York, Academic Press.

62 "a degree of belief"
I. J. Good, 1959. "Kinds of Probability." *Science* 129:443–447.

64 "Any theory of probability"
Myron Tribus, conversation with the author.

64 "maximally vague"
Tribus's words.

65 Views of Edwin Jaynes on probability and entropy
Edwin Jaynes, conversation with the author.

Chapter 5. Not Too Dull, Not Too Exciting

70 Shannon's word games
Claude E. Shannon, 1951. "Prediction and Entropy of Printed English." *Bell Syst. Tech. J.* 30(1):50–64.

72 redundancy in Black English
John Simon, 1978. "The Language. Pressure From Below." *Esquire* 89(11):90–91.

73 von Neumann on redundancy
John von Neumann, 1949. Lecture at University of Illinois. In Arthur W. Burks, ed., 1966. *Theory of Self-Reproducing Automata.* Urbana, University of Illinois Press.

74 "The first is too dull"
Fran Lebowitz, 1978. *Metropolitan Life*. New York, Dutton.

74 Isaac Stern interview
Louise Sweeney, 1980. "Isaac Stern, Concertmaster of the World."
Christian Science Monitor, September 30, p. 132.

Chapter 6. The Struggle Against Randomness

77 Shannon on secret codes
Claude E. Shannon, conversation with the author.

80 "second-theorem evolution"
Lila L. Gatlin, 1972. *Information Theory and the Living System*. New
York, Columbia University Press, p. 191.

Part Two. Nature as an Information Process

Chapter 7. Arrows in All Directions

83 The "arrow of time"
Sir Arthur Eddington, 1928. *The Nature of the Physical World*. Cambridge, England, Macmillan.

84 David Layzer's theory
David Layzer, 1975. "The Arrow of Time." *Scientific American* 223
(6):56–69.

89 "My view, however"
David Layzer, conversation with the author.

90 "In Laplace's world"
David Layzer, 1975. "The Arrow of Time." *Scientific American* 223
(6):59.

Chapter 8. Chemical Word and Chemical Deed

91 "Aristotle was correct"
B. G. Goodwin, 1972. "Biology and Meaning." In C. H. Waddington,
ed., *Towards a Theoretical Biology* 4:269. Chicago, Aldine-Atherton.

97 "The powers of invention"
Pierre-Paul Grassé, 1977. *Evolution of Living Organisms*. New York,
Academic Press, p. 3.

98 hitting the typewriter keys at random
Murray Eden, 1967. "Inadequacies of Neo-Darwinian Evolution as a Scientific Theory." In Paul S. Moorhead and Morton M. Kaplan, eds., *Mathematical Challenges to the Neo-Darwinian Interpretation of Evolution.* Philadelphia, Wistar Institute Press, pp. 5–19.

Chapter 9. *Jumping the Complexity Barrier*

100 "Languages have an internal rationale"
Robin Lakoff, conversation with the author.

101 "This is something completely new"
Ilya Prigogine, 1979. Quoted in Malcolm Browne, "Scientists See a Loophole in the Fatal Law of Physics." *New York Times,* May 29, pp. C1, C4.

102 "doom or destruction"
Ilya Prigogine, 1980. Quoted in Carol M. Thurston, "Ilya Prigogine— Towards a Unity of Science and Culture." *Christian Science Monitor,* October 8, p. 16.

102 language competence and biological complexity
Noam Chomsky, 1972. *Language and Mind,* enlarged ed. New York, Harcourt Brace Jovanovich.

102 a poem as emergent
T. S. Eliot, 1956. *The Frontiers of Criticism.* Lecture at University of Minnesota. Minneapolis, University of Minnesota Press, p. 13.

103 "which increases in complexity"
Ilya Prigogine, 1979. Quoted in Malcolm Browne, "Scientists See a Loophole in the Fatal Law of Physics." *New York Times,* May 29, pp. C1, C4.

103 von Neumann's brain
Robert Axtmann, 1976. "Superredundancy." Letter to *New York Times,* May 29. Pointing out that the redundancy of the normal human brain is such that it has ten times as many neurons as it "needs," Axtmann speculates that von Neumann's brain must have had ten times as many neurons as that of the average person. He recounts a conversation in 1957 with the physiologist Warren S. McCulloch, in which McCulloch wondered how von Neumann could drink a full quart of rye whiskey within an hour and then drive his car at ninety miles an hour without killing himself. McCulloch reasoned that it would take ten quarts of whiskey to impair von Neumann's driving ability, adding, "My guess is that Johnny simply doesn't like rye that much."

104 von Neumann on complexity
John von Neumann, 1949. Lecture at University of Illinois. In Arthur
W. Burks, ed., 1966. *Theory of Self-Reproducing Automata*. Urbana,
University of Illinois Press.

105 Ulam's games
Stanislaus M. Ulam, 1966. "Mathematical Problems with Growth of Fig-
ures." In Arthur W. Burks, ed., 1970. *Essays on Cellular Automata*.
Urbana, University of Illinois Press.

108 Goedel's paper
Ernest Nagel and James R. Newman, 1958. *Goedel's Proof*. New York,
New York University Press.

109 the word "nature" in classical and quantum mechanics
Aage Petersen, 1968. *Quantum Physics and the Philosophical Tradition*. New York, Belfer Graduate School of Science, Yeshiva University.

110 "For myself"
T. S. Eliot, 1956. *The Frontiers of Criticism*, p. 13.

Chapter 10. Something Rather Subtle

112 Lila L. Gatlin, 1970–71. "Evolutionary Indices." In *Sixth Berkeley
Symposium on Mathematical Statistics and Probability*.
Held at the Statistical Laboratory, University of California, June and
July 1970, April, June, and July 1971. Berkeley, University of California
Press.
Lila L. Gatlin, 1971. "Comments on Papers by Reichert and Wong."
Journal of Molecular Evolution 3:233–238.
Lila L. Gatlin, 1972. *Information Theory and the Living System*. New
York, Columbia University Press.
Lila L. Gatlin, 1974. "Conservation of Shannon's Redundancy for Pro-
teins." *Journal of Molecular Evolution* 3:189–208.

116 if a trillion monkeys were to type ten keys a second
William R. Bennett, Jr., 1976. *Scientific and Engineering Problem Solv-
ing with the Computer*. Englewood Cliffs, N.J., Prentice Hall.

121 "the vertebrates and their ancestors"
Lila L. Gatlin, 1972. *Information Theory and the Living System*, p. 96.

122 "We cannot agree"
Lester King and Thomas Jukes, 1969. "Non-Darwinian Evolution." *Science* 164:788–798.

124 "Something rather subtle"
Quoted in Walter Sullivan, 1977. "Genetic Decoders Plumbing Deepest Secrets of Life Process." *New York Times*, June 20, p. 48.

Part Three. Coding Language, Coding Life

Chapter 11. *Algorithms and Evolution*

128 Chomsky exposed the folly
Noam Chomsky, 1957. *Syntactic Structures*. The Hague, Mouton and Co.

129 information stored in a law or rule
Michael S. Watanabe, 1960. "Information-Theoretic Aspects of Inductive and Deductive Inference." *IBM Journal of Research and Development* 4(2):208.

131 algorithms must impose constraints
Murray Eden, 1967. "Inadequacies of Neo-Darwinian Evolution as a Scientific Theory." In Paul S. Moorhead and Morton Kaplan, eds., *Mathematical Challenges to the Neo-Darwinian Interpretation of Evolution*. Philadelphia, Wistar Institute Press, pp. 5–19.

132 Edmund Lin's experiment
S. A. Lerner, T. T. Wu, E. C. C. Lin, 1964. "Evolution of a Catabolic Pathway in Bacteria." *Science* 146:1313–1315.

133 "We follow the view"
Roy Britten and Eric Davidson, 1971. "Repetitive and Non-repetitive DNA Sequences and a Speculation on the Origins of Evolutionary Novelty." *Quarterly Review of Biology* 46(2):111–138.

134 anagenesis
Bernhard Rensch, 1960. *Evolution Above the Species Level*. R. Altevogt, trans. New York, Columbia University Press.

135 The ideas of Morris Goodman that are briefly summarized here can be explored in much greater depth and detail in the following publications:
Morris Goodman, 1969. "Molecular Anthropology, Its Approach to Mental Retardation." *Michigan Mental Health Research Bulletin* 3(1):7–16.
Morris Goodman, John Barnabus, Genji Matsuda, and G. William

Moore, 1971. "Molecular Evolution in the Descent of Man." *Nature* 233:604–613.

Morris Goodman and G. W. Moore, 1975. "Darwinian Evolution in the Genealogy of Haemoglobin." *Nature* 253:603–608.

Morris Goodman, Richard E. Tashian, and Jeanne H. Tashian, eds., 1976. *Molecular Anthropology.* New York, Plenum Publishing.

Morris Goodman, 1977. "Molecular Evolution and Natural Selection in the Descent to Man." *Primate News* 15(7):3–7.

Morris Goodman, 1978. "Contrasting Forms of Natural Selection Affecting Biomolecular Evolution in the Descent to Man." Paper presented at the Symposium on Natural Selection at Liblice, Czechoslovakia, June 5–9.

Chapter 12. Partly Green Till the Day We Die

137 only about one percent
Mary-Claire King and Allen Wilson, 1975. "Evolution at Two Levels in Humans and Chimpanzees." *Science* 188:107–116.

138 Emile Zuckerhandl, 1976. "Programs of Gene Action in Progressive Evolution." In Morris Goodman, Richard E. Tashian, and Jeanne H. Tashian, eds., *Molecular Anthropology.* New York, Plenum Publishing, pp. 387–447.

138 our "abysmal" ignorance
Roy Britten, 1978. "The Sources of Variation in Evolution." In Ronald Duncan and Miranda Weston-Smith, eds., *The Encyclopedia of Ignorance.* New York, Pocket Books, p. 217.

139 For a detailed explanation of neoteny see Stephen Jay Gould, 1977. *Ontogeny and Phylogeny.* Cambridge, Mass., Belknap Press of Harvard University Press.

140 an endearingly combative figure
J. Huxley, A. C. Hardy, and E. B. Ford, eds., 1954. *Evolution as a Process.* London, George Allen and Unwin.

142 the brain of a six-year-old
Dr. Peter Huttenlocher, 1979. Quoted in Carol Kleiman, "Brain Is More than Ready For School." *Chicago Tribune*, September 4, Section 2, pp. 1, 8.

144 technology was a sort of extension of play
Jerome S. Brunner, 1972. "Nature and Uses of Immaturity." *American Psychologist* 27(8):687–708.

145 children's flights of fancy
Howard Gardner and Ellen Winner, 1979. "The Child Is Father to the Metaphor." *Psychology Today* 12(12):81–91.

146 "must always substantially remain"
John Fowles, 1978. *The Magus.* Revised with foreword by the author. Boston, Little, Brown, p. 10.

146 "we will understand the nature of life"
Roy Britten, 1978. "The Sources of Variation in Evolution." *The Encyclopedia of Ignorance,* p. 211.

Chapter 13. No Need for Ancient Astronauts

148 "convinced me of the infinite superiority"
Charles Darwin, 1887. *Autobiography.* With original omissions restored, edited with appendix and notes by his granddaughter, Nora Barlow, 1958. New York, Norton Library.

148 "Paleontologists have documented"
Stephen Jay Gould, 1978. "Evolution: Explosion, Not Ascent." *New York Times,* January 22, p. E6.

149 the thesis of gene duplication
Susumu Ohno, 1970. *Evolution by Gene Duplication.* New York, Springer-Verlag.
Susumu Ohno, 1972. "An Argument for the Genetic Simplicity of Man and Other Mammals." *Journal of Human Evolution* 1:651–662.

151 "Did the genome"
Susumu Ohno, 1970. *Evolution by Gene Duplication,* p. 144.

152 early use of symbolism
Alexander Marshack, 1972. "Cognitive Aspects of Upper Paleolithic Engraving." *Current Anthropology* 13(3–4):445–477.
Alexander Marshack, 1972. "Upper Paleolithic Notation and Symbol." *Science* 178:817–828.
Alexander Marshack, 1976. "Implications of the Paleolithic Symbolic Evidence for the Origin of Language." *American Scientist* 64:136–145.
Alexander Marshack, 1977. "The Meander as a System." In Peter J. Ucko, ed., *Form in Indigenous Art.* Australian Institute of Aboriginal Studies.
Alexander Marshack, 1979. "Upper Paleolithic Symbol Systems of the Russian Plain." *Current Anthropology* 20(2):271–311.

152 Björn Kurtén, 1981. *Dance of the Tiger.* New York, Berkley Books.

153 "It is no longer sufficient"
Clive Gamble, 1980. "Information Exchange in the Paleolithic." *Nature* 283:522–523.

157 "One of the underlying effects"
Jacquetta Hawkes, 1973. *The First Great Civilizations: Life in Mesopotamia, the Indus Valley, and Egypt.* New York, Knopf, p. 7.

Chapter 14. The Clear and the Noisy Messages of Language

160 "real inner core of the communication problem"
Warren Weaver, 1949. In Warren Weaver and Claude E. Shannon, *The Mathematical Theory of Communication.* Urbana, University of Illinois Press, p. 25.

160 The evolution of Chomsky's ideas can be traced in these major writings:
Noam Chomsky, 1957. *Syntactic Structures.* The Hague, Mouton and Co.
Noam Chomsky, 1965. *Aspects of the Theory of Syntax.* Cambridge, Mass., MIT Press.
Noam Chomsky, 1966. *Cartesian Linguistics.* New York, Harper and Row.
Noam Chomsky, 1971. *Language and Mind: Problems of Knowledge and Freedom.* New York, Pantheon Books.
Noam Chomsky, 1975. *Reflections on Language.* New York, Pantheon Books.
Noam Chomsky, 1977. *Essays on Form and Interpretation.* New York, North-Holland.
Noam Chomsky, 1979. *Language and Responsibility.* Based on conversations with Mitsou Ronat. John Viertel, trans. New York, Pantheon Books.
Noam Chomsky, 1980. *Rules and Representations.* New York, Columbia University Press.

162 John is easy to please
Noam Chomsky, 1962. "Explanatory Models in Linguistics." In Ernest Nagel, Patrick Suppes, and Alfred Tarski, eds., *Logic, Methodology and the Philosophy of Science.* Proceedings of the 1960 International Congress. Palo Alto, Calif., Stanford University Press, pp. 528–550.

163 Who do you want to choose?
Noam Chomsky, 1976. "On the Nature of Language." *Annals of the New York Academy of Sciences* 280:46–57.

167 "We must not seek"
Immanuel Kant. *Prolegomena to Any Future Metaphysics*. Introduction by Lewis White Beck. New York, Bobbs-Merrill, 1950, p. 66.

168 "the more abstract the principles"
Noam Chomsky, 1977. *Essays on Form and Interpretation*, p. 16.

169 Einstein letter
Quoted in Gerald Holton, 1973. *Thematic Origins of Scientific Thought*. Cambridge, Mass., Harvard University Press, p. 243.

Chapter 15. A Mirror of the Mind

170 closely compatible with the ideas of modern psychology
Robin Lakoff, 1978. Book review of Marshall Edelson, 1975. *Language and Interpretation in Psychoanalysis*. New Haven, Yale University Press. *Language* 54(2):377–393.

170 "a mirror of the mind"
Noam Chomsky, 1975. *Reflections on Language*. New York, Pantheon Books, p. 4.

174 "More significantly, why are there no six-legged vertebrates?"
Boyce Rensberger, 1980. "Recent Studies Spark Revolution in Interpretation of Evolution." *New York Times*, November 4, p. C3.
Neil Smith and Deidre Wilson, 1979. *Modern Linguistics: The Results of Chomsky's Revolution*. Harmondsworth, England, Penguin Books.

178 "What has happened is that people realized"
Ray Jackendoff, conversation with the author.

179 "it is the theory which decides"
Werner Heisenberg, 1971. *Physics and Beyond: Encounters and Conversations*. New York, Harper and Row, p. 63.

180 "the patterns jump out"
Megan Marshall, 1981. "Musical Wunderkinds." *Boston Globe Magazine*, July 26, p. 28.

180 a universal grammar of music
Leonard Bernstein, 1973. *Leonard Bernstein at Harvard: The Norton Lectures*. Sound recording, Columbia M2X 33017, M3X 33020, 33024, 33028, M4X33032.

181 atonal music
Michel P. Philippot, "Arnold Schoenberg and the Language of Music." *Perspectives of New Music*, Spring-Summer 1975. Philippot believes that to call Schoenbeıg "a grammarian" is to pay him an enormous

compliment, because Schoenberg excelled at inventing a new syntax of
music rather than changing the "alphabet" as, say, Edgar Varèse did.
The chief function of rules in musical composition, Philippot argues, is
to maintain a flow of information in which the predictable is balanced
by the unpredictable. He writes:

> Since we know that the rules changed several times in the course of
> the centuries, that one era's music was consequently very different
> from that of another, but that all were accepted, it therefore seems
> that the *nature* of these rules is, in the end, of relative importance,
> but that, on the other hand, their *quantity* is very important and
> approximately constant throughout the course of time. Thus, the ge-
> nius of Schoenberg was to have succeeded in conceiving and apply-
> ing new rules, directly issuing from those which preceded them in
> *music's then current* state, and to have been able to maintain, within
> his system, an indispensable equilibrium between freedom and con-
> straint.

181 "Tonality is not simply man's response"
Ray Jackendoff, 1977. Book review of Leonard Bernstein, 1976. *The
Unanswered Question.* Cambridge, Mass., Harvard University Press.
Language 53(4):883–894.

182 an archetype of order
C. G. Jung, 1952. In C. G. Jung and W. Pauli, *Naturerklärung und
Psyche.* Studien aus dem C. G. Jung-Institut, IV; Zurich. *The Structure
and Dynamics of the Psyche.* R. F. C. Hull, trans., 1960. New York,
Pantheon Books, p. 456. Jung argues that the sequence of natural numbers turns out to be unexpectedly more than a series of identical units
succeeding one another. Indeed, it contains all of mathematics, both
what has been discovered in the past and everything that will be discovered in the future. In a sense, therefore, the sequence of natural
numbers is an unpredictable entity. Jung adds, "Number helps more
than anything else to bring order into the chaos of appearances. It is the
predestined instrument for creating order, or for apprehending an already existing, but still unknown, regular arrangement or 'orderedness.'
It may well be the most primitive element of order in the human mind."

183 "a system of rules and forms"
Noam Chomsky, conversation with the author.

186 "gives form and sense"
Robin Lakoff, 1978. Book review. *Language* 54(2):386. Discussing the
view that the mechanisms by which we unconsciously, as infants, come
to intuit grammatical processes are the same as those used unconsciously to construct dreams, appreciate jokes, write and understand

poetry, "and to protect ourselves, characteristically, from internal and external realities which we cannot confront directly," Lakoff writes:

> Language is thus just one way in which the human mind uses a single set of rules, and these rules underlie all our psychological capacities. Language-learning is then not the isolated and unique function that Chomsky thought it was, nor is cognitive ability something apart from other aspects of psychological capacity. It is important to think of ALL these powers as potentially creative: language, symptom formation, defence, dream, poem—in the sense that all allow the user to give form and sense to his universe, where without them there would be none.

I am grateful to Deborah Tannen, of the Georgetown University Linguistics Department, for bringing this article to my attention.

Part Four. How the Brain Puts It All Together

Chapter 16. *The Brain as Cat on a Hot Tin Roof and Other Fallacies*

189 Shannon on computers and human intelligence
Claude E. Shannon, 1953. "Computers and Automata." *Proceedings of the Institute of Radio Engineers* 41:1234–1241.

192 three types of events
Steven Rose, 1976. *The Conscious Brain*, rev. ed. Harmondsworth, England, Penguin Books.

193 distinction between power engineering and communication engineering
Norbert Wiener, 1966. *I Am a Mathematician*. Cambridge, Mass., and London, MIT Press.

194 "simply and fundamentally wrong"
Robert W. McCarley and J. Allan Hobson, 1977. "The Neurobiological Origins of Psychoanalytic Dream Theory." *American Journal of Psychiatry* 134(11):1211–1221.

197 collapse of the bullet theory
Wilbur Schramm, 1973. "Mass Communication." In George A. Miller, ed., *Communication, Language and Meaning*. New York, Basic Books.

Chapter 17. The Strategies of Seeing

201 the innocent eye does not exist
Ernst Gombrich, 1961. *Art and Illusion: A Study in the Psychology of Pictorial Representation.* New York, Pantheon Books.

202 the brain as building and testing hypotheses
Richard Gregory, 1976. *Eye and Brain: The Psychology of Seeing.* New York, World University Library/McGraw-Hill.

203 James J. Gibson's major writings on perception are:
James J. Gibson, 1950. *The Perception of the Visual World.* Boston, Houghton Mifflin.
James J. Gibson, 1966. *The Senses Considered as Perceptual Systems.* Boston, Houghton Mifflin.
James J. Gibson, 1979. *The Ecological Approach to Visual Perception.* Boston, Houghton Mifflin.

206 an archeologist at the site of a lost city
James R. Newman, 1956. In James R. Newman, ed., *The World of Mathematics.* New York, Simon and Schuster, p. 1536.

209 a few perspectives only are enough
Robert Shaw and Buford Wilson, 1977. "Abstract Conceptual Knowledge. How We Know What We Know." In David Klahr, ed., *Cognition and Instruction,* Hillsdale, N.J., Lawrence Erlbaum Associates.

210 "Ideas are not in the mind"
Robert Shaw and Michael McIntyre, 1974. "Algoristic Foundations to Cognitive Psychology." In Walter B. Weimer and David S. Palermo, eds., *Cognition and the Symbolic Processes.* New York, Lawrence Erlbaum Associates/Wiley, p. 360.

210 "core concepts"
Robert Shaw and Buford Wilson, 1977. "Abstract Conceptual Knowledge."

210 "One important insight"
Ibid.

211 "A perceiver is a *self-tuning* system"
James J. Gibson, 1966. *The Senses Considered as Perceptual Systems,* p. 271.

211 "There does seem to be evidence"
Robert Shaw and Michael McIntyre, 1974. "Algoristic Foundations to Cognitive Psychology," p. 357.

212 Some American schoolchildren
E. Paul Torrance, 1972. "Tendency to Produce Unusual Visual Perspective as a Predictor of Creative Achievement." *Perceptual and Motor Skills* 34(3):911–915.

213 "an ideal decoder"
Claude E. Shannon, 1956. "The Bandwagon." Institute of Electrical and Electronics Engineers. *Transactions on Information Theory* IT-2(3):3.

Chapter 18. The Bottom and Top of Memory

215 The banquet scene is described in Francis Yates, 1966. *The Art of Memory*. Chicago, University of Chicago Press.

217 Shannon's experiment with redundancy
Claude E. Shannon, 1949. In Claude E. Shannon and Warren Weaver, *The Mathematical Theory of Communication*. Urbana, University of Illinois Press.

218 a better memory for context-sensitive redundancy
G. A. Miller and J. A. Selfridge, 1950. "Verbal Context and the Recall of Meaningful Material." *American Journal of Psychology* 63:176–185.

218 John is eager to please
A. Blumenthal and R. Boakes, 1967. "Prompted Recall of Sentences: A Further Study." *Journal of Verbal Learning and Verbal Behavior* 6:674–675.

219 Bransford points out
John D. Bransford, 1979. *Human Cognition: Learning, Understanding and Remembering*. Belmont, California, Vanderbilt University/Wadsworth Publishing.

220 expert and novice strategies of recall
Paul Johnson, conversation with the author.

220 tend to have breezy titles
James J. Jenkins, 1974. "Remember That Old Theory of Memory? Well, Forget It." *American Psychologist* 29:785–795.

222 "*All* analyses eventually 'sheer away' "
James J. Jenkins, 1974. "Remember That Old Theory . . ."

223 this apparent paradox
James J. Jenkins, 1974. "Can We Have a Theory of Meaningful Memory?" In R. L. Solso, ed., *Theories in Cognitive Psychology: The Loyola Symposium*. Hillsdale, N. J., Lawrence Erlbaum Associates.

224 experiment to test abstract memory for ideas
John Bransford and Jeffrey Franks, 1971. "The Abstraction of Linguistic Ideas." *Cognitive Psychology* 2:331–350.

225 "Any study of knowledge structure"
James J. Jenkins, conversation with the author.

226 and still pass a lie detector test
John D. Bransford, 1979. *Human Cognition.*

228 "I think we will eventually conclude"
James J. Jenkins, 1973. "Language and Memory." In George A. Miller, ed., *Communication, Language and Meaning: Psychological Perspectives.* New York, Basic Books, p. 170.

Chapter 19. The Information of Dreams

231 "Every dream is an organ of information and control."
C. G. Jung, 1934. "Die Praktische Verwendbarkeit der Traumanalyse." In *Wirklichkeit der Seele.* Zurich. *The Practice of Psychotherapy.* R. F. C. Hull, trans., 1954. New York, Pantheon Books, p. 153.

231 "are the essential message carriers"
C. G. Jung, 1964. "Approaching the Unconscious." In Carl G. Jung, M.-L. von Franz, Joseph L. Henderson, Jolande Jacobi and Aniela Jaffé, *Man and His Symbols.* New York, Dell, p. 37.

232 "They seem to hang together"
C. G. Jung, 1945. "Vom Wesen der Traüme." *Ciba-Zeitschrift* 9:99. *The Structure and Dynamics of the Psyche.* R. F. C. Hull, trans., 1954. New York, Pantheon Books, p. 289.

233 brain generates its own information for dreams
J. Allan Hobson and Robert W. McCarley, 1977. "The Brain as a Dream State Generator: An Activation-Synthesis Hypothesis of the Dream Process." *American Journal of Psychiatry* 134(12):1335–1348.

236 a "hidden observer"
Ernest Hilgard, 1977. *Divided Consciousness: Multiple Controls in Human Thought and Action.* New York, Wiley, p. 185.

Chapter 20. The Left and Right of Knowing

239 it seems that in evolution
Marcel Kinsbourne. "Hemisphere Specialization and the Growth of Human Understanding." *American Psychologist,* in press.

240 "Objectively measured"
Robert K. Yin, conversation with the author.

241 a man's left brain was put to sleep
This experiment is described in Michael S. Gazzaniga and Joseph E. Le Doux, 1978. *The Integrated Mind*, New York, Plenum.

241 list of left- and right-brain styles of knowing
Joseph E. Bogen, 1977. "Some Educational Implications of Hemispheric Specialization." In M. C. Wittrock, ed., *The Human Brain*, Englewood Cliffs, N. J., Prentice-Hall.

243 the right is almost speechless
The disconnected right hemisphere has been known to speak with difficulty short words such as *clap, cup,* and *six*. It has a certain amount of comprehension of spoken language. In 1981, Jeffrey Elman, Kunitoshi Takahashi, and Yasu-Hiko Tohsaku reported ("Lateral Asymmetries for the Identification of Concrete and Abstract *Kanji*." *Neuropsychologia* 19(3):407–412) that the different writing systems of Japanese, *Kanji* and *Kana*, are not processed the same way in the brain. *Kanji* is ideographic. Its characters represent individual words and have no systematic relationship with sound. *Kana*, on the other hand, is a phonetic system in which each element represents a syllable, and there is a close relationship with the way a word is pronounced. The right hemisphere does better with *Kanji* than with *Kana* if the word in question is a noun.

243 an entire syllable in a single stream of sound
A. M. Liberman, 1974. "The Specialization of the Language Hemisphere." In F. O. Schmitt and F. G. Worden, eds., *The Neurosciences: Third Study Program*. Cambridge, Mass., MIT Press, pp. 43–56.

245 "minor" hemisphere and stories, jokes
Howard Gardner and Suzanne Hamby, 1979. "The Role of the Right Hemisphere in the Organization of Linguistic Materials." Paper presented at the International Neuropsychology Symposium, Dubrovnik, Yugoslavia.

247 "A heavy heart can really make a difference"
Howard Gardner and Ellen Winner, 1977. "The Comprehension of Metaphor in Brain-Damaged Patients." *Brain* 100:717–729.

249 Imagine a traffic jam in a mass-transit system
Robert R. Hoffman and Richard P. Honek, 1976. "The Bidirectionality of Judgments of Synonymy." *Journal of Psycholinguistic Research* 5(2):173–184.

250 Verbrugge attracted to the study of metaphor
Robert Verbrugge, conversation with the author.

251 "crystallized" intelligence
Eran Zaidel, 1980. Quoted in Harold M. Schmeck Jr., " 'Two Brains' of
Man: Complex Teamwork." *New York Times*, January 8, pp. C1–C3.

251 "When a skill or task is new"
Eran Zaidel, conversation with the author.

252 passages from schizophrenic compositions
W. Ross Winterowd, 1980. "Brain, Rhetoric and Style." *Language and
Style* 13(3):151–181.

Chapter 21. The Second-Theorem Society

255 "We must go beyond the temptation"
Ilya Prigogine, 1980. Quoted in Carol M. Thurston, "Ilya Prigogine—
Towards a Unity of Science and Culture." *Christian Science Monitor*,
October 8, p. 16.

255 ". . . the behaviour of an organised system"
E. H. Hutten, 1975. *Information, Explanation and Meaning.* Unpublished in English. Published in Italian trans. as *Informazione, Spieta-
zione e Significato*, Rome, Ermando.

257 "John's smoking bothers me"
Suzette H. Elgin, linguist, conversation with the author.

258 *kosmos* and *taxis*
F. A. Hayek, 1960. *The Constitution of Liberty.* Chicago, University of
Chicago Press.
F. A. Hayek, 1973. *Law, Legislation and Liberty*, vol. 1, *Rules and
Order.* Chicago, University of Chicago Press.

259 primary and secondary rules of society
H. L. A. Hart, 1975. *The Concept of Law.* Oxford, Clarendon Press.

260 "Man is as much a rule-following animal"
F. A. Hayek, 1973. *Law, Legislation and Liberty*, vol. 1, p. 11.

261 "it has always been the recognition"
Ibid, p. 8.

261 "If we succeed in finding our place"
Noam Chomsky, 1979. *Language and Responsibility.* Based on conver-
sations with Mitsou Ronat. John Viertel, trans. New York, Pantheon
Books, p. 70.

261 artificial languages a failure
Mario Pei, 1966. *The Story of Language*. New York, Mentor/New American Library.

Afterword: Aristotle and DNA

267 "Aristotle's viewpoint and approach"
John Herman Randall, 1960. *Aristotle*. New York, Columbia University Press, p. 126.

270 "A monstrosity, of course"
Aristotle. *Generation of Animals*. A. L. Peck, trans., 1942. Cambridge, Mass., Harvard University Press, p. 425.

271 "Aristotle contended that from substance alone"
B. G. Goodwin, 1972. "Biology and Meaning." In C. H. Waddington, ed., *Towards a Theoretical Biology* 4:268. Chicago, Aldine-Atherton.

271 "A given germ does not give rise"
Aristotle, *Parts of Animals*. In Richard McKeon, ed., 1941. *The Basic Works of Aristotle*. New York, Random House, p. 649.

272 Max Delbrück proposes Aristotle for a Nobel Prize
Max Delbrück, 1976. "How Aristotle Discovered DNA." In Kerson Huang, ed., *Physics and Our World: Symposium in Honor of Victor F. Weisskopf*. New York, American Institute of Physics.

Index